Young Children's Play and Crea

This book draws on the voices of practitioners, academics and researchers to examine young children's play, creativity and the participatory nature of their learning. Bringing together a wide range of perspectives from the UK and internationally, it focuses on the level of engagement and exploration involved in children's play and how it can be facilitated in different contexts and cultures. This new reader aims to challenge thinking, promote reflection and stimulate further discussion by bringing together research and practice on play and creativity.

Divided into two parts, Part I is written by researchers and academics and explores key themes such as creative meaning making, listening to children's voices, risk and spaces, children's rights, play and technology. Part II is authored by Early Childhood professionals and reveals how practitioners have responded to the issues surrounding play and creativity. Each chapter is contextualised by an introduction to highlight the key points and a list of follow-up questions is also included to encourage reflection and debate.

Drawing on the wide-ranging writing of academics, practitioners and researchers, this book is an invaluable resource for students, practitioners and all those who are interested in the essence of play and creativity, what it means for children and the far-reaching benefits for their well-being, learning and development.

Gill Goodliff is a Senior Lecturer in Education and Programme Leader for Early Years at The Open University. She has a background in social work with young children and families, primarily in the voluntary sector, and has extensive experience of teaching practitioners. She represents The Open University at the Early Childhood Studies Degree Network.

Natalie Canning is a Senior Lecturer in Education, Early Years at The Open University. Her background is in playwork and social work, particularly in supporting children to explore personal, social and emotional issues through play.

John Parry is a Lecturer in Education at The Open University, where he has written and chaired courses on inclusion, primary and early years practice. He has a background of extensive work experience in the early years sector, primarily as a teacher and co-ordinator of educational support services for pre-school children.

Linda Miller is Emeritus Professor, Early Years at The Open University. She has worked both with and for young children throughout her professional life as a practitioner and teacher/practitioner educator.

Anna Craft
1961–2014
Friend and colleague, inspiring teacher and researcher, and
passionate advocate for children's creativity in education.

This Reader forms part of the 120 credits studied in Stage 1 of The Open University BA (Hons) Early Childhood. This degree is for practitioners working with young children (birth to seven years) or adults interested in learning more about young children's lives and experiences. Details of this and other Open University modules can be obtained from Student Recruitment, The Open University, PO Box 197, Milton Keynes MK7 6BJ, United Kingdom (tel. +44 (0)300 303 5303; email general-enquiries@open.ac.uk)'

Young Children's Play and Creativity

Multiple Voices

Edited by
Gill Goodliff, Natalie Canning,
John Parry and Linda Miller

Routledge
Taylor & Francis Group
LONDON AND NEW YORK

The Open University

First published 2018
by Routledge
2 Park Square, Milton Park, Abingdon, Oxon OX14 4RN

and by Routledge
711 Third Avenue, New York, NY 10017

Routledge is an imprint of the Taylor & Francis Group, an informa business

Published in association with The Open University, Walton Hall,
Milton Keynes, MK7 6AA, United Kingdom

British Library Cataloguing in Publication Data
A catalogue record for this book is available from the British Library

Library of Congress Cataloging in Publication Data
Names: Goodliff, Gill, editor.
Title: Young children's play and creativity : multiple voices / edited by
    Gill Goodliff, Natalie Canning, John Parry & Linda Miller.
Description: Abingdon, Oxon ; New York, NY : Routledge, 2018.
Identifiers: LCCN 2016058669| ISBN 9781138214064 (hardback) |
    ISBN 9781138214071 (pbk.) | ISBN 9781315446844 (ebook)
Subjects: LCSH: Play. | Creative ability in children. | Early childhood
    education. | Child development.
Classification: LCC LB1139.35.P55 Y68 2018 | DDC 372.21—dc23
LC record available at https://lccn.loc.gov/2016058669

ISBN: 978-1-138-21406-4 (hbk)
ISBN: 978-1-138-21407-1 (pbk)
ISBN: 978-1-315-44684-4 (ebk)

Typeset in Bembo
by Swales & Willis Ltd, Exeter, Devon, UK

MIX
Paper from
responsible sources
FSC® C013056
www.fsc.org

Printed and bound in Great Britain by
TJ Books Limited, Padstow, Cornwall

Contents

Part II
Practitioners responding to young children's play and creativity   163

Illustrations

Figures

Tables

Acknowledgements

We wish to thank all those who have written chapters for this Reader or who have given permission for us to edit and reprint writing from other publications.

A special thank you to Christine Ashby for her invaluable administrative support, and to Gill Gowans for her ongoing involvement and support in preparation of the final manuscript for handover to the publishers.

Grateful acknowledgement is made to the following sources for permission to reproduce material in this book. Chapters not listed below have been specially commissioned.

Albon, D. (2010) 'Reflecting on children "Playing for real" and "Really playing" in the Early Years', in Moyles, J. (ed.), *Thinking About Play: Developing a Reflective Approach*, Maidenhead: Open University Press.

Brooker, L. (2010) 'Learning to play, or playing to learn? Children's participation in the cultures of homes and settings', in Brooker, L. and Edwards, S. (eds) (2010) *Engaging Play*, Maidenhead: Open University Press.

Cameron, C.A., Pinto, G., Gamannossi, B.A., Hancock, R. and Tapanya, S. (2011) 'Domestic play collaborations in diverse family contexts', *Australian Journal of Early Childhood*, Vol. 36, No. 4. Early Childhood Australia: www. earlychildhoodaustralia.org.au (accesed 17 March 2017).

Canning, N. (2013) 'Where's the bear? Over there!' – creative thinking and imagination in den making', *Early Child Development and Care*, Vol. 183, No. 8, pp. 1042–53. http://dx.doi.org/10.1080/03004430.2013.772989 (accessed 17 March 2017).

Cremin, T., Glauert, E., Craft, A., Compton, A. and Stylianidou, F. (2015) 'Creative little scientists: exploring pedagogical synergies between inquiry-based and creative approaches', in *Early Years Science Education 3–13*, Vol. 43, No. 4, pp. 404–19.

Green, C. (2014) '"Because we like to": Young children's experiences hiding in their home environment', in *Early Childhood Education Journal* Vol. 43, pp. 327–36.

Waller, T. (2014) 'Voices in the park: researching the participation of young children in outdoor play in early years settings', *Management in Education*, Vol. 28, No. 4, pp. 161–6, British Educational Leadership, Management and Administration Society (BELMAS).

Introduction

Young children's play and creativity – multiple voices

Gill Goodliff and Natalie Canning

In choosing and commissioning chapters for this edited book, *Young Children's Play and Creativity: Multiple Voices*, a primary concern has been that it should reflect children's play and creative experiences. The chapters reflect children's engagement and explorations in playing and being creative, and how play and creativity can be facilitated in different contexts and cultures. Some of the challenges faced by adults, whether it be Early Childhood professionals or parents and carers, emerge in the debates surrounding play and creative environments. These challenges are similar throughout the world and the chapters in this book reflect international researchers and professionals concerned with the debates surrounding play and creativity.

This book has a dual function: not only to draw together research and practice on play and creativity, but also to enrich the study experience of students registered on modules in the first stage of The Open University BA (Hons) Early Childhood. This degree is for both experienced practitioners, volunteers working in early childhood contexts, and adults simply interested in learning more about young children's lives and experiences. We bring together a range of perspectives on children's play, creativity and learning which are intended to challenge thinking, promote reflection and stimulate discussion.

There are recurring themes that run through the book and also the Open University modules for which it is a companion. These include how play and creativity is valued, not just in organised and regulated establishments, but more widely in society, in communities and in families. The chapters, although focused on particular research and practice, consider how children make sense of their world through play and by being creative, and the significance this has for their ongoing learning and development. Children's play and creative experiences are explored, provoking questions such as 'What is it like to play and be creative?' and 'What do children bring or take away from those experiences?'

Inclusion is another key theme, and the chapters in Part 2 of the book, which focus on practice, consider how play and creative experiences encourage children's participation. Children's right to play and creativity is another important theme underpinned by the United Nation's Convention on the Rights of the Child (UNCRC) and is reflected in the discussions presented through the chapters. The book explores children's experiences, but also how adults are positioned in supporting and facilitating play and creativity. The chapters ask you to reflect on your own experiences, values and beliefs, and questions to help you do this are asked at the end of each chapter. If you are particularly interested in a chapter, further reading suggestions are also recommended by authors.

The book is organised in two parts. In Part 1, entitled 'Researching young children's play and creativity', the twelve chapters are authored by researchers and academics. Some of the chapters are previously published journal articles but have been included here because they are significant in developing the dialogue around children's play and creativity. Just as children experiment and explore in play, you may find yourself dipping into some chapters and immersing yourself in others. Here is a brief overview of the chapters in Part 1.

Chapter 1 by Deborah Albon uses narrative observations as a basis for reflecting on 'playing for real' and 'really playing' through her research on children's meal and snack time. Chapter 2 by Liz Brooker interrogates accepted ideas about play and explores practitioners' values and beliefs, and their impact on children's experiences and play opportunities. Chapter 3 by Catherine Cameron and an international team of researchers considers very young children's domestic play and how caregivers directly and indirectly encourage and support play. They argue that professionals educating young children can learn from an increased appreciation of the way children and their caregivers sustain and participate in play at home. Chapter 4 by Natalie Canning explores opportunities for creative thinking and imagination through den making. Chapter 5 by Teresa Cremin and a research team explores teaching, learning and assessment of science through creative approaches based on children's interests in everyday events. Chapter 6 by Gill Goodliff explores how young children express their spirituality and the challenges for practitioners in recognising and facilitating this often unspoken aspect of children's creative and imaginative play.

Chapter 7 by Penny Hay uses arts-based action research with young children to show how participation in creative environments supports critical thinking and the wider well-being of children and adults. Chapter 8 by Lisa Kervin and Irina Verenikina draw on their research exploring pre-school children's use of technology in their play and the seamless transition between on-screen and off-screen interaction. Chapter 9 by John Parry explores how playing with others creates opportunities for friendship and what they tell us about providing support for peer relationships. Chapter 10 by Alison Street discusses a range of theoretical perspectives that have informed research related to babies and young children's musicality. Chapter 11 by Tim Waller looks back at the shifts and developments in an outdoor learning project and discusses the many influences that have impacted on children's levels of participation. Chapter 12 by Elizabeth Wood extends our thinking about observing and listening skills, emphasising that they are integral to being attentive to children's voices and perspectives.

Part 2, 'Practitioners responding to young children's play and creativity', is a collection of ten chapters written by Early Childhood professionals, passionate about what they do and how they facilitate children's play and creativity. In both parts of the book, different research approaches are used depending on the size and scale of the project. This may be of interest if you are planning your own research with young children.

Chapter 13 by Babette Brown outlines how and why the Persona Doll approach provides an effective, stimulating and non-threatening way to combat discrimination, empower young children and promote social justice. She suggests that children need to be able to build a deep sense of self-worth and clarity in their cultural identities in order to be proud of where they come from. Chapter 14 by Tara Copard looks back on the way she established cross-agency, family-focused practices in her setting in order to support parent understanding and enhance young children's language and literacy learning. Chapter 15 by Donatella Giovannini reflects on the role of environments and spaces in the education of young children in Pistoia, Italy. Chapter 16 by Menna Godfrey draws on observations of children in her setting to discuss the rich experiences that a 'Mud Kitchen' and playing with mud offers young children. Chapter 17 by Carie Green researches 3- and 5-year-olds' hiding places and experiences in their home environment. She advocates opportunities for play and creativity where young children are recognised as active agents in creating their own culture and place in the world.

Chapter 18 by Karen Horsley draws on her study which uses photographs to listen to children and find out about their experiences. She considers the different relationships children have with practitioners and family members and how talking about photographs provides insight into their interests and preferences. Chapter 19 by Linda Pound gives examples of everyday play situations that can be linked to mathematical explanations. She considers the significance of children being able to create and investigate through ideas and discovery and how that promotes flexible, playful and challenging thinking. Chapter 20 by John Oates and Nóra Ritók explains the work of The

Real Pearl Foundation and Art School in Hungary which works towards developing self-worth and optimism for positive change for children and their families through art activities. Chapter 21 by Lee Robertson explores the value of learner-led projects where children are encouraged to develop their creativity through dance, music, movement and creative exploration of natural resources. Chapter 22 by Philippa Thompson, Jenny Bulloss and Steven Vessey considers the value of Forest School and how the natural environment can support and enhance young children's experiences. They suggest that Forest School is a way in which children's play and creativity can be nurtured in a risk benefit environment. Chapter 23 by Vanessa Young discusses a research project that worked with baby room practitioners to explore ways in which singing and song can influence the development of more intimate interactions between practitioners and the babies in their care.

As you read the chapters in Part 1 and Part 2 you will become aware that there are wide-ranging and contested views about play and creativity. This book explores and challenges some of these perspectives and encourages you to take a questioning approach as you reflect on your own understanding and the implications for supporting young children's play and creativity. However this text is ultimately a celebration of the essence of play and creativity, what it means for children and the far-reaching benefits for their well-being, learning and development.

Researching young children's play and creativity

Chapter 1

Reflecting on children 'playing for real' and 'really playing' in the early years

Deborah Albon

Chapter introduction

The observations in this chapter by Deborah Albon, Senior Lecturer in Early Childhood Studies at London Metropolitan University, are drawn from her research looking at 'food events' (as in meals and snack times) in four early years settings over a three-year period. Using the narrative observations as a basis for reflection on play, she proposes it might be categorised on a continuum of 'playing for real' and 'really playing'. She concludes that both categories of play are valuable, and encourages further reflection as the key to considering children's own experiences and the role of practitioners.

Introduction

There is a range of ways in which to categorize types of play. Indeed, the topic 'play' has undergone thorough examination and continues to do so, such is its importance in the field of early years education and care. Examples of such categorizations include Hutt et al.'s (1989) taxonomy of play as involving either 'epistemic behaviour', which relates to activity that involves problem solving and exploration, and 'ludic behaviour', which is more playful, repetitive and/or symbolic. In thinking about young children's pretend play, Hendy and Toon (2001) make a distinction between 'socio-dramatic play' and 'thematic-fantasy play', arguing that the former involves the child in pretend activities such as cooking a meal and the latter relates to imaginary worlds that children have invented for themselves, sometimes drawing on cultural narratives available to them and other times derived purely from their imaginations.

This chapter draws on five observations from three early years settings. It should be noted from the outset that I do not claim that *all* play episodes can be categorized exclusively as falling within one of the terms I have called 'playing for real' or 'really playing' and will also include play episodes that are not food-related. Possibly these terms are best thought of as opposite ends of a *continuum* with the observations discussed here viewed as towards the two opposite extremities of this continuum. In addition, as play is often shifting in its focus, a play episode that starts as 'playing for real' can turn into something akin to 'really playing' in a moment – such is the *beauty* of play.

'Playing for real'

The episodes of play that I am characterizing as 'playing for real' are those that seem highly imitative of real life, where the conventions that children may have witnessed at home, nursery, cafés or elsewhere are often highly recognizable to the observer. Hendy and Toon (2001) describe such activity as 'socio-dramatic play'. I have often observed this type of play when children have access to real objects such as real food or cooking equipment and when they have access to a range of materials that they use to stand very directly for something else (as noted in Vygotsky, 1978). Children engaged in episodes of 'playing for real' tend to appear to be 'purposefully' engaged – sometimes for long periods – and seem to be performing an activity in their play at a higher level than might be expected from someone of their age and experience, such as cooking the dinner. I use the term 'purposefully' in inverted commas because it is the type of play that practitioners I have observed and spoken to tend to view highly. It is the kind of play where children seem to want to encounter reality (Moyles, 1989) rather than playfully pushing the boundaries of what is 'real' as we will see in the play episodes I am describing in terms of 'really playing'.

In 'playing for real', children are able to explore aspects of the 'real' world from different angles but without the emotional stress that goes with real life. This is not to say that strong emotions are absent from play but that children are not *really* trying to feed a small baby and get it to sleep and can choose to come out of role when they wish to. When 'playing for real', children may take on different but recognizable roles. In so doing, they are able to experience the world from different vantage points, particularly those of people who have control over them such as parents (Mead, 1967).

In order to illustrate what I mean by 'playing for real', I will now reflect on two observations. The first involves a group of 3-year-old children, one of whom is making roti using play dough in the home corner. The second observation involves a group of 4-year-old children who are using real potatoes as part of their play in the home corner. We will see in these two observations that the play is very recognizable from the real world of cooking and serving food.

Observation 1: Making roti (observation of children aged 3 in a nursery class)

Sarbjeet takes a lump of play dough into the home corner and uses it to make roti, speaking to me in Punjabi but interspersing it with 'special for you'. She demonstrates a high level of skill in forming the flat, round shapes with her hands. Sarbjeet increases the heat on the cooker by turning the knob. Then she stands with her hands on her hips as if waiting for time to pass by, seemingly annoyed at the length of time the roti are taking to cook. To cook them, she places the dough directly onto the 'heat', pressing them down slightly as if they are bubbling up. As she does this, she piles the cooked roti onto a plate very carefully and carries on cooking.

Daspurnima comes over to join her and they both stand at the cooker cooking roti, saying 'wait' as the roti cooks. Sometimes they have their arms folded, chatting together as if gossiping. When all the dough is cooked and a huge pile of roti is made, they bring it over to the table and I am invited to join the group (a group of five children including Sarbjeet and Daspurnima). Sarbjeet gives me a roti on a plate and spoons an imaginary blob next to it saying 'chutney'. She is concerned her roti are too hot to eat at the moment and says 'careful – hot' to make sure we all take care.

Observation 2: Play with potatoes (observation of children aged 4 in a private day nursery)

Today there are real potatoes in the home corner. This is interesting because the children run over to the cook in the kitchen with them and say they have found them and they belong in the kitchen. The cook seems a bit confused about this initially but then laughs and says 'That's OK!' It is very noticeable in this setting that the kitchen is visible to all the children and the children are able to watch the meals being cooked or engage in conversation with the cook about the food they are going to eat.

The children seem to have a very strong sense of real and pretend in the home corner as evidenced by the potatoes. Once they realize that they can have the real potatoes in the home corner, I notice a marked change in the play. Mary gets the toy knife and starts to cut one of the potatoes into pieces and puts the pieces into a saucepan. This is tricky given the lack of a sharp edge. Other children do this too but with a lesser degree of ability and there is a very purposeful air in the home corner. The cook supplies extra potatoes at the request of the children, who run over to the kitchen and tell her what they are doing.

The nursery manager brings over some real knives from the kitchen and the children become engrossed in cutting the potatoes and filling pans. Once full, Mary and Eva say that they need water in the pans to boil the potatoes. They have clearly seen this being done. A practitioner does not question this and puts some water in the water tray to enable the children to fill their pans with water (on top of the cut potatoes). The children are unable to access water from taps themselves owing to the building design. The children spend a long time at play – preparing, cooking and serving up food. The children comment on how the water is dirty now and talk about the need to peel the potatoes. Later, Mary says that she needs to get the water out of the pan like her mum does at home and takes the pans over to the water tray. Mary selects a sieve from a couple offered to her by the cook and takes it over to the water tray and drains her potatoes successfully. She then returns to the home corner.

What follows are some questions to reflect on in relation to these observations:

- How willing are practitioners to allow materials to be moved from one part of the room to another, even if it causes a degree of mess?
- How 'real' are practitioners willing to make play activities? In a play situation – one that is likely to be less regulated than a cooking activity, for instance – how willing are we to allow *real* knives, *real* sieving and *real* food, for example, in the home corner?

We might also question the extent to which the second observation, in particular, constitutes play. Arguably, these observations could be likened to an 'in-between activity' (Gura, 1996: 60) as they share many elements from the world of work as much as play. Certainly the skills developed in cutting the potatoes in Observation 2 appear more work-like than play-like (Wing, 1995; Gura, 1996).

- How willing are practitioners to allow children to eat food that has been placed in a play situation? My many observations in this area show that inevitably some children eat what is there.
- If we do allow such activity but are worried about the potential risks for health and safety, are we in danger of regulating such play to the extent that it becomes something that is not play?
- Can staff other than early years practitioners become involved in children's play as in Observation 2? In this example, the cook was involved in the children's play.

- Should real food be used as a play material? There are decisions to be made regarding whether this is ethical, given the experience of some people in the world of food insecurity. Alternatively, by having the opportunity to play with real food, children may be able to alleviate any anxieties they experience in relation to food and eating in a relaxed environment (Albon and Mukherji, 2008).

In my observations, the use of real food tends to result in children 'playing for real' whereas plastic food tends to result in play that might be regarded in terms of 'really playing'. Maybe this points to the need for both real *and* pretend items in play situations alongside the ability to mix media from around the play space(s). An example of this might be the child I observed putting dried pasta onto a plate that was available in the home corner and then carefully selecting a piece of red fabric from the workshop area to act as tomato sauce on top of it.

'Really playing'

'Really playing', I wish to argue, differs from 'playing for real' because here, children appear to be stretching conventional boundaries. In my data this relates to *what* food is eaten, but more usually, *how* it is eaten and the kinds of unwritten cultural rules that exist about what is acceptable behaviour during food events. It is play that can be likened to Hendy and Toon's (2001) thematic-fantasy play, but more than this, it is often characterized by its humour and playfulness. For Parker-Rees (1999: 61), playfulness enables us to cope with 'the tension between personal freedom and social constraints that characterizes all forms of interaction'. Further to this, 'really playing' can be linked to 'ludic' behaviours (Hutt et al., 1989) and Kalliala's (2006) notion of 'dizzy' play that turns the world upside down. It should be noted that the *Early Years Foundation Stage* (*EYFS*) (DfES, 2007) lacks reference to such humour and playfulness – the few references there are seem to relate to babies.

'Really playing' can be contrasted with 'good' play, which is encouraged by practitioners as it emphasizes turn-taking and following approved rules (e.g. King, 1992). Bakhtin (1984) discusses the important role played by the carnivalesque in subverting and making fun of authoritarianism, order, officialdom, narrow-minded seriousness, dogma and 'all that is finished and polished' (p. 3). Carnival is a time when there is temporary liberation from the established order of things and it is always accompanied by laughter. Thus, my conceptualization of some play episodes as 'really playing' seems to fit well with this.

Such playfulness is important as we can see in many examples in this book. Corsaro (1997) argues that playful activity is indicative of children's ability to create and participate in their own peer cultures. In addition to this, the sharing of comic situations and the camaraderie that this engenders may be significant as a precursor to forming close relationships (Dunn, 1988). Given the centrality of developing and sustaining positive relationships in early childhood practice (Elfer et al., 2003; Manning-Morton and Thorp, 2003), it would seem that practitioners should be seeking to maximize opportunities for 'really playing' in their settings.

But are there other benefits to playfulness? Meek (1985) builds on the work of Bateson, who believes that play is important in freeing children from the rigidity of rule-bound games and messages, and that this playfulness is essential from an evolutionary perspective as it enables the child to be adaptable and imagine 'What if?' In a similar way, Chukovsky (1968: 97) celebrates the 'intellectual effrontery' and 'topsy-turvy' nature of play. These topsy-turvies have educational value because, as Chukovsky (1968: 99) notes, 'The more aware the child is of the correct relationship of things, which he violates in his play, the more comical does this violation seem to him'.

Thus, in stretching the boundaries of what is possible, children are demonstrating their understandings of 'what might be' and, in so doing, generating new and creative understandings of the world. It would seem, then, that the playfulness and humour indicative in 'really playing' are important in the child's developing awareness of 'sense and nonsense', 'fact from fiction' and that which is 'socially tolerated' (Meek, 1985: 48). Similarly, Egan (1991) argues that in exploring the fantastic, children are able to discover the limits of their world and thus develop a greater understanding of reality.

What follows now are three observations of children 'really playing' where the play bears little relation to what we might, on reflection, view as 'usual conventions' – or are only recognizable in as much as they are opposite to what is usual. In reading these, you will see examples of carnivalesque behaviour and, in Observation 5, children exploring the unthinkable.

Observation 3: Feeding the pets (observation of children aged 3 and 4 in a nursery class)

Hanan gets a doll and takes it out of the high chair and then puts it to bed saying 'She's asleep now'. This paves the way for the toy cat to come onto the high chair. This results in peals of laughter from Hanan, Sarah and Ben, who has just arrived in the home corner. Ben gets the toy dog and puts it into the larger of the two high chairs and both he and Hanan feed their animals using spoons. All are laughing as they seem to know that this is not how you feed pets. I make a comment about Hanan's cat being in a high chair and Ben jokes 'That's not a high chair, silly – that's a low chair!' This play on words seems highly appropriate in a topsy-turvy world where pets eat at high chairs!

Ben and Hanan have their respective pets in the high chairs and are feeding the pets a range of foods. After trying each one, Ben says 'He [*i.e. the pet*] likes it'. Hanan is copying him. This becomes increasingly bizarre, with ice creams, cups of tea, chocolate cake, babies bottles of milk and, later, a clock and some clothing (etc.) offered and sometimes force-fed to the pets. The laughter increases as the food items get increasingly outrageous – as if each child is egging the other on to find something more and more inappropriate. Each time this is reinforced with the language 'He like it' accompanied by laughter at how preposterous this is. After a while a practitioner comes over and tells the children to be quieter.

Observation 4: Sicking up food mum has cooked at a party (observation of a group of children aged 3 and 4 in a nursery class)

In the home corner, Charlie, James, Nina and Furqan are playing together. Charlie says 'Let's pretend we are all eating this food at a party – you're the mum, Nina, and we don't want to eat it 'cos it's horrible and makes us sick'.

Every time Nina, as 'mum', presents food to her 'children', they are sick. James and Charlie shout 'Ugh – horrible' with Charlie making sick noises, with everyone accompanying this with laughter. Sarah and Zara join in as other 'mothers', putting on aprons as if to denote this status. All three girls serve up food only to have it refused and a pretence of regurgitation made. Sarah and Zara add a new dimension to the play because they make a pretence of being very offended by this action, telling the 'children' off. 'You just eat it all up and do what I say' says Zara. The more the 'children' are sick or refuse food, the more she and Sarah tell them to 'Eat it'. Their remonstrations with the 'children' are accompanied with wagging fingers and mock cross faces. Maybe the children are also playing out very real anxieties that occur during mealtimes, not least being told to eat foods even when they are not deemed palatable.

The play continues for a while and gets quite raucous. All the children – a cross-language/cultural group – seem to recognize that it is funny to refuse food in this way and that being sick – almost forcing this – is not to be borne. The biggest affront to civility and acceptance is to refuse food or let the cook feel it is horrible in some way. Some-how this is further intensified in the context of a party.

Observation 5: 'Pretend real' eating the dough baby (observation of children aged 3 and 4 in a nursery class)

Farrah is sitting at the dough table where some home corner equipment has been taken and makes a dough baby. She says 'I'm going to make a baby and cut it up and put it in my stew'. I obviously look disgusted and shocked, so she says 'You know it's not real – it isn't even pretend – it's *pretend real*'.

Maybe pretend is pretend, but it *is* real; 'pretend real', it seems, is when all sense of being real is suspended. At least I think this is her meaning. Farrah cuts the dough baby into pieces and puts it into the saucepan. She stirs the pan and Hamid laughs saying it's a 'nice baby' (taking a spoon to the pan).

I will now reflect on some of the challenges contained in these last three observations.

* Should practitioners get involved in this type of play?

For Edmiston (2008), when adults and children participate in pretend worlds *together*, there is an opportunity to co-author ethical identities as such play facilitates the exploration of different actions and ways of being in the world. Therefore, in play we can imagine identities that we might like to be or that make us fearful and in doing this, not only *enact* the socially unacceptable, such as sicking up food, but *evaluate* those actions. This is also useful when reflecting on the many observations collected of Farrah's play (such as Observation 5) because as well as exploring the unthinkable in making baby stew, there are many observations of her playing roles where she cares for babies and saves them from 'near death' experiences. When considering Observation 5 now, I wonder what might have happened if I had participated playfully with Farrah and Hamid – maybe as someone with special powers coming to save the baby. As Edmiston (2008) notes, when adults participate directly in children's pretend play, children are not abandoned to think ethically about the actions and feelings explored in their play on their own.

* But do *all* practitioners see such playfulness as valuable? Moreover, my observations show a tendency for some practitioners to become overly concerned with the level of noise and the possibility of chaos. One practitioner I observed was very concerned that children were using a plastic orange as something other than a food item eaten by humans and

some others were dismissive of such play as lacking any real educational purpose and as only valuable for the immediate sense of fun it engenders. In reflecting on play in this way, we need to ask ourselves whether play is valuable purely in terms of its future benefits for children or whether we should also be valuing the lived-time of children now (Polakow, 1992).

Grace and Tobin (1997) seem to address this issue when they draw on the work of Barthes in relation to pleasure. Barthes distinguishes between *plaisir* and *jouissance*, with the former signifying the more conservative, conformist notions of pleasure and the latter relating to the more playful, anti-authoritarian forms of pleasure. *Jouissance* happens less often in the classroom (or play-space) than *plaisir* as it is focused on the moment. Grace and Tobin (1997: 177) argue that in *jouissance*-like moments in the classroom 'the teacher temporarily disappeared, and the children were united in a spirit of camaraderie, a celebration of "otherness" organized around laughter'.

This seems a useful way to think about joining in when children are 'really playing': a temporary liberation from the usual order of things. Certainly, in my own playful rejection of food and drink in the play episode outlined earlier, I felt a strong sense of truly sharing in the 'dizziness' of the children's play (Kalliala, 2006) in ways that cheerful acceptance of a cup of tea, keeping to the general order of things and 'playing for real' would not have engendered. However, it is interesting to reflect on *when* we might think it is acceptable and if it *is*, the *extent* to which we fully engage with this type of play.

- Is it possible to plan for such play? Would it cease to be 'really playing' if preplanned by adults? I suspect that it would cease to be play. Like Gura (1996), I am suspicious of adult constructs such as 'structured play' and think it is possible to plan for episodes of 'playing for real' more than 'really playing'!

Conclusion

My intention in writing this chapter has been to encourage reflection on play, which I have suggested might be categorized on a continuum of 'playing for real' and 'really playing'. In doing this, my wish has been to highlight the need to preserve both types of play. Each has value and exposes its own challenges for early childhood practice as I have outlined.

My observations and reflections on these show a tendency for practitioners to prize 'playing for real' more highly than 'really playing'. This may be because it is easier to plan for such play and, consequently, it may be more amenable to adult control. Possibly this makes it a more comfortable activity for practitioners to engage in with children when compared to 'really playing'. However, I hope this chapter has encouraged readers to reflect on the challenges 'playing for real' poses for practitioners, not least how 'real' play can be made to be and still be called 'play'.

By way of contrast, engaging in 'really playing' may mean vanquishing the usual order of things. In order to truly be part of such play, practitioners may need to suspend, albeit momentarily, their more powerful position when compared to young children. The *EYFS* (DfES, 2007) contains little reference to such playfulness – to the mercurial ability to turn the world on its head and laugh at it. Maybe this is a good thing, because such playfulness resists easy documentation. But its omission ignores the importance of humour and the role it plays in communality and ongoing relationships.

Questions for further thinking and reflection

1. Reflecting on your own attitudes, which kinds of play do you feel most comfortable with and why?
2. Reflect on observations you have made of young children's play. Where would you put them on a continuum of 'playing for real' and 'really playing'?

Acknowledgement

I am indebted to the practitioners, parents and children who made this research possible and who shared their reflections on practice with me.

References

Albon, D. and Mukherji, P. (2008) *Food and Health in Early Childhood*. London: Sage Publications.

Bakhtin, M. (1984) *Rabelias and His World* (trans. by H. Iswolsky). Bloomington, IN: Indiana University Press.

Chukovsky, K. (1968) *From Two to Five*. Berkeley, CA: University of California Press.

Corsaro, W. (1997) *The Sociology of Childhood*. London: Sage Publications.

Department for Education and Skills (DIES) (2007) *The Early Years Foundation Stage*. Nottingham: DfES.

Dunn, J. (1988) *The Beginnings of Social Understanding*. Oxford: Blackwell.

Edmiston, B. (2008) *Forming Ethical Identities in Early Childhood Play*. Abingdon: Routledge.

Egan, K. (1991) *Primary Understanding: Education in Early Childhood*. London: Routledge.

Elfer, P., Goldschmeid, E. and Selleck, D. (2003) *Key Persons in the Nursery: Building Relationships for Quality Provision*. London: David Fulton.

Grace, D. and Tobin, J. (1997) Carnival in the classroom: elementary students making videos, in J. Tobin (ed.) *Making a Place for Pleasure in Early Childhood Education*. New Haven, CT: Yale University Press.

Gura, P. (1996) *Resources for Early Learning: Children, Adults and Stuff*. London: Hodder & Stoughton.

Hendy, L. and Toon, L. (2001) *Supporting Drama and Imaginative Play in the Early Years*. Buckingham: Open University Press.

Hutt, S.J., Tyler, S., Hutt, C. and Christopherson, H. (1989) *Play, Exploration and Learning: A Natural History of the Pre-School*. London: Routledge.

Kalliala, M. (2006) *Play Culture in a Changing World*. Maidenhead: Open University Press.

King, N. (1992) The impact of context on the play of young children, in S. Kessler and B. Swadener (eds) *Reconceptualising the Early Childhood Curriculum: Beginning the Dialogue*. New York: Teachers College Press.

Manning-Morton, J. and Thorp, M. (2003) *Key Times for Play*. Maidenhead: Open University Press.

Mead, G.H. (1967) *Mind, Self and Society*. Chicago, IL: Chicago University Press.

Meek, M. (1985) Play and paradoxes: some considerations of imagination and language, in G. Wells and J. Nicholls (eds) *Language and Learning: An Interactional Perspective*. Lewes: Falmer Press.

Moyles, J.R. (1989) *Just Playing? The Role and Status of Play in Early Childhood Education*. Milton Keynes: Oxford University Press.

Parker-Rees, R. (1999) Protecting playfulness, in L. Abbott and H. Moylett (eds) *Early Education Transformed*. London: Falmer Press.

Polakow, V. (1992) *The Erosion of Childhood*. Chicago, IL: University of Chicago Press.

Vygotsky, L.S. (1978) *Mind in Society: The Development of Higher Psychological Processes*. Cambridge, MA: Harvard University Press.

Wing, L.A. (1995) Play is not the work of the child: young children's perceptions of work and play, *Early Childhood Education Research Quarterly*, 10(2): 223–47.

Chapter 2

Learning to play, or playing to learn? Children's participation in the cultures of homes and settings

Liz Brooker

Chapter introduction

Liz Brooker is Reader Emerita in Early Childhood at University College London Institute of Education. Liz was an early years teacher for many years, and her interest in children's home experiences and transitions to school stemmed from her own work with children and families. In this chapter, she interrogates accepted ideas around play and suggests that practitioners must examine their conscious and unconscious beliefs. She examines how beliefs about play are communicated and how they might provide 'bridges' for children, families and communities.

A time when play was king

> There was a time when play was king and early childhood was its domain.
>
> (Paley 2004: 4)

This time, like most golden-age theories, proves hard to define and demonstrate despite its vivid presence in the mind. Theories of *learning* have evolved wherever human communities have had sufficient leisure and luxury to turn their attention away from the primary goals of subsistence and survival towards the decidedly secondary goals of improving the minds of their children; but theories of *play* are both recent and anomalous. Modern educational theory is often described as commencing with Locke's (1690) account of the child as a *tabula rasa* or 'blank slate' to be inscribed with adult knowledge, an account that went unchallenged until the publication of the Romantic proposals of Rousseau (in *Emile*, 1762) and the subsequent pioneering efforts to establish child-centred education, initiated by Pestalozzi and Froebel (Nutbrown et al. 2008). These early kindergartens were characterized, not by the 'free-flow play' advocated by late-twentieth-century educators, but by carefully sequenced learning activities such as Froebel's 'occupations', along with virtuous habits such as gardening and handicrafts (Anning 1997). Montessori's (1912) manual prescribing her 'scientific pedagogy' was precise as to the types and sequencing of 'didactic material' which should be presented to children, and the 'intellectual work' (not play) which was to occupy their day.

The belief that 'well-planned play . . . is a key way in which young children learn' (QCA 2000: 25) not only arrived relatively late in the history of theories of instruction, but has remained relatively 'local' to European and English-speaking communities. Its appearance marked the convergence of a number of emergent streams of thought: streams originating in the child study movement and the growth of developmental psychology as a discipline (Smith 2006); in the radical democratizing proposals of Dewey (1916) and the experimental learning environment created by Susan Isaacs (1929); in the ethological studies in the 1950s which prompted the first experimental studies of the impact of play on the cognition of human children (Sylva et al. 1976) and in the gradual dissemination of the work of both Piaget (1951) and Vygotsky (1933). In England, once the liberal-progressivism of the 1960s had taken hold (CACE 1967), the orthodoxy that children 'learn through play' seemed unassailable, even if actual practice rarely matched the rhetoric (Bennett et al. 1997). By the early 2000s, belief in play as an instrument of early learning dominated the pre-school curricula of European, American and Australasian nations, and had begun to infiltrate the curricula of former colonies with very different cultural traditions (Hamza 2009).

These then are the kingdoms where, for a brief historical period, play has been king, and these are the early childhood domains where it has reigned. In other eras and in less privileged parts of the world such ideas have had little purchase, but the scientific knowledge which informs dominant discourses pays little attention to such places – a fact which, as educators, we should always keep in mind.

Learning as participation: a more inclusive stance?

This Western advocacy of 'learning through play' has been located by socio-cultural theorists (Rogoff et al. 1996) within a broader pendulum swing of ideas which is characterized by periodic shifts in preference from adult-led to child-led theories of instruction. The trajectory of this pendulum is bounded by the oppositional beliefs in learning as *transmission* (adult-led) and learning as *acquisition* (child-led). The adult-led mode is universally recognized as *pedagogy* – intentional actions to bring about learning – while the child-led mode will be generally recognized as *play* – voluntary, exploratory and spontaneous (Smith 2006), but may or may not be viewed as instructional.

The persistent tension between these opposed models can be resolved, Rogoff suggests, by defining learning differently: as the *transformation of participation in cultural activities*. Such a transformation sees a child's performance in culturally valued activities change over time from that of novice to that of expert, as a result of drawing on the affordances of the environment, under the guidance of more experienced individuals:

> Guided participation involves adults or children challenging, constraining and supporting children in the process of posing and solving problems – through material arrangements of children's activities and responsibilities as well as through interpersonal communication, with children observing and participating at a comfortable but slightly challenging level.
>
> (Rogoff 1990: 18)

Cognitive development, in other words, occurs in the course of 'children's everyday involvement in social life' (1990: 18), including their intent participation in all the activities which they see other children, and adults, performing. Such participation, Rogoff argues, depends for its effectiveness on the *intersubjectivity* or 'shared understanding' which exists between the expert and the novice (1990: 71). The activities may include 'play' (as in most Western childhoods) but they may equally include some form of 'work', or of didactic instruction. Research into this broader conception of learning was until recently associated with the non-formal learning activities of children in developing societies such as Kenya (Harkness 1980), Liberia (Lave and Wenger 1991) or Cameroon (Nsamenang and Lamb 1998) rather than with the learning of children in industrial nations. When the research gaze shifts to Western societies, and to institutions such as schools and pre-schools, a tension emerges: is the apprenticeship model described by Rogoff and others equally effective in developing school-related knowledge such as literacy, mathematics or science, or is it only applicable to learning skills such as fishing or weaving, childminding or goat-herding? Socio-cultural theory challenges us to attempt to answer that question through looking carefully at what children learn, and how they learn it, in environments such as schools and pre-schools, where different cultural activities prevail.

The following sections propose that a model of learning through participation in cultural activities can encompass a pedagogy of play, along with other pedagogical models, and thus can accommodate the diverse cultural contexts in which children learn.

Whose culture, whose activities?

Rather than attempt to explore the multiple meanings and implications of 'culture', it can be helpful to revert to the simple reminder, by the English cultural critic Raymond Williams, that 'Culture in all of its early uses was a noun of process: the tending of something, basically crops or animals' (1973: 87). By extension, as Michael Cole argues, it often describes the construction of an environment for growing up in: 'an artificial environment in which young organisms could be provided optimal conditions for growth' (Cole 1998: 15). Since families and communities, and the caregivers and educators charged with bringing up young children, hold implicit goals and values for the kinds of adults these children will become, and implicit theories of how to achieve these goals, the 'cultures' provided for young children are inevitably shaped towards these ends. Family and community cultures, like school and pre-school cultures, are fashioned to bring about the desired outcomes for children, although these outcomes will vary from one group to another. Different families may provide an environment which prioritizes play, or one which prioritizes work, as the appropriate activity for children; one which fosters deference and compliance, or assertiveness and challenge; conformity or non-conformity; independence or interdependence (Göncü et al. 2000). Thus, children's enculturation in their home communities will have taught them distinctive participation repertoires.

Educators, similarly, build their environments and their practice on their conscious or unconscious beliefs about what is best for children: the knowledge and skills they should acquire, and the optimal ways to acquire them. The early learning environments beloved of Western educators communicate a coherent system of beliefs about young children's learning. Children 'need' (we tend to believe) sand and water, paints and crayons, blocks and climbing structures, These 'material arrangements of children's activities and responsibilities' (Rogoff 1990: 18) are the physical embodiment of our beliefs about learning, and are very often grounded in the importance of play for childhood.

In consequence, as children enter their first group care setting, or make the transition to a subsequent one, they encounter a plethora of new cultural activities and new ways of learning. They must, in Rogoff's terms, gradually transform their participation in these new activities in order to become an expert in the setting. Learning how to learn in a new setting is a major challenge for children, especially when the values, goals and cultural activities of the setting contrast starkly with those of the home (Brooker 2008).

The status and function of play, for the different stakeholders in any setting – peers, parents, practitioners – are factors which inform the range of cultural activities in which children must acquire expertise.

Practitioners, parents and the pedagogy of play

In England, despite the powerful mantra of learning-through-play (Bennett et al. 1997), early educators complain of top-down pressures from statutory subject-based curricula for school-aged children, and increasingly for pre-schoolers (Soler and Miller 2003), prompting ongoing struggles to incorporate traditional early childhood ideologies into the recommended pedagogy. Tensions lie along several axes: between free choice and compulsion for children; between adult-initiated and child-initiated activities; between structured and unstructured learning tasks; and between convergent and divergent forms of knowledge.

Ultimately, the 'struggle' described by Soler and Miller (2003) is not simply between different theories of learning but between different views of children: as immature, inexperienced and ignorant people whose learning depends on the tutoring of more mature, experienced and knowledgeable adults, or as competent individuals who are capable of making meaning from their experiences of the world, in collaboration with others and with the support of cultural tools. And since such views are themselves fundamentally *cultural*, in the sense that they have been constructed through experience from the beliefs of previous generations, and transmitted through early experiences in the family and community, these tensions have their roots within families and education systems, and are made visible when children pass from their home culture to that of the pre-school. As a result, practitioners often describe pressure from parents to 'sit them down and teach them' as the most pressing constraint on their practice, while at the same time, many parents feel disappointed that their educational aspirations for their children are unmet (Brooker 2002). Where are children in this debate, and what do they make of their experiences?

Learning through cultural activities at 2, 3 and 4

This section presents examples of children's early learning – their participation in cultural activities within different play-based contexts – in a range of English settings. They illustrate some of the ways that children learn through participation in the environments they experience before school, and in their first encounter with formal schooling; and the extent to which practitioners' understandings of this learning may be aligned with those of parents.

The episodes have been chosen to illustrate some of the complexity surrounding this issue. In the case of younger children, for instance, there may be a broad consensus between parents and practitioners on the goals for their development: most adults want children to develop at their own pace, to demonstrate well-being and to display a positive sense of self. As children approach school age, however, there may be a growing concern for children to show they are acquiring academic knowledge and skills; a growing division between a focus on the 'basics' of literacy and numeracy, and a recognition of the value of broader life-skills; and a growing polarization in beliefs about the most effective ways for children to learn. The children and parents presented here exemplify some of these issues.

All three observations were undertaken in the course of studies of children's transitions (Brooker 2002, 2008). The first two snapshots occurred in the pre-school environment of a London children's centre offering early education in a free-play setting for children from 6 months to 5 years, as well as family and community support services. The third case study was located in the 'reception' classroom of a primary school in an English provincial town, in which 'play-based learning' was directed towards planned curriculum objectives. The parents and teachers of all three children were interviewed in the course of these studies, and their perspectives highlight the different ways that play and learning may be interpreted by adults from different backgrounds.

Davey appropriates the outdoor environment

Davey, aged 2 years, was observed in his fifth week in the toddler room of a children's centre. Until recently he had spent most of his time, in his dad's company, in a small flat with no access to the outdoors, so the encounter with an open-plan environment full of strange adults and children presented him with many new learning challenges and a range of unfamiliar cultural activities – climbing and building, painting and modelling, music groups, malleable materials and simply digging outdoors. The observation was as follows:

> In the garden
> He is pushing a very heavy wooden cart, making a real effort to push, then stop and re-direct the steering, then move forward again. He looks in to check the contents: two paint brushes; moves forward a bit further then removes the brushes from the truck and walks purposefully to the back of the garden to the shed, which he then 'paints' with the brushes. Turns round, beaming with confidence and self-importance,

and addresses other children (apparently to tell them what he is doing), pointing to the shed wall. Moves away a few feet to 'paint' the low posts round the sand pit, and then walks away to the slide.

Davey's growing participation in the cultural activities offered by the nursery environment is clear. The garden contains many affordances which Davey is identifying for himself, through observation of other children or simple experiment. These resources, which are typical of a traditional 'free-flow' nursery environment, obviously make sense to Davey, and to his dad, who reflected that

> He teaches himself a lot of things I think because he's quite inquisitive and he tries to find out how things work and if he can't he'll go and ask someone.

Davey's play, could be described as work-like and potentially gendered. His mode of exploration is an approved *cultural activity* in the nursery environment, and is actively promoted by his key worker:

> I know that Davey likes his outdoor space and he doesn't have it at home, he doesn't have access to it . . . so the first thing I do is go outside, let them be where they want to be – and he's got the things he likes – the sand, the trucks, the tractor.

Larissa: regulating peer relationships

In the kindergarten section of the same children's centre, 3-year-old Larissa was another subject of the transitions study. Larissa and her friends were also regularly found playing out of doors, and the goals of their 'cultural activity' were those of their peer culture. This observation was made in Larissa's fourth week in kindergarten.

> Larissa prances across the open space, followed closely by Saskia, and at a distance by Millie, Eva and finally Cara. Larissa and Saskia sit on a bench and the next two join them while Cara hangs back. All except Cara now begin to skip and dance in a circle, apparently spontaneously, although they stop, confer and start up again more than once. At some point the activity becomes 'My Little Pony' as they toss imaginary manes ('Mine is pink' says Larissa).
>   Following Larissa's lead, the four girls now sing 'Horsey, horsey, don't you stop' as they skip in a circle with knees raised, tossing

their pony heads. But Cara intervenes, apparently making a bid for leadership: 'This is a butterfly song, right? Everybody, this is a butterfly song!'

Larissa stops, stares briefly and loudly begins, 'Horsey, Horsey, don't you stop . . .'; Saskia, Millie and Eva join in, with some giggling and sideways glances suggesting that they are aware of the way that power is being exercised.

Larissa's key worker, Anessa, is aware of the power relationships in the peer group:

I knew from the start she was quite a popular child, everybody wanted to be her friend and they'd fight over her, it's like she's the leader of the pack and everyone does what she says.

If Anessa is concerned by this, she doesn't say so, because her goal has been to build Larissa's confidence. Like the staff in this setting, Larissa's mother describes 'learning social skills' as a priority of early education,

In this centre, parents talk daily to their child's key worker, and meet regularly to review a portfolio of documented activities, so that their goals for the children are discussed and shared. For the 3–year–olds, these shared goals include establishing a secure sense of identity, and making friends. To a superficial gaze, Larissa and her friends are 'learning' in the ways that the setting promotes, although a closer view prompts concerns as to what is actually being learned: the 'pleasure' of playing is here closely bound up with the exercise of power within the peer group. For now, however, Larissa's social learning – accomplished through participation in traditional, girl-group outdoor games – satisfies the expectations of her mother as well as her professional educators.

Khiernssa: 'Learning cultures' at home and school

Khiernssa was one of sixteen 4–year–old children whose home and school learning was observed during their first year in an English primary school, as part of a study of the culture and pedagogy experienced by children of diverse cultural backgrounds (Brooker 2002). As the youngest child of highly aspirational Bangladeshi parents, she had experienced a formal 'home' curriculum which included explicit tuition in school-like knowledge, and was also steeped in the cultural activities of her family and community.

With regard to the former, she received daily tutoring from her father and siblings and was learning to recite alphabets in Bengali, Arabic and English, as well as to count, add and subtract. In terms of family and community knowledge, Khiernssa was apprenticed to her father's traditional activities (growing vegetables on an allotment, tending pigeons and chickens in the back yard) as well as to the activities of the mosque and mosque school; and she was equally at home in the world of the Bollywood films which she watched with her mother every day, joining in the songs. Within her own community context, she was an active and accomplished participant.

On entry to school – a colourful welcoming environment whose play-based pedagogy was rooted in an ethos of 'having fun' – Khiernssa was assessed against the school entry profile, and by additional research instruments (Brooker 2002). On the former she appeared rather 'unready' for the learning activities that were on offer: she was indisposed to engage actively with toys, games and picture books, unwilling to get dirty or messy, and unresponsive to adult invitations to 'play' or 'choose'. On more formal assessments she achieved some high scores, the direct result of her home instruction. But her transformation in participation in the learning culture of the classroom was slow and reluctant. When interviewed at the end of her first term, she expressed her resistance to some important learning opportunities:

Researcher: Can you think what you like best about school?
Khiernssa: Home corner! They got babies! – I like real babies, I like Rufia's baby, I like Amadur's baby . . .
Researcher: Is there anything at school you really *don't* like?
Khiernssa: I don't like play water: they boys. And sand: they boys.

(see Brooker 2006)

Conversations with her mother confirmed that her views of learning were at one with her daughter's, and at odds with the preferred pedagogy of the classroom:

She has to work harder, you have to stop her playing . . .

The setting offered many different opportunities for learning, both formal (instructional) and informal (adult-led or child-initiated), but most of these opportunities fell outside Khiernssa's cultural repertoire. Her teacher's carefully planned strategies for experiential learning made little sense to her.

The most challenging examples of the 'play pedagogy' in this setting occurred when the staff made the greatest effort to be playful and 'child-friendly': setting up an area as a 'monster pit' in which children were intended to scare and excite each other, or a 'jungle' in which they could roar and play with furry tiger toys; outings to a park or playground where children were encouraged to swing high, spin fast and race down hills. Khiernssa and her girlfriends viewed such activities with a mixture of fear and disdain, yet they were at the heart of the setting's playful pedagogy, a visible demonstration of a belief in childhood as a time for fun and excitement, and children as motivated by novelty and challenge. The classroom's learning activities at no point resembled those of Khiernssa's home, and in consequence her parents' own instructional efforts remained largely invisible and unacknowledged.

Learning cultures

Documenting children's learning through documenting their participation in cultural activities is an idea which proves highly problematic in practice, because of the very different cultural activities, beliefs and values which make up the complex worlds of children living in plural societies. The activities found in children's home cultures change over time, and vary with children's age as well as their gender and ethnicity; and over time, children construct their own hybrid cultures, which incorporate the values of their families, peers and school. But the critical moments, like the start of school, when children encounter new and strange 'learning cultures' are times when some children fail to understand the rules for participation, or choose to participate in avoidant activities, using the solidarity offered by their peer culture to resist the agenda offered by adults.

If children are to continue learning in all the cultural contexts they experience, and make connections between the ways they participate in each, the adults who construct these environments must allow some of their most deeply-held convictions to be challenged by other views: beliefs about childhood and the role and status of children; about goals and values for children's present and future lives; and about the nature of learning itself. Research on the pedagogy of play, since the 1970s, has moved from the laboratory into the classroom, and from the classroom into the family and community. We could now try, in Rogoff's terms, to 'provide bridges from known to new' (1990: 65), for the adults as well as children whose learning is at issue.

Questions for further thinking and reflection

1.   What set of beliefs do you think the early years setting in which you work (or one that you are familiar with) communicates about young children's learning?

2.   How might early years settings enable smoother transitions for young children from the context and culture of home and family?

References

Anning, A. (1997) *The First Years at School*, 2nd edn. Buckingham: Open University Press.

Bennett, N., Wood, E. and Rogers, S. (1997) *Teaching through Play*. Buckingham: Open University Press.

Brooker, L. (2002) *Starting School: Young Children Learning Cultures*. Buckingham: Open University Press.

Brooker, L. (2006) From home to the home corner: observing children's identity-maintenance in early childhood settings, *Children & Society* 20(2), April: 116–27.

Brooker, L. (2008) *Supporting Transitions in the Early Years*. Maidenhead: McGraw-Hill.

CACE (Central Advisory Council for Education) (1967) *Children and Their Primary Schools [The Plowden Report]*. London: HMSO.

Cole, M. (1998) Culture in development, in M. Woodhead, D. Faulkner and K. Littleton (eds) *Cultural Worlds of Early Childhood*. London: Routledge/The Open University.

Dewey, J. (1916) *Democracy and Education*. New York: Basic Books.

Göncü, A., Mistry J. and Mosier, C. (2000) Cultural variations in the play of toddlers, *International Journal of Behavioural Development*, 24(3): 321–9.

Hamza, S. (2009) *Contextualising Policy in Early Childhood Education*. Jos, Nigeria: University of Jos.

Harkness, S. (1980) The cultural context of child development, in C. Super and S. Harkness (eds) *New Directions for Child Development*, 8: 7–13.

Isaacs, S. (1929) *The Nursery Years*. London: Routledge & Kegan Paul.

Lave, J. and Wenger, E. (1991) *Situated Learning: Legitimate Peripheral Participation*. Cambridge: Cambridge University Press.

Locke, J. (1690) *An Essay Concerning Human Understanding*, reprinted 1841, London: Tegg.

Montessori, M. (1912) *The Montessori Method: Scientific Pedagogy*. London: Heinemann.

Nsamenang, B. and Lamb, M. (1998) Socialization of Nso children in the Bamenda Grassfields of Northwest Cameroon, in M. Woodhead, D. Faulkner, and K. Littleton (eds) *Cultural Worlds of Early Childhood*. London: Routledge/The Open University.

Nutbrown, C., Clough, P. and Selbie, P. (2008) *Early Childhood Education: History, Philosophy and Experience*. London: Sage.

Paley, V.G. (2004) A *Child's Work: The Importance of Fantasy Play*. Chicago: University of Chicago Press.

Piaget, J. (1951) *Play, Dreams and Imitation in Childhood*. London: Routledge & Kegan Paul.

Qualifications & Curriculum Authority (QCA) (2000) *Curriculum Guidance for the Foundation Stage*. London: QCA.

Rogoff, B. (1990) *Apprenticeship in Thinking: Cognitive Development in Social Context*. Oxford: Oxford University Press.

Rogoff, B., Matusov, E. and White, C. (1996) Models of teaching and learning: participation in a community of learners, in D. Olson and N. Torrance (eds) *The Handbook of Education and Human Development: New Models of Learning, Teaching and Schooling*. Oxford: Blackwell.

Rousseau, J-J. (1762) *Emile* (Book 2), reprinted 1974. London: Dent.

Smith, P. (2006) Evolutionary foundations and functions of play: an overview, in
A. Goncii and S. Gaskins (eds) *Play and Development: Evolutionary, Sociocultural and
Functional Perspectives*. Mahwah, NJ: Lawrence Erlbaum Associates.

Soler, J. and Miller, L. (2003) The struggle for early childhood curricula: a comparison of
the English Foundation Stage Curriculum, *Te Whaariki* and Reggio Emilia, *International
Journal of Early Years Education*, 11(1): 57–67.

Sylva, K., Bruner, J. and Genova, P. (1976) The role of play in the problem-solving
of children 3–5 years old, in J. Bruner, A. Jolly and K. Sylva (eds) *Play: Its Role in
Development and Evolution*. Harmondsworth: Penguin.

Vygotsky, L. (1933) Play and its role in the mental development of the child, reprinted,
in J. Bruner, A. Jolly and K. Sylva (eds) *Play: Its Role in Development and Evolution*.
Harmondsworth: Penguin.

Williams, R. (1973) *Keywords*. London: Fontana.

Chapter 3

Domestic play collaborations in diverse family contexts

Catherine Ann Cameron, Giuliana Pinto, Beatrice Accorti Gamannossi, Roger Hancock and Sombat Tapanya

Chapter introduction

The international study described in this chapter stems from a collaboration involving researchers across five countries. Videos of the domestic play of five 30-month-old girls were analysed along with field notes and parental interviews. The observations of this five little girls study contribute to greater understanding of the domestic play of very young children and the different ways in which they are supported by their caregivers. The authors conclude by considering the implications of the study for professionals working with children in early years settings, highlighting the importance of culture and context in providing play opportunities.

Introduction

Play has been described as the 'work' of children: Paley (2004) offers engaging, persuasive demonstrations of fantasy play as the medium, bar none, for working through questions of social developmental import, solving both intellectual and relational problems in a preschool classroom. Many theorists, researchers and practitioners agree that play creates building blocks for cognitive, linguistic and socio-emotional development, reduces stress and enhances problem solving (Bornstein, Haynes, Legler, O'Reilly & Painter, 1997; Dube et al., 2009; Elkind, 2007; Roskos & Christie, 2000; Singer, Golinkoff & Hirsh-Pasek, 2006). Berk, Mann and Ogan (2006) highlight the efficacy of play in the development of self-regulation, a critical predictor of academic success; and Nicolopoulou, McDowell and Brockmeyer (2006) and Trionfi and Reese (2009) report significant benefits of pretend play for narrative development, also a critical academic feat. Language may also set off a process of differentiation between planning and enacting early pretence play (Musatti, Veneziano & Maye, 1998).

Studies of very young children's play are disadvantaged because researchers, being adults, have difficulties 'seeing' what they are studying from a child's point of view. Studies of younger children therefore rarely generate 'inside information' as can studies of older children's play, where participants might provide some information on their perspectives. Fromberg and Bergen (1998) carefully and fully laid out a wide range of perspectives on play across the developmental spectrum, the large variety of contexts in which play can be identified, and the meaning that can be made of play in all its formats in healthy development. Following Gomez and Martin-Andrade (2005, p. 140), we treat diverse forms of symbolic play (imaginative, pretence, make-believe and fantasy play) synonymously.

The present socio-ecological study of toddlers in their homes sheds light on variations on themes they draw. This chapter focuses on the domestic play of five children: their play-related interactions with caregivers and the play of very young children at home. We additionally explore caregivers' roles as supporters of the play. Our observations and analysis are influenced by Haight and Miller's (1993) view of how caregivers guide pretend play, and Lillard's (2007) report of mothers entering into such play with their very young children. We selected play episodes the children freely engaged in (although they might be influenced by a caregiver in some small way, even by simply providing a toy or receptacle or just showing an interest). We examined engagements where the children acted 'as if', focusing on symbolic play, partly because it is relatively easily agreed upon as different from other play forms, simply requiring that the child be engaged in representational activity with adult reality held more or less at bay.

Methods

Participants

Five families with 30-month-old girls were contacted by local researchers in Thailand, Italy, Peru, the US and Turkey. These toddlers were selected in their local communities by members of an international team of researchers investigating strong and thriving early childhood beginnings.

Procedures

Following a preliminary home visit to explain the visual methods of the study and potential limitations to anonymity, caregivers were interviewed about their approaches toward childrearing, and provided with information in advance of the filming of a *day in the life of their child*. Each child was filmed for a full waking day by two researchers who additionally took field notes and drew maps of the home context. Colleagues then selected 'significant' segments from these videos to make a half-hour compilation video containing five or six illustrative clips of the child's day for parents to reflect upon.

Analytic procedures regarding play

Two team members reviewed the video footage, field notes and home plans, identifying all instances of play. These examples were then considered for their potential to reveal: 1) the diverse roles the children played in their self-selected activities, 2) efforts made to enlist participation of other family members, 3) the locations and 4) the materials chosen for the play. The selected play passage from each day was first analysed by one of the investigators most closely allied with the local context, and then these passages were conjointly analysed by the whole team, bringing a range of cultural perspectives to an understanding of children's play.

Findings

The following observations were selected from the play during the five days to provide a sense of the many ways the children played within their domestic contexts, and the situations giving rise to this.

Italy

Doll-feeding play.
    After lunch Beatrice, in her play, furnishes the small balcony of her family's apartment and carefully positions a low seat near her large doll 'Coccolone'. A doll-feeding sequence ensues.
    Beatrice calls her mother's attention to her doll-feeding. Mother, entering into the play, makes a suggestion ('Shall we put his bib on?') that Beatrice accepts. Mother leaves the balcony to find a bib, asking Bea from the kitchen if she wants to put the bib on the doll herself. Beatrice hurries to the kitchen to get the bib and makes several attempts to put it on the doll, but without success. Ultimately, she asks her mother to do it. Mother helps by holding the doll in her arms while Bea puts the bib on, and says, 'I'll pick him up, put it on. His head is too big! Pull! Look, he has an ear . . . Here he is! Shall we put him here?'
    Mother places the doll back on the chair and hands Beatrice a small bowl and spoon.
    Moving towards an equal involvement in the play, Beatrice and her mother collaboratively establish a common goal of feeding the doll. They assemble the accoutrements and create a suitable context, fully engaging Beatrice while

her mother frees herself to proceed with cooking the family meal. Beatrice shows no discomfort in not managing to get the bib on the doll.

> Mum: *That's his food. Listen, Mum is busy now: won't you feed him?* (Entering into play.)
> Bea: *His food* (starting feeding the doll with the spoon). *Gnam!*
> Mum: *How hungry that little boy is!* (Continuing in the child's world of play.)

Beatrice feeds Coccolone, then pretends she is eating too.

> Mum: (going back and forth to the kitchen): *I am hungry too!* (Linking Beatrice's play to real needs.)
> Bea: *It's finished.*
> Mum: *Such a good boy! Who is the best at eating, Beatrice or Coccolone?* (Again linking play to real needs.)

Beatrice goes in the kitchen then comes back onto the balcony, continuing to feed the doll. She wipes the doll's mouth with the bib. Then she pretends that some food fell on the floor – 'The food, yes! That's ice cream!' – 'pretends to pick it up and put it in the bowl and then continues feeding.

> Bea: (feeding Coccolone): *Here you are!* (Still playing.).
> Bea: *I eat! I eat! Mum, I eat!* (Leaving play to address her own needs.)

Beatrice stands up and follows her mother into the bedroom, still carrying the bowl and spoon.

This example shows Beatrice internalising values connected with eating events in her family culture. When she carefully applies the bib on the doll and feeds her with precise hand movements, gently wiping away imaginary mess from the face, she evinces skills in play, potentially standing 'a head taller' (Vygotsky, 1967). It is as though she is being inducted into the norms and values of a gourmet approach to food, often perceived as particularly Italian. When she ate her midday meal with her parents, the qualities and origins of food were discussed; the parents recognise Beatrice's likes and dislikes. Encouragement to articulate such values has been noted in a study of families in urban Italy, where the researchers reported the active role the children played in their own socialisation (Pontecorvo, Fasulo & Sterponi, 2001), proposing the concept of 'mutual apprentices'. So, she is encouraged in pretend play with food both by parents' interactions and traditions (mother is preparing a real meal while Beatrice feeds the doll), and by their providing a context rich in materials and cues for playing.

Thailand

Cooking with earth.

Earlier in the day, while playing in parallel, Gai observed her sister stirring and grinding earth with a mortar and pestle in the family's outdoor cooking area. During this earlier play, Gai sat alongside a table where her sister was using a small shovel to put earth into a toy truck and boat.

After her nap, Gai is encouraged to go outside and she returns to the table pictured above. Her grandmother and sister encourage her with verbal directives from the sidelines. Gai plays on her own, stirring earth in the mortar and creating a dish for a muddy meal. The earlier parallel play had engaged her for almost 15 minutes. Her more solitary (yet monitored by Grandmother) play on the tabletop lasted four minutes.

> Grandmother: *Come sit over here, child. Don't use the water. Mom will spank you. Dad is coming. He will ask 'Have you been playing with water?'* . . . *You look busy.* (Not actually playing, but stimulating play by suggesting Gai is busy.)

(Gai adds ingredients and engages in pounding with pestle.)

> Grandmother: *Use the small spoon to scoop it.* (Support for Gai's skills within play.) *It is where [the dog] Kae is lying. Don't add water. It will splash on your face.*

(Gai stirs and lifts ingredients with spoon.)

> Grandmother: *It's better to pound.* (Again, a focus on skill but serving to maintain play.)

(Gai pounds with a cup in the mortar.)

In Thai households a mortar and a pestle are commonly used to prepare chili paste for making a curry, a chilidish, or papaya salad. Gai is likely envisioning one of these as she plays.

> Grandmother: *Take the cup out or you will break it.*

(Grandmother walks over to remove the white plastic cup from the mortar.)

> Grandmother: *Scrape it with a spoon. Don't drop it on your foot* . . .

Gai not only observed her older sister's mortar and pestle play earlier, but is also likely to be imitating female activities in her home.

> Grandmother: *Take the spoon out and scrape with your hand. There it is, right there (Gai sits down to pick up the spoon where the dog is lying).*

In this segment, Gai receives numerous instructions, suggestions and practical advice from her grandmother, who indicated in her interview that she likes Thai girls to practise their female-typical roles, mostly through cooking and doll 'mastery play' (Piaget, 1953). Her support seems to enhance Gai's enjoyment of a serious household role. In this sequence Grandmother does not directly enter into play with Gai; rather, she encourages her to acquire certain domestic skills. Thus her grandmother, through watching Gai from a distance, took the opportunity to teach her the desired skills both through restrictions and encouragement. This is an adult role familiar to many professional educators who elect to be on the periphery of children's play, stimulating skills rather than actually playing alongside them—seeing play in the service of other learning rather than valuable in itself.

Peru

Many faces of childcaring arts.

While the adults engaged in Juanita's care at the time (her Aunt Lina and her grandmother) are reading, knitting and doing a little housework in the family's communal courtyard, Lina sets out a basket with various small objects including cards, a small doll and pieces of cloth. A baby doll and toy stuffed rabbit are on the ground nearby. Grandmother passes by, putting down a mat; Juanita places her doll on the mat, pulls up a chair to use as a table-top, and organises toys on the mat beside her, including the rabbit which she pats as she positions it on the mat. She arranges the available domestic objects, lining them up much as her mother's shop is meticulously arranged. During the next 15 minutes Juanita entertains herself with the materials at hand but also searches for and finds other artefacts related to her play. She takes one of the dolls to her aunt, seeming happy to share with her.

The adults continue with their own activities: knitting, reading and tending the yard, animals and child. Prompted by her aunt's claim (entering into the play) that the doll is crying, Juanita takes it, wraps it in a blanket and comforts it. Looking up, she notes a manta (a large, colourful cloth used by Peruvian mothers to wrap their babies), shakes it out and places it carefully on the ground. Looking around, she picks up her rabbit, gently places it

on the manta, wraps it and carries it around the courtyard. This bundle
is too much to manage for long; the rabbit is dropped on its head, almost
unnoticed. The adults present seem engaged in their own activities but
pause briefly to comment or encourage until Juanita wanders off to her next
'projects': reading and colouring with her aunt.

USA

Playing for time: A working parent's day is almost never done.

Gearing up for bedtime, having announced, 'Ready for bed!' after
brushing her teeth, Katy's day is only gradually winding down, as her
busy mind is still generating ideas of things yet to be done. En route from
the dining room to her bedroom, she retrieves a blanket and a purse.
On reaching the bedroom, she picks up a notebook and wanders to her
playroom to get a pencil for her play idea.

Her father enters the bedroom as Katy is engaged with items on her bed
and she hands him the notebook and pencil, directing him to use them . . .
an invitation to play, perhaps. Dad obliges by drawing while reminding her
that she has only a little playtime before getting ready for bed, Katy appears
to hear but pays scant attention. She is focused on playing, and she walks
toward her dolls' crib, saying 'Let me show you my babies!' She hands dolls to
everybody in her bedroom—her father and two researchers (inviting them to
play)—and takes a stuffed monkey for herself, declaring that she needs to sing
it a lullaby and rock it to sleep. As that activity wanes, Katy abruptly declares,
'I need to go to work!' and, grabbing a bag from her bedside table, bids
farewell to Dad. She trundles down the hall (as in Hancock & Gillen, 2007)
to the playroom, getting another purse, into which she puts more pencils.
Not playing, her father trails behind her, trying to persuade Katy to return to
her 'ready for bed' theme, yet he finds himself recruited back into Katy's play
to help pack her workbags. Eventually Katy returns to her bedroom, carrying
two bags, with work still in mind, but Dad persuades her to change into
pyjamas. This serves for a short time to pull her away from her world of play
into his world, which is about 'bedtime'.

Nevertheless, Katy is still not ready to acquiesce. She commences the long
trek back to her room with a superfluity of paraphernalia. The demands on
a working parent are overwhelming, Katy discovers, as she struggles with
both stroller and outsized bag. She eventually cries out, 'I'm falling!', seeking
Dad's assistance. At this point, Katy seems finally to tire of her play and,
re-entering her bedroom, succumbs to Dad's suggestion of a bedtime story.

Both parents are working professionals who highlight their priority of
providing a relatively open environment for their child to learn to make

personal choices for herself, Their large, single-family home affords extensive space for many kinds of play.

Turkey

Kitchen water-play.

Turkish toddler Selin has had an energetic 'rough-and-tumble' game of jumping on her parents' bed with her father, who has declared himself entirely worn out. After trying to convince him that the game could continue, she finally admits that she will not make headway with that activity, so wanders into the kitchen where she finds her sister playing at cooking.

Selin pauses and places the gum she is chewing into a container—a pretend cooking pot. Her mother notices and places a large wooden fork inside the container, which Selin uses to mash her gum. A moment later, she uses the fork to pick up the gum, enthusiastically saying 'Mmm!' to her mother. This 'cooking with gum' is repeated, and this time Mother responds with a positive 'Mmm mmm mmm!' Selin stirs the invisible contents of her 'pot' with her fork, but quickly gives up on 'cooking' and wears the container on her head as a hat instead, eliciting laughter from her mother. One sister turns each pot upside down as the other stacks them. They stack a tower four pots high and then kick it, shrieking with delight.

After being distracted for a few minutes by a small toy on the floor, then by watching her father playing the piano in the living room, Selin returns to the kitchen, where her sister continues to play on her own. Their mother, having returned to her initial reason for being in the kitchen, is now cooking. Given her own water bottle, Selin returns to 'cooking' and begins to squirt water into various pots and a plastic saucepan, drinking water from each container after pouring it in. Selin's water-play with containers continues for a few moments before she discovers the fun of squirting water from her bottle onto the tiled floor. She thoroughly wets her own hands and socked feet as she experiments with splashing the water all over the floor. When her mother brings a cloth to wipe up the water, she offers Selin a plastic saucepan as a distraction, serving to maintain the play.

Throughout the activity, few words are spoken. Selin's mother watches with only intermittent intervention to supply play resources.

Selin's parents, both physicians, commented in our interviews that they were 'non-traditional' in providing an open environment for natural play, believing that being non-interventionist would afford their children the best scope for thriving. The data seem also to demonstrate that the parents (by their involvement and patience) see the spontaneous activities of their daughters as important. Selin is seen to be self-directed but also to join in activity originated by her sister and supported by her mother as an observer.

Discussion and conclusion

From our observations of five active little girls in their respective family contexts in five locations around the world, play is their preferred way of engaging with and being in the world; indeed, it is their childhood 'culture' (James, Jenks & Prout, 1998, p. 81).

Selin in Turkey, after vigorous co-play with father, wanders in to see her sister 'cooking' with pots of water on the kitchen floor. The girls play partly side-by-side and partly collaboratively. Their maintaining the flow of play in a joint and intuitive way is striking, and their mother's close proximity and occasional support seems to sustain the play.

Beatrice in Italy organises balcony space as she wants it, with mother's help both as co-player and sometimes supporter of the play: putting a bib on the doll, setting it in a chair, and feeding it with a small spoon. Gai in Thailand has a 'cooking' session in her family's courtyard. Grandmother, although on the periphery, would seem to be significant in supporting Gai's play.

In Peru, Juanita, given toys, books, a blanket, a manta and other objects, weaves books and writing implements into her caretaking play initiatives

Katy in the USA develops an elaborate 'going to work' routine of journeying up and down a long hall from 'home' to 'work' and back, collecting containers with writing utensils and pushing a stroller in the process. Although aiming that Katy gets ready for bed, Dad provides support for the continuation of her play.

For the caregivers in our selected sequences, we have identified several kinds of play involvement. First, they provide background and peripheral help in a way that doesn't involve them directly as players. These actions come as advice, suggestions, the provision of play resources and practical help. This kind of involvement can be important for play to be sustained. Second, caregivers might enter in a child's play as a co-player. This is evident in our sequences, but it tended not to be prolonged; it was often a momentary pretence involvement after which the caregiver returned to more pressing domestic commitments. Such fleeting adult participation seems important in terms of play being reinforced and extended and, moreover, a child's feeling secure in its play.

During play, the five children re-enact roles that are meaningful from their own cultural perspectives. The exchanges between the child and the family are valued early socialisation experiences. Communication and imaginative play seem to enhance one another (Mayer & Musatti, 1992).

The play discussed here was a dominant activity in all five children's days. It appeared to be both a cause and an effect of family culture. Play is an expression of a particular culture; it is important for cultural learning/transmission, as well as a reflection of a child's development (Schwartzman, 1978).

The wide variety of what appeared acceptable resources for play engagement, whether it be Thai earth and cooking implements available from older children's play, or, as in the US and Italy, a multitude of toys and space for the co-existence of adult and child activity and interests. In Turkey, ordinary kitchen storage devices were as enthusiastically drawn upon as much as the many available toys and musical instruments. The Peruvian family courtyard was a backdrop for engagement in wrapping, tending and distributing items provided by caregivers, including books and writing materials Juanita used in her play.

Importantly, not only can play assist children in their own emotion regulation (Berk et al., 2006) but may also afford positive interactions with caregivers and playmates.

Spending a full working week watching videos of the days of five 30-month-old girls convinces us that these children are impelled to spend as much of their days in play as they possibly can. The familiar adult-defined categories of play (language-, physical-, social- or solitary-, dramatic- or fantasy-play) all emerged in seamless and integrated ways. When at all possible, the toddlers turned mealtimes, domestic engagements and bedtimes into fertile occasions for the dramatic actions of their thoughts. They employed artefacts and raw materials that came to hand; they used purpose-built toys when available, but they constructed likenesses of objects to incorporate into their play if none other was handy. Their caregivers reported often finding it better to acquiesce to, rather than resist, their child's play imperative. On occasion, caregivers initiated and joined in play activities; at other times they set out toys so children could 'amuse themselves', and occasionally they simply tolerated certain playful engagements (Fiese, 1990).

The importance of context in studying play (Roopnarine, Johnson & Hooper, 1994) raises questions about the significance ascribed to play in early childhood education; that is in childcare centres and kindergartens specifically designed for children. The ways the carers in our study observe, support and sometimes participate in their children's play is potentially of interest to, and can possibly inform, professional early years educators, who seek to encourage children to play in both 'unstructured' and 'structured' ways. In viewing the play of these children in diverse home contexts, two common threads predominate. The first is the ubiquity of the wish to engage in play, the second is the play's apparent intensity of purpose. The little girls appear impelled to enact play with whatever and whomever comes to hand. It is their means of engaging with and understanding the world around them. Efforts to divert this energy and enthusiasm to other ends would seem to call for respectful caution.

Questions for further thinking and reflection

1. Consider the way in which, in each cultural context, the five children use the spaces and artefacts around them to engage in creative pursuits. How would it be if these caregivers held back from participating in the play of the children?
2. If play is something that children naturally do and need to do *in their own ways*, what right do adults have to intervene in play?

References

Berk, L. E., Mann, T. D., & Ogan, A. T. (2006). Make-believe play: Wellspring for development of self-regulation. In D. G. Singer, R. M. Golinkoff, K. Hirsh-Pasek (Eds), *Play = Learning: How play enhances children's cognitive and socio-emotional growth* (pp. 74–100). New York: Oxford University Press.

Bornstein, M. H., Haynes, 0. M., Legler, J. M., O'Reilly, A. W., & Painter, K. M. (1997). Symbolic play in childhood: Interpersonal and environmental context and stability. *Infant Behavior and Development, 20*(2), 197–207.

Dube, S. R., Fairweather, D. L., Pearson, W. S., Felitti, V. J., Anda, R. F., & Croft, J. B. (2009). Cumulative childhood stress and autoimmune diseases in adults. *Psychosomatic Medicine, 71,* 243–250.

Elkind, D. (2007). *The power of play.* Cambridge, MA: Da Capo Press.

Fiese, B. (1990). Playful relationships: A contextual analysis of mother-toddler interaction and symbolic play. *Child Development 61,* 1648–1656.

Fromberg, D. R, & Bergen, D. (Eds). (1998). *Play from birth to twelve and beyond: Contexts, perspectives, and meanings.* New York: Garland.

Gomez, J-C., & Martin-Andrade, B. (2005). Fantasy play in apes. In A. D. Pellegrini & P. K. Smith (Eds), *The nature of play: Great apes and humans* (pp. 139–172). New York: Guilford.

Haight, W. L., & Miller, P. J. (1993). *Pretending at home: Early development in sociocultural context.* Albany NY: SUNY Press.

Hancock, R., & Gillen, J. (2007). Safe places in domestic spaces: two-year-olds at play in their homes. *Children's Geographies, 5*(4), 337–351.

James, A., Jenks, C., & Prout, A. (1998). *Theorizing childhood.* Cambridge: Polity Press.

Lillard, A. (2007). Guided participation: How mothers structure and children understand pretend play. In: A. Göncü and S. Gaskins (Eds) *Play and development: Evolutionary, sociocultural and functional perspectives,* (pp. 131–153). New York: Erlbaum.

Mayer, S., & Musatti, T. (1992). Towards the use of symbol: play with objects and communication with adults and peers in the second year. *Infant Behavior & Development* 15(1), 1–13.

Musatti, T. E., Veneziano, E., & Maye, S. (1998). Contributions of language to early pretend play. *Cahiers de Psychologie Cognitive/Current Psychology of Cognition,* 17(2), 155–184.

Nicolopoulou, A. J., McDowell, J., & Brockmeyer, C. (2006). Narrative play and emergent literacy: Storytelling and story-acting meet journal writing. In G. D. Singer, R. M. Golinkoff & K. Hirsh-Pasek (Eds), *Play = Learning: How play enhances children's cognitive and socio-emotional growth* (pp. 124–144). New York: Oxford UP.

Paley, V. G. (2004). *A child's work: The importance of fantasy play.* Chicago: U Chicago Press.

Piaget, J. (1953). *Play, dreams and imitation in childhood.* London: Routledge, Kegan Paul.

Pontecorvo C., Fasulo A., & Sterponi L. (2001). Mutual apprentices: the making of parenthood and childhood in family dinner conversations. *Human Development, 44,* 340–361.

Roopnarine, J. L., Johnson, J. E., & Hooper, E H. (Eds). (1999). *Children's play in diverse cultures.* Albany: SUNY Press.

Roskos, K. A., & Christie, J. F. (Eds). (2000). *Play and literacy in early childhood: Research from multiple perspectives.* Mahwah NJ: Erlbaum.

Schwartzman, H. (1978). *Transformations: The anthropology of children's play.* New York: Plenum.

Singer, D. G., Golinkoff, R. M., & Hirsh-Pasek, K. (Eds). (2006). *Play = Learning: How play enhances children's cognitive and socio-emotional growth.* New York: Oxford UP.

Trionfi, G., & Reese, E. (2009). A good story: children with imaginary companions create richer narratives. *Child Development,* 80(4), 1301–1313.

Vygotsky L. S. (1967). Play and its role in the mental development of the child. *Soviet Psychology, 5,* 6–18.

Vygotsky, L. S. (1978). *Mind in society: The development of higher psychological processes.* Cambridge, MA: Harvard UP.

Chapter 4

'Where's the bear? Over there!' Creative thinking and imagination in den making

Natalie Canning

Chapter introduction

In this chapter Natalie Canning explores opportunities for creative thinking and imagination through den making. A woodland accessed by a private day nursery provides a stimulating context for supporting young children's imaginative and creative play. The research focuses on a group of three and four year old children in peer social groups and the way in which early years practitioners facilitated the children's imaginative and story making about 'bears in the wood'.

Introduction

Creativity is a key factor when children interact with their environment and their peers. When children experiment with new thoughts and ideas, or are curious to find out new things or take risks, they are open to creative thinking and doing. Jeffrey and Craft (2006) see children's engagement with creativity involving open adventures where they explore and develop knowledge and learning through trial and error. Children mainly have opportunities for exploration and developing their creativity through playing, exploring and interacting with their environment. Play gives children the opportunity to use their imagination, create complex stories which are fluid, can change in a moment and can also be remembered or associated with a place or play space. Creativity in play is also perpetuated by the interplay between children in social group interactions (Sawyer, 1997). The context of children's experiences – how they make sense of what they are doing and engage with other children in the same play – is another contributing factor in how creative play develops and is sustained (Pramling Samuelsson & Carlsson, 2008). The physical factors associated with creativity such as a flexible environment and reusable resources, coupled with human factors such as social interactions and communication children engage in with their peers, contribute to the sustainability of creativity. The way in which early years practitioners support children's engagement in creative thinking through their response to children's ideas is also important. When all of these factors come together, children's engagement in a construction of knowledge, ideas and meanings result in creative responses and opportunities to revisit and extend their creative thinking and experiences (Loveless, 2009).

The research draws on sociocultural theory which considers the interrelationship between developing social interactions and existing cultural traditions. Children are active participants in their communities as they are not only dependent on their caregivers and the transmitted experiences they gain from those around them, but also the nature of learning means that they are influenced by their social and cultural surroundings. The process where children come together to share their imagination and consequently develop their creativity relates to their past experiences and existing interpretations of the world. Beghetto and Kaufman (2007) highlight the important relationship between learning and creativity and refer to this as 'mini-c creativity' where a transformation of existing knowledge takes place to support creative expression. In play, children are able to explore social aspects of their lives and Rogoff (2003) argues that a child's cultural background can shape their preferences. She explains that not only are children alert to learning from the cultural opportunities and reactions of others around them, but also that children's relationships with other children and adults shape their future experiences and allow for further interpretation of their social context.

What children create as well as how they create it is important as being creative, developing ideas and turning them into something meaningful relies on making judgements about the value of creative thinking for children. Duffy (2006) recognises that perceptions of creativity vary according to individual experiences and personal interpretation of what being creative means and what it involves. The significance of exploration, curiosity, being motivated to follow an interest and experimenting with ideas in developing and sustaining creative thinking for children relies on early years practitioners embracing child-led play. Rogers (2000) suggests that creative connections are made while children play, stimulating opportunities for self-expression, problem solving, communication and building social relationships. She also suggests that an aspect of creativity is about making meaningful connections and using ideas and resources in new ways. This not only supports sharing experiences with others, but also widens children's ability to feel able to participate.

Methodology

This small scale ethnographic study aimed to explore creative thinking and imaginative responses generated through social play in the context of den making. The research question was 'How does den making support creative thinking in young children?' The qualitative research method (James, Jenks, & Prout, 1998) explored the social worlds of children, to examine their social interactions, sharing of ideas and creativity. In seeking to understand 'meaning and action . . . in a lived situation' an interpretative tradition of social enquiry was employed (Carr & Kemmis, 1986, p. 83).

The setting

The setting is a rural private day nursery on the border between England and Wales in the UK. As well as its indoor provision, it has a large outdoor space and access to a secure woodland area with a small stream running through it, set in approximately 3000 square meters. There are well-established trees and an abundance of leaves and other natural debris covering the woodland floor. The area is enclosed by a fence on two sides, a steep bank and a farm track. The woodland is a short walk from the nursery but children are familiar with the space the woodland offers as the setting frequently uses den making as part of their early years practice.

Method

The research was built on previous research in den making (Canning, 2010) and consisted of non-participant observations recorded as field notes at the time of observation. Particular attention was given to the conversations between children, the way in which the den-making resources and the woodland environment was used by the children and the extent to which they utilised the early years practitioners in this context. The observations were collected during den-making sessions lasting 2 hours per week, over a four-week period. There were opportunities to talk to practitioners after the den-making sessions and these informal conversations were also recorded as field notes immediately after the discussion. They focused on the practitioners' views about children's social interaction, engagement with the woodland area and creative responses to the space and resources.

Ethical considerations

Informed consent was gained from parents and staff in the setting for the non-participant observations and purpose of the research. A mutual day was identified with the setting when den making could be incorporated into their planning and observations could be carried out. Children were already familiar with each other and played together on a regular basis in the setting. The names of the children have been changed to protect their anonymity.

Ethical considerations ensured that the British Educational Research Association (BERA, 2011) revised guidelines were adhered to in relation to researching children's perspectives. At the first meeting with children, practitioners facilitated circle time where the research was explained in child-friendly terms.

The early years practitioners acted as gatekeepers for the children's participation in the research. It was important that children had a choice about their participation and Alderson and Morrow (2004) consider gatekeepers as a way in which safeguards can be put in place to ensure that children are able to express if and when they want to take part. Alderson (2004) warns that children may find it difficult to tell an adult that they no longer want to participate because of the power relationship between the researcher and child. Therefore, children were made aware that they could go to a practitioner if they felt unsure of being observed.

Participants

On each of the visits, there were five children who were consistently present at all observations, three boys and two girls aged between three and four years old. On the third visit, there were eight children taking part in the den making. On the other visits, there were between five and seven children. Den making was a regular activity in the setting and the children knew that they could explore the woodland, but that they would always find a practitioner at the 'square' (a collection of logs arranged in a square where practitioners started and ended each session) if they needed help or support. Each visit to the woodland started in the square with practitioners discussing with children what they wanted to do and if they wanted any help.

The ethos of the setting is child-centred play, where children are able to make choices and create their own play with support from practitioners. The idea of the 'square' reflects the traditions of Reggio Emilia and the focus of the plaza as a meeting and coming together point (Malaguzzi, 1998). Reggio places great emphasis on the environment, and in the same way, the woodland area at the nursery aspires to a dynamic and changing landscape where children can actively engage with what and who is in it.

Findings

From the observations and recording of discussions with practitioners, content analysis which consisted of looking for reoccurring themes within the data revealed the 'bear in the wood' story. Over a four-week period, a creative narrative from the children emerged about a family of bears living in the woods. The story was adapted each time the children visited the woodland, with different children adding new dimensions to what might happen and children already familiar with the story telling and showing new children what had happened. There was lots of discussion amongst the children at the start and end of each session in the square about the family of bears which was initiated by the children and facilitated by the practitioners. The initial idea of 'bears in the wood' evolved from a casual comment made by an early years practitioner on the way to a den-making session. She commented to a child, 'Perhaps we'll see bears in the woods today' which became the focus of conversation for two four-year-old children during their den-making play. As the session progressed, bears were mentioned by these two children on several occasions:

> 'Don't make a hole big . . . bear could get in' (Amy, 4 years old),
>   'I saw a bear and I've got a stick now . . . when he comes back . . . I've got him' (Ben, 4 years old).

These conversations were picked up by other children involved in the den-making session with comments such as, 'Where's the bear?' and 'I'm making bears tea'. The selected extracts from the observations and discussions with practitioners give examples of how the 'bears in the wood' story was sustained.

Extract 1

Week 2 – Molly ($3\frac{1}{2}$ years), James (4 years), Ed (4 years)
Ed looking into a partly constructed den left over from last weeks (Week 1) session: 'I can see my bear, he's there, hiding' Ed crawls into the den.
Molly tugs at Ed's leg: 'Don't scare him, it's quiet time'
Ed starts to back out of the den on his tummy: 'He doesn't want to come out'

James:	'Why?'
Ed shrugs:	'Sleeping'
Molly:	'I said quiet time'
James:	'I'm going to find my bear – where is he?'
Ed:	'This way James'

All three children move away from the den.

Extract 2

Week 3 – There are eight children in the wood and Katie (4 years) is talking to Jo the practitioner

Katie is standing near the square on her own

Jo: 'Are you ok Katie?'
Katie: 'All the bears – gone'
Jo: 'Have they? Where do you think they have gone?'

Katie shrugs her shoulders and kicks the leaves with one foot

Jo: 'Maybe they have gone for a rest?'
Katie: 'In bed'
Jo: 'Maybe – where do you think their beds are?'
Katie: 'In trees' pointing at the nearest tree trunk
Jo: 'Shall we see?'

Jo offers Katie her hand and they walk to the nearest tree. Jo puts her ear to the trunk.

Jo: 'Can you hear them?'

Katie puts her ear to the trunk and Jo starts to make snoring noises. Katie laughs, 'They're snoring asleep!'

Extract 3

Week 4 – Katie (4 years) and Molly ($3\frac{1}{2}$ years)
The girls are adding sticks to a partially constructed, pyramid shaped den when it starts to drizzle with rain.

Katie: 'I'm wet'
Molly: 'Let's go inside' (she feels the ground inside the den with her hand) 'It's dry in here'

The girls crouch down, side by side on the floor at the entrance to the den

Katie: 'Is there room for Pepper? (an imaginary bear)
Molly: 'Already here' (she points to the back of the den) 'I saw her come in . . . doesn't like rain'
Katie: 'Warm for her in here, she can have my blanket too'
Molly: 'Do you want a blanket Pepper? (there is a pause) 'Ok then' (Molly turns to Katie)

'She said she is ok. Let's stay here for a bit.'

Extract 4

Week 4 – James (4 years) and Jack ($3\frac{1}{2}$ years)
Jack is moving sticks and stacking them into a pile in the middle of a small clearing

James: 'What are you doing?
Jack: 'Got to move sticks'
James: 'Why?'
Jack: 'Bears want them for their tea'
James: 'To eat?'
Jack: 'They crunch them up' (makes noises and gestures as if putting lots of food into his mouth) 'and it fills them up' (rubs his tummy)
James: 'With big teeth' (pretends to eat a small stick) 'it tastes' (pause) 'Chocolate!' (jumps up and down)
Jack: 'And ice cream!' (Jack joins in jumping up and down)

The boys laugh then continue to move the sticks into a pile.

Extract 5

Discussion with Kerry (early years practitioner) walking back from the den making session (Week 3), talking about how the children had used their imagination in the session.

'The boys used fantastic imagination today when they were imagining they were climbing up to the top branch [of a tree] to look out for bears. They really seemed to focus on what they wanted to achieve and used the sticks to actually layout a ladder and then pretended to climb it. They all contributed as well – even Jack ($3\frac{1}{2}$ years) who sometimes gets a bit left behind by some of the bigger, older children. He reminded the other boys – 'We're going to look for bears' and that comment seemed to trigger the others to include him in the game . . . Their language as well was delightful – James said 'I can see my bear, he's got a blue coat' and this is all in his imagination. For him that creative thinking is quite rare to hear; he is usually more practical'.

Extract 6

Discussion with Jo (early years practitioner) at the end of the research on the impact of the bear story for her practice.

'Certainly the story [bears in the wood] and creativity that has come from it has made me think about what I am doing and how as a team we can build on it. I don't know if it is because you are here or whether it [bears story] would have happened anyway but the children's persistence with the story and the way they have used the environment and the resources to keep it going has made us as a team reflect on what we want children to get out of their experiences with us and has reminded me of why I came into childcare in the first place.'

Discussion

An overriding factor in the research was that children found ways to use the woodland environment to fulfil their own curiosity, motivation and creative thinking to revisit 'bears in the wood' and to develop their creation, adding new dimensions each time they played in the woods. The den-making material and dens themselves became a way for children to express an imaginary world and develop their creative thinking and responses linked to the environment. Practitioners engaged in possibility thinking with children, asking 'what if?' questions to support the imaginary play and children sustained their 'what if' curiosity extending the possibilities for the 'bears in the wood' idea (Craft, 2001). The relationship between practitioners and children was a significant factor in the analysis of the observations as this determined the way in which children interacted with the woodland in terms of their confidence to be independent of the practitioners, to make their own choices and to develop the bear story. The nature of the outdoor environment also gave an insight into children's social group play and how they negotiated and used strategies to sustain their imaginative play. Their shared experience of creativity promoted communication and further learning as the bear theme extended into other nursery activities.

Children's play space and the outdoor environment

Langston and Abbott (2005) believe that children's play is influenced by their immediate environment as they use the resources available to them to develop and master skills, explore and problem solve, be creative and use their imagination. Outdoor play and particularly woodland environments provide a context where children are able to create a world of make believe. Some children become increasingly inspired through interacting with a woodland environment because it gives them the opportunity to try new things and have different experiences (O'Brien, 2009). The children moved the play beyond simply constructing dens, developing ideas and sustaining their own imaginative play agenda over a period of time. Consequently, Lester and Russell (2008) suggest that emphasis should be placed on valuing different types of spaces for children to play and explore and not just the content of resources in the space. Children used their environment of the woodland area and resources for den making to influence and direct their play in pursuit of 'bears in the woods' and because of this demonstrated to practitioners' future possibilities for planning children's personal development, risk taking and problem solving.

The outdoor environment provides children with opportunities for new ways of seeing the world, experimenting and developing skills (Dahlberg, Moss & Pence, 2007). The nursery regularly uses den making as an opportunity for children to create space for themselves whilst providing a focus for communication and building social relationships, which Knight (2009) believes is an important aspect of den making. The outdoor space in the woodland meant that den making was an opportunity for children to be in charge of their environment changing their space and recycling materials for different play at different times. Brown (2003) suggests that children need flexibility in their environment to be pro-active in the play they create by themselves. He argues that a flexible environment creates a flexible child who can adapt and be resourceful in other situations. Therefore, when an environment has flexible potential, it is able to facilitate a child's potential for curiosity, problem solving and creative thinking. In the same way, Nicholson (1971) introduced a theory of 'loose parts' which linked the degree of inventiveness and creativity that children engage within their environment to the different resources provided within it.

The children adapted their play at each of the visits to the woodland, using the space as a platform for their imagination. Laris (2005) considers children as inventors of their play space and suggests that observing what children do in their environment and listening to what children say to each other reveals the extent to which environments are flexible for different age groups. It was interesting to note that each den-making session in the square started in a similar way. One of the children would say, 'Where's the bear?' and another would answer 'Over there!' Then all of the children would run into the woodland and continue their play from that point. Fjørtoft (2001, p. 111) states that 'intuitively children use their environment for physical challenges and play . . . they perceive the functions of the landscape and use them for play'. This was true in the observations of children interacting with the woodland environment. They utilised the outdoor space in their imaginary play, for example, a rabbit hole one of the children found became a 'trap for tigers so they can't eat the bears' (Amy, 4 years old). Two of the children became fascinated with the trees and choosing certain ones where the bears would live. 'My bear lives here . . . he's the only one who can fit in the door

and there's stairs inside so he can get up there [pointing to a high branch]'
(Darren, 4 years old).

Social interactions and children's communication

Children used the initial introduction of the den-making session as a basis
for extending their imaginative play about bears. Amy and Ben's interest in
the early years practitioner's initial comment about perhaps seeing a bear
in the wood sparked play which extended and involved other children in
the same imaginary world. As the play and den-making sessions progressed,
children built on each other's ideas to extend and sustain their play. Their
actions and engagement enabled a creative environment where children
established a purpose for their play (Duffy, 2006). Pramling Samuelsson
and Johansson (2006) identify that in order to be creative, children have to
communicate so that their play is able to evolve and take new directions
to satisfy all involved in play. Qualities such as flexibility, compromise
and negotiation are all elements of creative thinking and social group
play, and were essential in sustaining the 'bear in the woods' idea amongst
the children. This was especially significant as it was not always the same
children involved in the play.

In each visit to the woodland, children revisited and explored materials
in different ways within the theme of bears. Skar and Krogh (2009) argue
that children structure their experiences based on their own socialisation
and on earlier encounters with their surroundings. The continuation and
sustainment of the bear story may have happened because children wanted
to maintain the social interactions and relationships they had begun to build
through their creative and imaginative play. The practitioners also facilitated
the social interactions initiated in the woodland by supporting the bear
theme in other areas of the nursery such as craft activities and role play. They
posed 'what if' questions around the theme of bears encouraging children
to make links between what they were doing in the den-making/woodland
area and everyday nursery activities, to encourage them to problem solve
and think creatively within the context of an imaginary world. Cremin,
Burnard and Craft (2006) suggest that the way in which practitioners engage
with children's interests, alongside internal and external factors which
enable play, shape pedagogic practice and support possibility thinking. The
practitioners were aware of the significance of the external factors influencing
children's play and communicated to parents the nursery's sustained interest
in everything related to 'bears'. This resulted in a planned teddy bears picnic,
which parents were invited to attend and children brought their teddy bears

from home. The holistic nature of the theme supported practitioners in thinking about their strategy for future planning in the nursery. The use of possibility thinking and starting with 'what if' provided practitioners with a starting point for engaging with children's interests and allowing their curiosity and creativity to direct the nature and content of a play-based curriculum.

However, the practitioners had to consider what had sparked and sustained such an interest in 'bears'. Kadis (2007) believes that children's interest is maintained if they are given choice and freedom in the materials they choose to revisit. The den–making and woodland environment facilitated children's choice because the materials to a large extent were flexible to be used in different and imaginative ways, and children were able to fulfil their own play objectives. The children's interest was also maintained to a certain extent by the way in which the practitioners made a conscious effort to keep the bear theme the focus of 'what if' questions and integrated the idea of 'bears' into daily aspects of the nursery.

Practitioners' response to children's ideas

In den making, the practitioners placed significance on the natural environment as a resource for learning and stood back from the children's play to enable them to follow their own interests. Cremin et al. (2006, p. 113) consider that standing back from children's engagement in play is central for learner ownership which can 'foster autonomy and the opportunity for children to follow their own interests and shape their learning so that it is individually tailored'. The children responded positively to practitioners standing back, quietly observing from a distance and not becoming involved unless prompted by a child. The result was when a child did require a practitioner to help or answer a question the practitioner had a better understanding of the children's engagement with creative thinking and imagination of the 'bear' narrative. Standing back allows practitioners not only to notice behaviour and actions, but also to apply their knowledge and understanding of child development to support ways of encouraging future learning (Cremin et al., 2006).

Children will not necessarily use a play space that has been designated by practitioners for a particular play activity in the way they have planned (Armitage, 2001). Consequently, children's perceptions of outdoor spaces may differ from practitioners' in terms of both activity and interaction. This is what happened over the period of research. The practitioners did not initially encourage or expect the bear theme to generate such interest or sustain its motivation. However, Mooney (2000) suggests that when children are active and interactive in their environment, they explore possibilities for creativity which practitioners may not have entertained. She argues that when children have time and space to play in physical environments, which are different from children's normal expectations and routine, they are able to experiment and experience different aspects of learning through creativity.

Conclusion

The way in which children initiated and sustained the 'bears in the wood' theme through their imagination and creative thinking in the den-making sessions surprised the early years practitioners. It stimulated their reflection on practice with regard to how they support children to communicate their preferences and interests. The children's ability to revisit their creative play, involve other children in the same play and develop the bear story over a period of time demonstrated to the practitioners the significance of offering flexible resources and opportunities which support imaginative and creative thinking. The combination of the outdoor environment, the den-making resources, the ability of practitioners to stand back and use possibility thinking in responding to children enabled a space which nurtured children's imagination and creativity. The ability of the practitioners to allow the 'bears in the wood' theme to permeate through everyday practice ensured that the creativity generated remained child centred and focused on the children's agenda and motivation for their play. Following the child's lead and ideas meant that practitioners not only had to be flexible in their practice, but also creative in their own responses to support play and creative thinking in the pursuit of continued learning and development.

Questions for further thinking and reflection

1.   What are the benefits and challenges of promoting outdoor play and exploration for children's imagination and creativity?
2.   What is the role of the adult in facilitating outdoor play opportunities for young children?

References

Alderson, P. (2004). Ethics. In S. Fraser, V. Lewis, S. Ding, M. Kellett & C. Robinson (Eds.), *Doing research with children and young people* (pp. 97–112). London: Sage.

Alderson, P., & Morrow, V. (2004). *Ethics, social research and consulting with children and young people*. Barnardos: Ilford.

Armitage, M. (2001). The ins and outs of playground play: Children's use of play spaces. In J. Bishop & M. Curtis (Eds.), *Play today in the primary school playground* (pp. 21–37). Buckingham: Open University Press.

Beghetto, R., & Kaufman, J. (2007). Toward a broader conception of creativity: A case for 'mini-c' creativity. *Psychology of Aesthetics, Creativity and the Arts, 1*(2), 73–79.

British Educational Research Association (BERA). (2011). Revised Ethical Guidelines for Educational Research (2004). Retrieved July 21, 2012, from http://www.bera.ac.uk/files/guidelines/ethical.pdf

Brown, F. (Ed.). (2003). Compound flexibility. In *Playwork: Theory into practice* (pp. 51–65). Maidenhead: Open University Press.

Canning, N. (2010). The influence of the outdoor environment: Den making in three different contexts. *European Early Childhood Education Research Journal, 18*(4), 555–566.

Carr, W., & Kemmis, S. (1986). *Becoming critical: Education knowledge and action research.* London: Falmer Press.

Craft, A. (2001). Little c creativity. In A. Craft, B. Jeffrey, & M. Liebling (Eds.), *Creativity in education* (pp. 45–61). London: Continuum.

Cremin, T., Burnard, P., & Craft, A. (2006). Pedagogy and possibility thinking in the early years. *Thinking Skills and Creativity, 1,* 108–119.

Dahlberg, G., Moss, P., & Pence, A. (2007). *Beyond quality in early childhood education and care* (2nd ed.). London: Routledge.

Duffy, B. (2006). *Supporting creativity and imagination in the early years* (2nd ed.). Buckingham: Open University Press.

Fjortoft, I. (2001). The natural environment as a playground for children: The impact of outdoor play activities in pre-primary school children. *Early Childhood Education Journal, 29*(2), 111–117.

James, A., Jenks, C., & Prout, A. (1998). *Theorising childhood.* Cambridge: Polity Press.

Jeffrey, B., & Craft, A. (2006). Creative learning and possibility thinking. In B. Jeffrey (Ed.), *Creative learning practices: European experiences* (pp. 73–91). London: The Tufnell Press.

Kadis, A. (2007, November). 'The risk factor', *Play Today,* 60.

Knight, S. (2009). *Forest schools and outdoor learning in the early years.* London: Sage.

Langston, A., & Abbott, L. (2005). Quality matters. In L. Abbott & A. Langston (Eds.), *Birth to three matters* (pp. 68–78). Maidenhead: Open University Press.

Laris, M. (2005). Designing for play. In M. Dudek (Ed.), *Children's spaces* (pp. 3–20). London: Architectural Press.

Lester, S., & Russell, W. (2008). *Play for a change: Play, policy and practice, a review of contemporary perspectives.* London: Play England.

Loveless, A. (2009). Thinking about creativity: Developing ideas, making things happen. In A. Wilson (Ed.), *Creativity in primary education* (2nd ed., pp. 22–35). Exeter: Learning Matters.

Malaguzzi, L. (1998). History, ideas and basic philosophy: An interview with Leila Gandini. In C. Edwards, L. Gandini, & G. Forman (Eds.), *The hundred languages of children: Advanced reflections* (2nd ed., pp. 49–98). London: Ablex Publishing.

Mooney, C.G. (2000). *Theories of childhood: An introduction to Dewey, Montessori, Erikson, Piaget and Vygotsky.* St Paul, MN: Redleave Press.

Nicholson, S. (1971). How NOT to cheat children: The theory of loose parts. *Landscape Architecture, 62*(1), 30–35.

O'Brien, L. (2009). Learning outdoors: The forest school approach. *Education 3–13, 37*(1), 45–60.

Pramling Samuelsson, I., & Carlsson, M. (2008). The playing learning child: Towards a pedagogy of early childhood. *Scandinavian Journal of Educational Research, 52*(6), 623–641.

Pramling Samuelsson, I., & Johansson, E. (2006). Play and learning – Inseparable dimensions in preschool learning. *Early Child Development and Care, 176*(1), 47–65.

Rogers, N. (2000). *The creative connection: Expressive arts as healing.* Ross on Wye: PCCS Books.

Rogoff, B. (2003). *The cultural nature of human development.* Oxford: Open University Press.

Sawyer, K. (1997). *Pretend play as improvisation: Conversation in the preschool classroom.* Washington, DC: Lawrence Erlbaum Associates.

Skar, M., & Krogh, E. (2009). Changes in children's nature based experiences near home: From spontaneous play to adult controlled, planned and organised activities. *Children's Geographies, 7*(3), 339–354.

Chapter 5

Creative little scientists: exploring pedagogical synergies between inquiry-based and creative approaches in Early Years science

Teresa Cremin, Esme Glauert, Anna Craft[1], Ashley Compton and Fani Stylianidou

Chapter introduction

In this chapter Teresa Cremin from the Open University and the research team involved in the 'Creative Little Scientists' project report on a study exploring the teaching, learning and assessment of science with young children aged three to eight. Taking in settings across nine European countries the project provides insights into the connections between inquiry based science education and creative approaches in Early Years practice. It reports on how teachers developed rich physical environments for scientific exploration often linked to children's interests and everyday events.

Introduction

The project Creative Little Scientists (CLS) (2011–2014) was undertaken in nine European countries (Belgium, Finland, France, Germany, Greece, Malta, Portugal, Romania and the UK), representing a spectrum of educational, economic, social and cultural contexts. Across 30 months, the consortium explored the potential for creativity in the mathematics and science education of 3-8 year olds, combining comparative studies of policies and of teachers' views with case studies of classroom practice. The current chapter focuses solely on the pedagogical synergies identified between inquiry-based science education and creative approaches to education. The comparative dimension is reported elsewhere (Creative Little Scientists, 2014a).

The project was informed by five drivers. The first, the economic imperative, highlights the need for scientists in Europe's knowledge economy (European Commission, 2011). Framed within 21st century neo-liberal narratives, it demands flexible innovative thinkers who are knowledgeable and enthusiastic about science. The second highlights the development of responsible, scientifically literate citizens (Harlen, 2010). The third relates to the development of the child and citizen through creativity (Chappell and Craft, 2011) and the fourth to the technological imperative, since digital technologies support inquiry (Wang et al., 2010) enabling and demanding creativity (Craft, 2011). The final driver relates to changing perspectives on children and the importance of Early Years education. Children are now commonly viewed as active participants who have capabilities and interest in science (Duschl et al., 2007), and, it is argued, gain long-term benefit from early science education (Eshach and Fried, 2005; Harlen, 2010).

The CLS consortium shared a common encompassing purpose to explore the approaches used in the teaching, learning and assessment of science (and mathematics) in Early Years in the partner countries and the role, if any, that creativity might play in these. Through this focus it sought to further understanding of relationships between inquiry-based science education (IBSE) and creative approaches (CA) to teaching and learning. Although definitions of IBSE vary, internationally it is afforded value in both research and policy (Asay and Orgill, 2010). Its purpose is arguably to 'introduce students to the content of science, including the process of investigation, in the context of the reasoning that gives science its dynamic character and provides the logical framework that enables one to understand scientific innovation and evaluate scientific claims' (Drayton and Falk, 2001:25). Thus content knowledge and process skills are combined. Unlike IBSE, Creative Approaches to education are not as easily delineated. They tend to refer to repertoires of teaching strategies that allow practitioners to teach creatively and teach for creativity (Jeffrey and Craft, 2004), enabling learners to 'believe in their creative potential, to engage their sense of possibility and to give them the confidence to try' (NACCCE, 1999:90). As Dezuanni and Jetnikoff (2011: 264) note, creative pedagogies encompass 'the imaginative and innovative arrangement of curricula and teaching strategies in school classrooms and the development of students' creative capacities'. Whilst IBSE and CA differ in their purpose, origins and developmental histories, both are associated with child-centred philosophies from European and North American thinkers which foreground the child as an active curious thinker and meaning maker, and highlight the role of experiential learning.

In examining relationships between IBSE and CA, this paper seeks to explore the following research questions:

- What are the pedagogical synergies evidenced in the research literature between inquiry-based science education and creative approaches in the Early Years?
- Are these manifest in practice and if so in what ways?

In order to address these questions, the conduct of the CLS literature reviews is discussed and the identified pedagogical synergies presented. The fieldwork methodology is then explained and illustrative episodes from the dataset offered. This is followed by a discussion, consideration of differences observed in preschool and primary settings, and explication of the project's new definition of creativity in science.

Pedagogical synergies: Reviewing the relevant literature

A set of five thematic literature reviews were undertaken. These encompassed material identified by the nine partners in the consortium, and fed into the project's conceptual framework. The reviews focused upon: Early Years science, mathematics and creativity, teacher education across Europe and comparative education. Detailed analysis of the first three of research literatures highlighted the potential existence of a number of pedagogical synergies between IBSE and CA in the Early Years. The science and creativity literature reviews were thus re-examined in order to identify more closely these synergistic features of teaching and learning, and later empirical work was planned.

The pedagogical practices examined in this chapter, related to theorised and examined practices, spanning pre-school and the first years of primary education. The work focused on peer-reviewed journal articles from 1990–2013, although exceptions were made for 'landmark' studies and the work of significant theorists. Existing reviews within creativity (Davies et al., 2011) and science (Duschl, Schweingruber and Shouse, 2007; Minner, Levy and Century, 2010) were also consulted. To ensure consistency, members selected papers from the agreed period and produced rubrics encompassing attention to: research questions, methodological approaches, research design, sampling procedures and key findings. Advantageously, the consortium was able to draw on studies not published in English, ensuring more representative reviews. No particular theoretical perspectives were adopted; rather the authors sought to map the fields as comprehensively as possible, identifying broad themes. Methodologically, the studies, which numbered in excess of 400 papers ranged across interpretivist/positivist paradigms, both in terms of conceptual and empirical pieces.

It became clear that Early Years creativity and science education share in common recognition of children's exploratory and investigative engagement, and their consideration of ideas and conceptions. More specifically, the research literatures pertinent to IBSE and CA reveal that to different degrees both approaches profile particular pedagogical practices that seek to foster children's learning. The common pedagogical synergies identified across the two extensive reviews with regard to the Early Years include: play and exploration, motivation and affect, dialogue and collaboration, problem solving and agency, questioning and curiosity, reflection and reasoning, and teacher scaffolding and involvement. These are now examined. No hierarchy is intended.

Play and exploration. Widely recognised as inherent in all young children's activity, playful exploration represents the focus of considerable research within both approaches. It is argued playful hands-on experiences encourage children to make connections between science and their surroundings (Kramer and Rabe-Kleberg, 2011) and that sustained play increases children's creativity (Garaigordobil and Buerrueco, 2011). Empirical studies suggest open-ended exploratory contexts are well suited to fostering both learning and creativity (Burnard et al., 2006; Mitchell et al, 2002; Poddiakov, 2011). Supported by the pedagogic space and scope offered for exploration, it appears children in these studies often extended boundaries and explored with interest, commitment and a marked degree of openness that their teachers sought to build upon. Such openness, alongside objectivity, is recognised as a critical feature of the development of a scientific stance or attitude (Feng, 1987).

Motivation and affect. Research in both science and creativity indicates that such play-based contexts afford opportunities to develop positive attitudes and affective engagement. In particular Larsson and Halldén (2010) argue that playful experiences nurture children's motivation to understand their world and Milne (2010) contends that fascination, wonder and interest can prompt aesthetic engagement, spark curiosity and lead to the use of scientific inquiry to develop explanations of phenomena. Creativity focused research also highlights the importance of engaging children affectively (Craft et al., 2012; Millineaux and Dilalla, 2009) and the power of narrative has been shown to imaginatively involve children, fostering their creativity in different domains (Cremin et al., 2013).

Dialogue and collaboration. Research suggests dialogue is a critical feature of both IBSE and CA. In science learning it is claimed that it not only enables children to externalise, share and develop their thinking (Carlsen, 2008), but helps them consolidate their ideas (Chi et al., 1994) and develop verbal reasoning skills (Mercer et al., 1999). As Varela (2010) posits, the communication of scientific ideas and ways of thinking allows children to listen to others' strategies and ideas, developing increased awareness which may prompt a desire to restructure their own in the face of other more plausible or consensual ones.

Similarly creativity research increasingly recognises the essentially social and collaborative nature of creative processes and that dialogic engagement is characteristic of classroom creativity (Vass, 2007; Wegerif, 2005). Open dialogue between children and teachers, and space/opportunities for children to experiment alone and in peer groups, are prerequisites for learner creativity in science.

Problem–solving and agency. Problem-solving is widely recognised as central to both IBSE and CA, however there are debates in the literature concerning the teacher's role in IBSE and whether scaffolding children's inquiries constrains or enables learner agency (Asay and Orgill 2010; Cindy et al., 2007). It is argued that an inverse relationship exists between the amount of direction from teacher materials and learner self-direction over the problem-finding/problem-solving process in science (Barrow 2010). It is also claimed that children are competent in using problem-solving strategies and that structuring the learning environment appropriately offers them the space and agency to develop these (Barrow, 2010; Torbeyns et al., 2002).

In creativity research, engagement with problems has been shown to foster child agency, ownership of learning and the development of self-determination and control (Craft et al., 2012; Cremin et al., 2006; Lan and Marvin, 2002). These studies suggest that young children's engagement in finding their own problems is central to creativity, and that teachers' interest and respect for children's questions facilitates their sense of autonomy and agency as learners.

Questioning and curiosity. The role of questions, both children's and teachers', is another common research focus across these interrelated fields and recognised as central within IBSE and CA. Whilst it is widely accepted that children are innately curious and seek to explore the world around them, Nickerson (1999) suggests the educational process can inhibit their curiosity and their impulse to question and engage in mental play. Some studies indicate that teachers who use a lot of open questions achieve high-levels of pupil involvement and promote learning (Rojas-Drummond and Zapata, 2004). Others, focused on creative artists working in schools, note that they promote speculation by modelling their own curiosity (Thomson et al., 2012), potentially generating new questions on the part of the learners and 'developing intrigue' (Poddiakov, 2011), a core capacity of young scientists.

While Harlen and Qualter (2004) highlight diversity in the nature and purpose of scientific questions and Hmelo-Silver et al., (2007) stress their importance in driving inquiries, Harris and Williams (2007) show that if young children have little experience of open questions at home, they may find such questions in science difficult. Researchers also note children's curiosity and questions may be expressed through modes such as drawing, gestures and actions with materials, illustrating the focus of their investigation and 'intellectual play' (Wood and Hall, 2011).

Reflection and reasoning. Although synergies exist here too, there is rather more research evidencing the importance of these skills in IBSE than in CA. Kuhn (1989) argues children are intuitive scientists and as (Duschl, et al., (2007) and Eshach and Fried (2005) also claim, have an early capacity to reason scientifically. However Aleven and Koedinger (2002) assert children need support to develop metacognitively and Metz (2004) suggests they are biased towards interpreting evidence in terms of their existing theories, and do not develop scientific reasoning automatically from experience. Such reasoning, which usually involves differentiating between theories and evidence, and evaluating hypotheses, arguably connects to creativity conceptualised as the generation and evaluation of ideas, yet there is limited discussion of reasoning in Early Years creativity research literature. Although Bancroft et al., (2008) document children evaluating and Reggio Emilia schools profile reflection, this is rarely seen through a creativity lens. Nonetheless research into IBSE and CA suggests children employ diverse modes to record their ideas, potentially encouraging reflection, discussion and evaluation (Stevenson and Dumcumb, 1998; Wollman-Bonilla 2000).

Teacher scaffolding and involvement. Notwithstanding the recognition that IBSE and CA both include attention to problem-solving in playful exploratory contexts, in which questions, dialogue, motivation and reflection play a significant part, the efficacy of these two approaches depends largely on the teacher's role in scaffolding children's learning. As Fleer (2009) notes, teachers mediate children's thinking between everyday concepts gained through playful interaction and more formal scientific concepts. Such scaffolding is claimed to foster children's independence as inquirers and problem-solvers (Metz, 2004), their conceptual knowledge (Coltman et al., 2002), meta-cognitive strategies (Aleven and Koedinger, 2002) and their creativity (Craft et al., 2012). The research literatures also imply a central role for assessment to inform responsive teaching, and modes of assessment sensitive to young children's varied capabilities.

As has been shown, the research literature indicates a dynamic relationship exists between IBSE and Creative Approaches to teaching and learning;

inquiry-based science approaches link to the problem-finding/problem solving approach developed by those who teach for creativity and teach creatively. It was this synergistic relationship that the CLS project sought to explore further through empirical investigation.

Methods and data collected

Undertaken across four months, the project fieldwork focused on sites potentially offering 'exemplary practices' in fostering creativity and inquiry in early science (and mathematics), covering pre-primary and early primary education provision in each country. The sampling, which was purposive (Yin, 2009), was informed by information gathered from teacher surveys, school inspection reports, attainment records, local authorities and teacher education institutions.

The two main fieldwork foci were pedagogical, informed by Siraj–Blatchford et al., (2002:23):

- Pedagogical framing – including provision of resources, arrangements of space, daily routines to support cooperation, planning and assessment;
- Pedagogical interventions – face to face interactions.

The fieldwork was qualitative in nature, and conducted in 48 different sites across partner countries resulting in 71 case studies of practices in early science (and mathematics). Data was collected from:

- Wider site contexts: information potentially framing pedagogy from school policies, websites, inspection reports, national/local curriculum documents;
- Pedagogical contexts: information potentially framing pedagogy from teaching and learning policies, planning documents, assessment records, resources, a map of the space; teachers' reflections on practice in interview and during sessions;
- Observation: of face to face interaction and outcomes (episodes of learning involving children and teachers and children's reflections on this).

The core instruments included: field notes supplemented by transcribed audio recording; individual interviews (teachers); group interviews (children); child-led 'learning walks' and children's artefacts. To ensure consistency a training workshop including a fieldwork visit was organised for all researchers to introduce and trial methods and approaches to analysis.

Ethical issues

All partners followed ethical approval policies for their institution, school system, region and country as appropriate.

Data analysis

Qualitative analysis was carried out in two phases. Initially data from fieldwork in each country was analysed by local research teams. Regular online sub group meetings were held for analytic triangulation with partners to ensure consistency of coding. In this strand of the work, a deductive-inductive analytical approach was adopted. Country Reports[2] were created by each partner, consisting of a series of case studies.

The second analytic phase involved cross-analysis of the Country Reports. The cross country analysis highlighted the themes and issues discussed, as well as examples of opportunities for creativity in learning and teaching illustrated in episodes.

The pedagogical synergies in practice

The 218 episodes of learning and teaching reported by CLS partners provide an overview of the range of pedagogical approaches observed during fieldwork. The episodes offer strong evidence of the existence of the literature-derived synergies between IBSE and CA in both preschool and primary settings (CLS, 2013a). The extent to which particular synergies were evidenced in these two settings varied; this is discussed following presentation of extracts from the episodes. Three extracts from episodes documented in different countries have been selected as illustrative examples of the pedagogical synergies identified in the research literature.

Episode 1: "Gloop" (4–5 year olds), Northern Ireland

In this activity, children aged 4–5 years old were making and exploring 'gloop' – mixing water and cornflour in a large plastic tray on a table. Children were free to attend and leave the activity as they pleased. After a short time, the teaching assistant placed a number of different tools – for example spatulas of varying sizes, rubber paint brushes, a funnel – into the tray to further provoke interest and exploration.

One child, Ryan became immersed in this activity over a long period, observing the mixture and trying out different ways to use the tools and their effects, for example scooping it with spatulas or drawing in it with the rubber-tipped paint-brushes.

Curiosity was evident in Ryan's sustained engagement and questioning 'What can I do with this?' implicit in his actions. This was particularly apparent in his contemplation and subsequent use of tools in the tray. At one point, he was moving gloop across the tray with a wide spatula in his right hand, then trying to stop its return flow using a rubber paintbrush in his left hand. At another point he was scooping up the gloop with the spatula and slowly dribbling it on to his forearm and hand. Creativity was indicated in his sense of initiative and generation of alternative strategies in using the tools in different ways, providing often novel and unexpected outcomes.

(CLS, 2013b9: 280–285)

In this episode, adult provision of rich resources and sustained time for play and exploration fostered Ryan's motivation and interest. Adults largely stood back, occasionally intervening to provide additional materials or ask questions based on their observations of children's responses.

Episode 2: "The Wind" (5–6 year olds), Belgium

During this activity children experimented with putting different materials in front of a fan, to see if they moved with the wind. The children had been given a collection of objects to sort according to how they moved in the wind. They were then given greater agency to experiment with materials of their choice found in the classroom. The teacher joined in at times to extend their explorations as illustrated in the extracts below, sharing her own excitement in the inquiry.

A child puts a toy canoe in front of the fan.

Mathis: "Mrs X, the canoe doesn't move!"

At that moment the canoe goes sideways.

Teacher: "Oh, Mathis, look what's happening."
Mathis: "It moves sideways."
Teacher: "And if we place it in the other direction, will it move too?"

Mathis places the canoe in a different direction and notices it doesn't move.

Teacher: "How is this possible?"

. . .

Later Mathis places a sheet of paper in front of the fan.

Teacher: "Oh, should the paper always fly away?"

Mathis places the paper folded in two on the table in front of the fan.

Teacher: "Look, does the paper fly away now?"

All the children look at the sheet of paper.

Teacher: "How come it flew away before?"

Elise opens the sheet of paper and sees it is flying away then.

Teacher: "What did you do with the paper?"
Elise: "I have opened it!"
Teacher: "You had opened it".

Mathis picks up the paper and places it open in front of the fan, but pushes it flat against the table. The children and the teacher all look what will happen. The paper stays in place.

The children also discovered they could make the fan blow hard and soft, prompting experimentation with further materials.

(CLS, 2013bl: 81–84)

During this episode children were given space and time to explore and experiment with the available materials. The teacher fostered their curiosity by asking them questions about what they had observed. They were able to generate and test out their own ideas, building on evidence from their observations, promoting their agency.

Episode 3: "Building Blocks" (5 year olds), Germany

The teacher had observed that the class of 5-year old children enjoyed playing with wooden building blocks. To extend their learning she gave the children a book containing photographs of buildings. Inspired by these the children decided to build the 'Leaning Tower of Pisa' showing creativity in their sense of initiative and imagination in generating plans for a new building project. One child, Luca, started off with a plan but the tower tumbled down. The teacher encouraged him to reflect on the source of the problem and then stood back while he worked with Abel to find a solution.

Teacher: Why does it fall in again and again? What do you think?
Luca: Because there is no space . . . for this *(points to the tricky spot)*.
Teacher: Yes, it doesn't have enough support there, right? We have to think about something else there.

Luca starts to pile up bricks as a sort of supporting pillar.

Luca: We build a tower from below to fix it.

Abel starts to carefully slide bricks in the tower from the side.

Teacher: Ah, you're adding a supporting step!
Luca: Abel-Good idea!
Abel: And now it has to be unbuilt a little bit over here!
Teacher: What do you mean?
Abel: *(explains to Luca)* And here it has to support.
Luca: Yes, I know.
Teacher: Now you added a supporting construction. Now it is stable.
Luca: Luckily. At last.

The children demonstrated creative dispositions in making connections between observations and using reasoning skills in coming up with a solution.

(CLS, 2013b4: 19–21)

This activity, designed by the teacher, built on her observations of the children's interests and her provision of bricks and photographs. Children were encouraged to make their own plans for their building projects and to collaborate in solving problems. She provided opportunities for children to take the lead and, through her questioning, helped them to communicate and reflect on their observations and ideas, and to identify problems and offer alternative solutions and reasoned justifications for their actions. Her own interest and curiosity helped to create an environment in which children were confident enough to make mistakes and motivated to find alternative solutions.

Discussion

The fieldwork contributes new understandings about teaching and learning approaches in science and their relationship to teaching creatively and teaching for creativity. As the illustrative extracts evidence, teachers' planned motivating contexts for learning often linked to children's interests and everyday events. Teachers provided rich physical environments for inquiry in their classrooms, with the outdoors and with living things to generate children's interest and questions. Group work was commonly observed as a feature of teachers' practice and often prompted dialogue and collaboration. Very few of the teachers relied on published resources; they planned or adapted activities flexibly and in response to the children and wider curriculum framing. Thus the field work demonstrates that IBSE and CA to teaching and learning are closely connected in practice: they operate in a synergistic relationship.

Whilst these pedagogic practices were evidenced across the age span 3-8 years, several were documented more frequently in preschools than in primary settings. Synergies as well as differences were documented. Across all partner countries, opportunities to play were much less common as children got older. In pre-school settings there was greater evidence of encouragement of questioning on the part of adults. Teachers in pre-school settings in particular appeared to show sensitivity to questions implicit in children's actions and these were often voiced by teachers, mirrored back to the young thinkers and used to encourage conversation and reflection. In preschool contexts however, the potential for extending child–initiated inquiry and children's agency was not always recognised by teachers, although far more science inquiries were driven by pre-schoolers' questions than by older children's questions, and time for child-initiated inquiry was much more limited in the primary years.

Some teachers of older learners reported that time pressures and policy expectations acted as constraints on their professional practice, challenging their ability to balance the provision of both structure and freedom. Restrictions to child-initiated and child-led inquiries were also noted by Asay and Orgill (2010) who found these depended on the teacher's views of children's capabilities and the nature of the inquiry. However, in the CLS study even at the primary phase there were some opportunities for children to make decisions about the materials or approaches to be adopted, with varied levels of guidance. Regardless of the age of the children, there were few examples of teachers employing highly structured approaches to inquiry or problem-solving.

The differential employment of particular teaching and learning approaches at pre-school and primary appeared to be influenced by contextual factors such as wider policies, planning and assessment.

Significantly, the teachers involved in the fieldwork commonly expressed the view that they had not thought explicitly about opportunities for creativity in science: they planned science focused activities and creativity was either unrecognised or implicit in their planning and practice. Accordingly, the consortium developed a dual definition which combines little-c creativity: 'Purposive imaginative activity generating outcomes that are original and valuable in relation to the learner' with a definition specifically related to creativity in science (and mathematics): 'Generating ideas and strategies as an individual or community, reasoning critically between these and producing plausible explanations and strategies consistent with the available evidence.' (CLS, 2014b: 8). These new definitions have potential in identifying opportunities for creativity in learning in early science.

Conclusion

This research significantly furthers understanding of the relationship between inquiry based science education and creative approaches in the Early Years. Initially, the identified synergies were innovatively derived from the research literatures on science and creativity. Conceptual connections revealed numerous pedagogical synergies including: play and exploration, motivation and affect, questioning and curiosity, problem solving and agency, dialogue and collaboration, reflection and reasoning, and teacher scaffolding and involvement. Later their existence was examined empirically in 71 different classroom contexts across Europe: they were manifest across geographic and age contexts (3–8 years). Their existence affords a new contribution to the interrelated fields of inquiry and creativity-based approaches in the Early Years.

The research reveals that in playful motivating and exploratory contexts, young children, often supported by their teacher, engage with resources, ask questions, collaborate and find and solve scientific problems. In this way they are afforded opportunities to generate ideas and strategies, individually or communally, to reason between these and produce explanations consistent with the available evidence. They are afforded opportunities to be creative young scientists. The new definition of creativity in science developed through the work extends the project's contribution and may, alongside the episodes, enable the profession to recognise and capitalise upon opportunities for creativity in Early Years science.

Questions for further thinking and reflection

1. What opportunities are there in the setting in which you work (or know well) for children to be 'creative little scientists'?
2. What factors might inhibit or enhance opportunities for scientific exploration and creativity in Early Years settings?

Acknowledgments

The Creative Little Scientists project (2011–2014) received funding from the European Union's Seventh Framework Programme (FP7/2007–2013) under grant agreement no. 289081. The authors would like to acknowledge the work of all partners in the consortium.

Notes

1 Anna Craft was a member of the CLS project team until her untimely death in 2014.
2 Available at http://www.creative-little-scientists.eu/content/deliverables

References

Aleven, V. A. W. M. M. and Koedinger, K. R. (2002). An effective metacognitive strategy: *Cognitive Science*, 26(2), 147–179.

Asay, L. D. and Orgill, M. K. (2010). Analysis of essential features of inquiry found in articles published in The Science Teacher, (1998–2007). *Journal of Science Teacher Education*, 21(1): 57–79.

Bancroft, S., Fawcett, M. and Hay, P. (2008). *Researching children researching the world*. London, Trentham Books.

Barrow, L. H. (2010). Encouraging creativity with scientific inquiry. *Creative Education*, 1 1–6.

Bumard, P., Craft, A., Grainger, T. et al. (2006). Possibility thinking. *International Journal of Early Years Education*, 14(3), 243–262

Chappell, K. and Craft, A. (2011). Creative Learning Conversations *Educational Research*, 53(3), 363-385.

Chi, M. T. H., De Leeuw, N., Chiu, M.-H. and Lavancher, C. (1994). Eliciting self-explanations improves understanding. *Cognitive Science*, 18(3), 439–477.

Cindy, E., Duncan, R. G. and Clark, A. C. (2007). Scaffolding and achievement in problem-based and inquiry learning *Educational Psychologist*, 42(2), 99–107.

Coltman, P., Petyaeva, D. and Anghileri, J. (2002). Scaffolding learning through meaningful tasks and adult interaction. *Early Years*, 22(1), 39–49.

Craft, A. (2002). *Creativity and Early Years education*. London: Continuum

Craft, A. (2011). *Creativity and Education Futures*. Stoke on Trent: Trentham Books.

Craft, A., McConnon, L., & Matthews, A. (2012). Creativity and child-initiated play. *Thinking Skills and Creativity*, 71, 48–61

Creative Little Scientists (2013a) *Report on practices and their implications*. Deliverable D4.4. EU Project (FP7) (Coordinator: Ellinogermaniki Agogi, Greece). Leading Authors: E. Glauert, N. Trakulphadetkrai and J. Maloney.

Creative Little Scientists (2013b) *Country Reports on in-depth field work*. Deliverable 4.3 Addenda. EU Project (FP7) (Coordinator: Ellinogermaniki Agogi, Greece). Report 1 of 9: Belgium Lead Authors: H. Van Houte and K. Devlieger. Report 4 of 9: Germany Lead Authors: A. Scheersoi and L. Pohl. Report 9 of 9: UK Lead Authors: J. Johnston, A. Riley, A. Compton, E. Glauert, N. Trakulphadetkrai, J. Maloney, P. Barber, A. Manches, J. Clack, T. Cremin and A. Craft.

Creative Little Scientists (2014a) *Comparative Report*. Deliverable D3.4. EU Project (FP7) (Coordinator: Ellinogermaniki Agogi, Greece). Leading Authors: S. Havu-Nuutinen, D. Rossis and F. Stylianidou.

Creative Little Scientists (2014b) *Set of Recommendations to policy makers and stakeholders*. Deliverable 6.6. EU Project (FP7) Coordinator: Ellinogermaniki Agogi, Greece. Lead Authors: D. Rossis and F. Stylianidou.

Cremin, T., Burnard, P. and Craft, A. (2006). Pedagogy and possibility thinking in the Early Years, *Thinking Skills and Creativity* 1(2), 108–119.

Cremin, T., Chappell, K. and Craft, A. (2013). Reciprocity between narrative, questioning and imagination in the early and primary years, *Thinking Skills and Creativity* 9:136–151.

Dezuanni, M and Jetnikoff, A. 2011 Creative pedagogies and the contemporary school classroom. In J. Sefton-Green, P, Thomson, K. Jones and L. Bresler (eds.) 2011 *The Routledge international handbook of creative learning*. London: Routledge.

Drayton, B. and Falk, J. (2001). Tell-tale signs of the inquiry-oriented classroom. *NASSP Bulletin*, 856(23), 24–34.

Duschl, R. A., Schweingruber, H. A. and Shouse, A. W. (2007). *Taking science to school*, Washington: National Academy Press.

Eshach, H. and Fried, M. N. (2005). Should science be taught in early childhood? *Journal of Science Education and Technology*, 14(3), 315–336.

European Commission. (2011). *Science education in Europe: National policies practices and research* Eaceae9 Eurydice, Brussels: EACEA.

Feng, J. (1987). *Science, sciencing and science education* (ED319525). Retrieved from http://eric.ed.gov/PDFS/ED319525.pdf.

Fleer, M. (2009). Supporting scientific conceptual consciousness or learning in a roundabout way' in play-based contexts. *International Journal of Science Education*, 31 (8), 1069–1089.

Garaigordobil, M. and Berrueco, L. (2011). Effects of a play program on creative thinking of preschool children. *The Spanish Journal of Psychology*, 14(2), 608–618.

Harlen, W. (2010). *Principles and big ideas of science education.* Available from http://cmaste.ualberta.ca/eri/Outreacli/~/media/cmaste/Documents/Outreach/IANASInterAmericasInquirv/PrinciplesBigIdeasInSciEd.pdf [Retrieved 18th January 2014]

Harlen, W. and Qualter, A. (2004). *The teaching of science in primary schools*. London: David Fulton.

Harris, D. and Williams, J. (2007). Questioning 'open questioning' in Early Years science discourse from a social semiotic perspective. *International Journal of Educational Research*, 46(1–2), 68–82.

Hmelo-Silver, C., Duncan, R. and Chinn, C. (2007). Scaffolding and Achievement in Problem-Based and Inquiry Learning: *Educational Psychologist*, 42(2): 99–107.

Jeffrey, B. and Craft, A. (2004). Teaching creatively and teaching for creativity, *Educational Studies*, 30(1)77–87.

Kuhn, D. (1989). Children and adults as intuitive scientists. *Psychological Review*, 96(4), 674.

Lan, K. and Marvin, C., 2002. Multiple creativities? Investigating domain-specificity of creativity in young children. *Gifted Child Quarterly*, 46(2), 98–109

Larsson, Å. and Halldén, O. (2010). A structural view on the emergence of a conception *Science Education* 94, 640–664.

Mercer, N., Wegerif, R. and Dawes, L. (1999). Children's talk and the development of reasoning in the classroom. *British Educational Research Journal*, 25(1), 95–111.

Metz, K. E. (2004). Children's understanding of scientific inquiry, *Cognition and Instruction*, 222, 219–290.

Millineaux, P. Y. and Dilalla, L. F. (2009). Preschool pretend play behaviors and early adolescent creativity. *Journal of Creative Behaviour*, 43(1), 41–57.

Mitchell, 1., McCoy, J. and Evans, G. W.(2002). The potential role of the physical environment in fostering creativity. *Creativity Research Journal*, 14(3–4) 409–426.

Milne, I. (2010). A sense of wonder arising from aesthetic experiences should be the starting point for inquiry in primary science. *Science Education International*, 212, 102–115.

Minner, D. D., Levy, A. J., and Century, J. (2010). Inquiry-based science instruction: what is it and does it matter? Results from a research synthesis years 1984 to 2002. *Journal of Research in Science Teaching*, 47(4): 474–496

National Advisory Committee on Creative and Cultural Education (NACCCE) (1999) *All Our Futures: Creativity, Culture and Education*, London, DfEE.

Nickerson R.S. (1999). Enhancing creativity in Sternberg, R. J *Handbook of Creativity*, 392–430. Cambridge: Cambridge.

Poddiakov, N. (2011). Searching, experimenting and the heuristic structure of a preschool child's experience. *International Journal of Early Years Education*, 19(1): 55–63.

Rojas-Drummond, S. and Zapata, M. P. (2004). Exploratory talk, argumentation and reasoning in Mexican primary school children. *Language and Education*, 18(6): 539–557.

Siraj-Blatchford I., Sylva, K., Muttock, S., Gilden, R. and Bell, D. (2002). *Researching Effective Pedagogy in the Early Years*. DfES RR 356. Norwich: DfES.

Stevenson, J. N., and Duncum, P. (1998). Collage as a symbolic activity in early childhood. *Visual Arts Research,* 24(1): 38–47.

Torbeyns, J., Verschaffel, L. and Ghesquiere, P. (2002). Strategic competence *European Journal of Psychology of Education*, 17(3): 275–291.

Varela, P. (2010). *Experimental science teaching in primary school*, University of Minho, Braga.

Vass, E. (2007). Exploring processes of collaborative creativity *Thinking Skills and Creativity* 2(2): 107–117.

Wang, F., Kinzie, M. B., Mcguire, P. and Pan, E. (2010). Applying Technology to Inquiry-Based Learning in Early Childhood Education. *Early Childhood Education*, 37(5): 381–389.

Wegerif, R. (2005). Reason and Creativity in Classroom Dialogues *Language and Education* 19(3): 223–237.

Wood, E. and Hall, E. (2011). Drawings as spaces for intellectual play. *International Journal of Early Years Education*, 193(4): 267–281.

Wollman-Bonilla, J. E. (2000). Teaching science writing to first graders, *Research in the Teaching of English*, 35(1): 35–65.

Yin, R. K. 2009. Case study research: Design and methods. 4th ed. Thousand Oaks, CA: Sage.

Chapter 6

Young children's expressions of spirituality in creative and imaginary play

Gill Goodliff

Chapter introduction

In this chapter, Gill Goodliff from The Open University explores the question of how young children express their spirituality. A broader understanding of spirituality is discussed which extends beyond religious beliefs and traditions, and which for young children is revealed in their creative and imaginary play. The author draws on vignettes from her research in early childhood settings to illustrate young children's multi-dimensional expression of spirituality and in conclusion considers the challenges for practitioners in recognising and facilitating such expression.

> The most effective way to learn about children's spiritual experience is to pay attention – listening to words and silence, respecting what is expressed and being aware that much may *not* be expressed.
>
> (Crompton, 2009:23)

Introduction

This chapter explores the capacities of young children to express spirituality within their creative and imaginary play. A holistic understanding of young children's development generally includes recognition of a spiritual dimension. Internationally, early childhood education and care (ECEC) policies variously link spirituality to children's health and well-being, personal, social and emotional development, creativity and learning (Adams et al., 2015; Goodliff, 2016). Friedrich Froebel (1782–1852), one of the pioneers of play and early childhood education in the United Kingdom (UK) and beyond, argued that in play children operate at the highest level of learning and as such play is 'the most spiritual activity of the child' (Froebel, 1878 cited in Bruce, 2004:132). However, published resources and training supporting the professional development of early childhood practitioners in the UK tend not to explore definitions of the spiritual dimension of children's development, and offer little explanation of how young children's spirituality might be recognized or supported (Dowling, 2010). Whilst 'spirituality' is often closely related to religion and religious belief, and some (for example, Wright, 2000) argue it should only be considered within religious traditions, many today adopt the more inclusive definition taken in this chapter – arguing that spirituality is an attribute of all humanity (King, 2009) and not synonymous with religion (Adams et al., 2008). All have the capacity for spiritual awareness and expression regardless of religious affiliation or experience (Goodliff, 2013a).

Research studies into children's experiences and expressions of spirituality link it with their relationships (Bone, 2007; Goodliff, 2013a; Hay and Nye, 1998), imagination and creativity (Champagne, 2001; Fraser and Grootenboer, 2004; Goodliff, 2013a; McCreery, 1996) and a sense of wonder and wondering (Champagne, 2003; Hay and Nye, 1998; Hyde, 2005). Only three of the above studies (e.g. Bone, 2007; Champagne, 2003; Goodliff, 2013a) focused on how pre-school children (aged 2–6 years) experience or express spirituality. So although, arguably, more is understood about children's spirituality, there is less known about how very young children create and express dimensions of the spiritual.

This chapter draws on findings from a small-scale, ethnographic research study undertaken by the author with twenty children, five aged 2, and fifteen aged 3 years, in a day nursery (Goodliff, 2013a). The nursery is one of five privately owned and run children's nurseries in the Midlands area of England. Exploring the broader question of how young children express spirituality, focus here is on how, in their imaginative play, the children reveal a capacity for expressing meaning making and negotiating identity, key dimensions of the spiritual in childhood.

The chapter begins with a discussion of how spirituality and creativity is understood and linked within research literature. Three vignettes taken from the children's imaginary play and experiences in the nursery follow. Broader findings from the study (Goodliff, 2013a; 2016) that revealed the multi-dimensional nature of the 2- and 3-year-olds' expressions of spirituality and the significance of imaginative play as a context for listening to, and recognising, and documenting children's languages of spirituality, are also considered.

Understandings of spirituality

The word 'spirituality' has many meanings and finding one definition for it remains 'elusive' (Best, 2000; Eaude, 2005; Adams et al., 2015).

In predominantly secularised western cultures, such as that in the UK (Brown, 2001; Bruce, 2002), even using words such as 'spiritual' or 'sacred' can be treated with mild amusement, often due to embarrassment or suspicion (Abbs, 2003; Bone et al. 2007; Goodliff, 2013a). Spirituality is often automatically associated by teachers/practitioners with religious belief (Goodliff, 2006). This collapse of spirituality into issues of religion is an unhelpful confusion created in part by education policymakers. Whilst some policy statements do not do this, others have been confused. For example, in past policy statements for primary and early years provision, spirituality has been defined as 'fundamental to the human condition, transcending everyday experience and to do with issues of identity, death and suffering, beauty and evil' (SCAA, 1995:3). However, a slightly earlier definition of spirituality from the National Curriculum Council (1993) also includes the term 'beliefs' to imply an association with religion and religious practice as well as reference to human experience and personal identity, relationships and creativity.

As stated earlier, the understanding adopted in this chapter is that spirituality is ubiquitous and on the assertion that children have a natural capacity for spiritual awareness and expression regardless of any religious affiliation (i.e. as a member of a faith community) (Goodliff, 2013a).

McCreery, who talked to 4- and 5-year-olds in reception classes in England in order to gain an understanding of their conception of the spiritual, defined spirituality as an 'awareness that there is something Other, something greater than the course of everyday events' (1996:197). Like McCreery, Champagne (2003), a hospital chaplain in Canada, was interested in the spiritual awareness of young children. From her recorded observations of sixty pre-school children (aged 3–6 years) that focused on their talk, facial expressions and gestures, Champagne identified three spiritual facets of being: sensitive, relational and existential. Drawing on her observations as a teacher of young children in both primary classrooms and hospitals in America, Barbara Kimes Myers recognised how children brought 'all of their being – including the spiritual – into the so-called secular settings' (1997:x). Acknowledging the value of everyday story telling for young children and adults to explore questions about identity (who we are) and to create memories of connection and care, Myers defines spirituality as a 'depth dimension of human existence' (1997:18). As we shall see later, this points to a broader understanding of how young children's expressions of spirituality are shaped both by personal history – for example from home – and through participating in different experiences and environments.

Creativity and spirituality

The creativity of young children is most commonly defined as linked to play, particularly play involving the imagination (*imaginative play*) and fantasy (Claxton, 1997); to curiosity, the innate disposition to think creatively and actively explore possibilities (Craft, 2002; 2008) (*exploring possibilities*), and creative activity that connects thought, emotion and action (Bruner, 1996) in representations often (but not always) associated within the arts, e.g. a painting, song, or dance (*expressive and connecting representations*). In the research discussed in this chapter exploring expressions of young children's spirituality, each of these overlapping discourses of creativity – *imaginative play*, *exploring possibilities* and *expressive and connecting representations* contain potential synergies with recognising something of the spiritual dimension of children's lives.

Imaginative play

Imaginative play offers the young child agentive experiences (Erikson, 1965), where through pretending and exploring possibilities, a transitional or potential space is created between the child and his environment (Winnicott, 1971). Within this space, which Winnicott describes as 'sacred to the individual' (1971:6), the child draws on external experiences and the unique inner world of the imagination to express capacities for creativity and, it is argued, spirituality (Goodliff, 2013a). The process of negotiating, problem solving and imagining as a social activity demonstrates humane features which can be expressions by children of 'relational consciousness' (Hay and Nye, 1998) that indicates spirituality.

Paley documents the imaginative narratives created in the fantasy play of 3–5-year-olds, referring to the 'indomitable spirit of fantasy play' (2004:110) through which children are able to 'revise and replay the endless possibilities' (111) from their make-believe images. Imaginative play, alone or with others, provides a context for children to explore and reveal who they are and 'also who they would like to be' (Wright, 2011). Being imaginative and entering imaginative worlds is also a way of transcending everyday life, to explore 'mystery' (Hay, 2006:72) or to experience a sense of awe and wonder.

Exploring possibilities

Young children's search for meaning is situated in their everyday encounters and experiences: they 'live at the limit of their experiences most of the time'

(Berryman, 1985:126). The essence of transcendence, often associated with spirituality (Hay, 2006), is the sense or awareness of going through, crossing over, or moving beyond limitations or obstacles (Myers, 1997), and entering a space of mystery (Hay, 2006) – a 'what if?' space.

Acting 'as if' and posing the question 'what if?' in multiple ways is at the heart of understanding children's creativity as Possibility Thinking (Craft, 2002; Chappell et al., 2008). Imagining 'as if' and exploring 'what if I?' or 'what if we?' is also an element of transcendence, as children make the transition in thinking, or seeing, something in a new way. A particular category of sensitivity in children, identified as 'potentially spiritual' (Hay and Nye, 2006:68), is the awareness of experiencing 'flow' (Csikszentmihalyi, 1975), a state of deep absorption or immersion in creative activity where action and awareness somehow merge within to release a feeling of mastery (Csikszentmihalyi, 1988:367). For young children, not all their experiences of 'flow' in activity will necessarily be 'spiritual' moments, but there is the potential for aspects of their spirituality to be mediated within such creative spaces (see Goodliff, 2013b).

Expressive and connecting representations

Bone's concept of 'everyday spirituality' (2008:265) is an understanding of spirituality as a means of connection. From her research in three early childhood settings in New Zealand, exploring how young children's (age 3–6 years) spiritual experiences were supported, Bone proposes that there are spaces with potential for interpreting activity and reflection as mediating spirituality, situated within the everyday narratives of young children's lives – such as preparing or sharing food (Bone et al., 2007).

Creative explorations through the expressive arts, such as music, role play and drawing, enable young children to represent their thinking, feeling and knowing (Bruner, 1986) in ways that tell how they are making meaning of the world. In New Zealand, Fraser and Grootenboer (2004) report teachers' observations that 5–12-year-old children's deep engagement in such artistic endeavours seemed to motivate 'moments of spirituality' (p.315) that had a tangible effect on the classroom. The different voices of children's multimodal communication enable them to make 'cognitive, emotional and "spiritual" connections that are key to deep learning' (Wright, 2002:1). A key component of the multi-modal and embodied nature of children's creative expression and meaning making can be understood as somatic knowing (Wright, 2002), which links the body (soma), mind (psyche) and soul (Wright, 2011). Discussing the possibilities for learning offered by musical experience, Duffy more explicitly acknowledges the potential of music as a conduit for spiritual expression, stating that it 'is a form of communication that is spiritual, emotional and intellectual . . . music is more fundamental to humans than language' (2006:82). Young (2006:22) describes how the spontaneous singing by 2- and 3-year-old children 'was woven into the fabric of their play'. Spirituality, it has been argued, is an attribute of all humanity: it is a language of being and meaning making, in the same way that many argue that elements of creativity are characteristic of being human (see for example, Rosen, 2010, Duffy, 2010).

Although creativity was once recognised as divine inspiration within Greek, Judaic, Christian and Islamic traditions (Rhyammar and Brolin, 1999, cited in Craft et al., 2008), arguably, in secular western societies it no longer possesses an ethical or values base, particularly in education (Craft et al., 2008).

Imaginary play of 2- and 3-year-olds

Three vignettes of the children's imaginary play and experiences in the nursery follow. These detailed, narrative texts were created from transcribed observations, audio recordings and field notes containing reflections and conversations with adults and children. Each text includes children's actions, observations on their expressions and reflections and comments about each episode (in italics).

The interpretive reading (analysis) that follows each vignette considers the multiple meanings of what is happening.

Episode 1: Esther

Esther (2 years, 3 months) has only recently started attending the nursery for three sessions a week. In this seven-minute observation, she is playing in the role play area; two other children are playing close-by in the area, but Esther plays alone.

Esther is standing next to the 'cooker' and cupboard. She holds a mixing bowl with her left arm and is stirring objects in the bowl with a wooden spoon held in her right hand.

Esther is absorbed in the activity; she is aware I am there but is not distracted. She is concentrating on the task; she is a competent player; the bowl is held securely against her body and she stirs purposively.

She puts the bowl down and selects 'foods' from an egg box placed on the cupboard. Each item chosen is carefully placed in bowl; she shakes the box and turns round.

In the egg box are two plastic eggs, a small wooden brick and assorted plastic vegetables; I notice how carefully she selects items.

She stirs the items in the bowl again, then puts it down on the cooker – she looks at me, smiles and moves away from the role play area.

Esther completes her task; I reflect on whether it is the connections remembered with home – of who she is and what she can do – that has made this a significant activity for her – self-affirming.

Analysis

In this solitary imaginative and creative episode, Esther does not speak; she is one of the youngest children in the nursery and has only been attending for two weeks. In this role play, she imitates what she has perhaps witnessed at home. Is she remembering a recent cooking activity with a parent or her sister? Was it observed or did she participate? She has probably drawn on existing knowledge and skills from home. As she selects different 'foods', Esther appears to pose her own 'what if' questions as she independently initiates possibilities for the ingredients of her 'cake'. I suggest her demeanour throughout this episode demonstrates her individual agency. She has chosen and initiated the activity to which she brings a competence and confidence likely to have been gained from social and cultural learning in her home.

Although not articulated, by acting as if she is the cook or in charge, by exploring the 'ingredients' before her and selecting 'foods', she appears to pose, if only momentarily, 'what if?' questions that underpin the notion of creativity as Possibility Thinking (Craft, 2002). Through this activity in the nursery, she seems to make connections with her home and the significant relationships and experiences within that environment. This imaginative play is a means of helping her to interpret to herself her own identity. This connection to a special person (her mother or perhaps a sibling) gives meaning and purpose to her work here and is, I argue, an expression of her spirituality. It is evidence of the bi-directional (Bronfenbrenner, 1979) influence of Esther's 'ecological niche' (David, 1998:18) intersecting the two environments and creating a space for moments of imaginative role playing which express to the observer 'who I am'. Through narrative and embodied communication, Wright (2011:163) citing Geertz, asserts that children enter into an interpretive space where they can 'tell themselves about themselves' (Geertz, 1971:26). The solitary imaginative space can also be viewed as sacred – it is a private space Esther inhabits 'in which fantasy, daydreams, reflections, thoughts, meditations, anxieties find form in our consciousness' (Trotman, 2006:5).

Episode 2: Kirsty and Kirsten

In this text, Kirsty (K1) (3 years, 8 months) and Kirsten (K2) (3 years, 6 months) – who have both attended the nursery for more than two terms – make up a song as they role play the preparation and serving of food. To create some shade on a very hot day, the nursery staff have erected a tent made of sheets to cover the role-play area. Rachel (3 years, 2 months) is playing alongside them.

The girls are standing by the cooker which has two pans on it:

K2:   'Are you busy with your mother?' 'Can I have one chip please? – one chip gone now . . .'

The girls refer to 'your mother' – it is not clear to me who (if anyone) is taking the role –I reflect that 'mother' seems a person of significance.

K1:   'Ishy, wishy?' Both girls laugh . . .
K2:   'Lovely . . . La, la, la, la, la – la, la, la, la, la, la, la, la . . . there's your one; do you take sugar?'
K.1:   'All of the mudcakes in there . . .' Their vocalisation rises to a crescendo.

Rhythmic vocalisation extends to singing of the question re. the sugar . . . both girls take turns. Spontaneous vocalisation: a shared moment – which is fun/enjoyable.

Rachel imitates the song and attempts to join in.

R: 'There's an egg here, la, la, la nice cup of tea?'

I wonder if the tune or sounds are familiar from a TV programme – unknown to me? I reflect how much she is enjoying creating this 'song' – exploring and experimenting with the possibilities of rhythm and sound.

The other girls ignore Rachel and she stops singing but stays watching and listening. Kirsty returns to the earlier refrain – 'Ishy, wishy, wa'; she adds an additional phrase to extend the refrain:

K1:   'Ishy, wishy, wa . . . ishy, wishy, wa, ishy, wishy, wish was, ishy, wishy wish wa.'

Together Kirsty and Kirsten chant the 'song' they have composed together:

'Ishy, wishy, wa; ishy, wishy, wa; ishy, wishy, wish wa; ishy, wishy, wish wa.'

They smile at each other as they sing.

I reflect on how this playful exploration of sounds and words emerges from self-initiated role play; it seems to be an emotionally satisfying and meaningful episode for both.

Analysis

This playful spontaneous vocalisation emerges from self-initiated imaginative role play; as with Esther, the episode is linked to preparation and serving of food and creates connections with significant relationships ('your mother'), and experiences each brings to the nursery environment.

The shared rhythmic communicative activity between Kirsty and Kirsten demonstrates and marks a connection and intimacy between them. The self-creation of the musical rhyme seems to be emotionally satisfying and personally meaningful to them both (Young, 2011), a musical communication that perhaps draws on the spiritual as well as the emotional (Duffy, 2006).

I reflected that perhaps it was Kirsty and Kirsten's friendship and familiarity – they had both been attending the nursery for over six months – that prevented them from extending their exchange to acknowledge, or include, Rachel's contribution. They did not know her enough to trust her, or perhaps they were caught up in their own creative endeavour. However the younger girl did not protest and remained present, observing and smiling at their fun. It was my own sensing that she had wanted to join in – nothing was said. Perhaps even as an observer of Kirsty and Kirsten's collaborative creative play, Rachel had not been prevented from entering their imaginative space.

Episode 3: Billy and Amos

Billy (2 years, 10 months) and Amos (2 years, 3 months) are playing with cars on the carpet; Billy has been coming to the nursery for six months and attends every day. Amos has attended the nursery for two months, for four days each week.

Billy plays on his own with the cars; he lies on the carpet; he has a car in his hand; as he moves the car he vocalises the sound of the car to himself: 'Brrrm, brrrm . . . .'

Billy crashes the car into other cars − 'crashing' − vocalisation becomes louder − 'he's crashing into them . . . can't get out . . . .' Billy laughs.

Billy is totally absorbed. Although he knows I am there and observing, there is no acknowledgement − he inhabits his own imaginative space.

As he makes up his game, Billy acts as if he is the car − imagining. The sounds he makes imitate a car's engine and through his actions he is 'being' the car. I wonder has he watched the Grand Prix (on TV or with family), experienced the excitement and seen cars crashing?

Amos comes over to carpet; Billy welcomes and accommodates this interruption to his play. The boys smile at each other. Together they put cars in garage − run them up the ramp . . . self-initiated activity . . . .

Amos: 'I've got a red car . . . la, la, la, la . . . .'

Billy and Amos: 'Ah, ah, ah, eeeeh,' 'Ah, ah, ah, eeeeh . . .', their vocalisation is spontaneous − screeching rising to a crescendo.

I reflect on each boy's agency − each brings his own understanding, experiences and imagination to create and direct the game; they are collaborating in thinking what they can do as cars − a shared exploration in developing sounds for their cars.

They continue playing alongside each other − both hum and sing; no other interaction between the boys is observed now. Humming and singing, Amos moves over to the dinosaurs (also on carpet) . . . Billy continues playing with the cars vocalising to himself; 'mmm, aah, mmm, aah . . . .'

Listening later to the recording, I reflect on the happiness/exuberance expressed; how deeply satisfying Billy seems to have found this activity.

Analysis

In this imaginative play episode, both Billy and Amos demonstrate their agency. Billy chooses to be the car, acting as if he is the driver and mimicking the sounds the car makes as he drives it over the carpet and crashes it into other cars. There is evidence of somatic knowing (Wright, 2002; 2011), as Billy thinks through the car's direction, embodies its actions and creatively imagines his own narrative. Gestural and vocal representation is seen in Billy's crashing of the car.

I reflected on whether he had watched a recent Grand Prix on TV? In creating a story around the cars, both boys will have been influenced by personal experiences beyond the nursery – whether through first-hand experience or digital media.

In imaginative play, children can probe their emotions through felt responses to images (Trotman, 2006). When the two boys play together, I reflected that their enjoyment and exuberance seem palpable. The spontaneous vocalisation of humming and singing together, and alone, is calming and soothing (Young, 2006). When Amos briefly moves to another area of the carpet, Billy seems to be in his own solitary imaginative space – his quieter, reflective humming suggesting he is inhabiting his own private space for a few moments, an inner world that is personally meaningful (Beghetto and Kaufman, 2007).

Possibility Thinking is observed in the context of children's immersive play (Chappell, 2008). Billy and Amos act as if they are cars, and in their actions and exchanges pose questions that evidence 'what if?' thinking (Craft, 2002), which in turn, through engaging the mind, body and soul (Wright, 2011), suggests expressions of spirituality.

Conclusion

A major finding of the wider study from which the vignettes in this chapter are taken is that the expression of spirituality is multi-dimensional. The everyday spaces or environments of relationship and imagination, created and inhabited by the two- and three-year-olds and adults in the day nursery, were shown to be rich with potential for listening to and recognising languages of spirituality (see Goodliff, 2013a; 2016). The children's imaginative narrative, and solitary narrative spaces, revealed how: in private, *fantasy* worlds they *explored possibilities* – sometimes alone and sometimes with a companion and through *embodied communications* – sometimes vocalised and sometimes silent, they expressed connectedness to others and moments of remembering and stillness.

This chapter has considered the little discussed spiritual dimension of children's development and being. A key focus has been on creative play: play that involves the imagination, where questions are posed, possibilities explored and where young children's thinking, feelings and meaning making may be expressed through music, drawing, or other embodied ways, and where aspects of their spirituality – as an attribute of their humanity (King, 2009) – may be glimpsed or recognised. For practitioners the importance of working with a perspective that recognises young children's agency and capacity: to bring their spirituality, as a dimension of their humanity (Myers, 1997) into the nursery, and to create imaginative narrative spaces where dimensions of the spiritual should be recognised. To notice moments when young children create a space of inner reflection (perhaps in a day dream or solitary, silent withdrawal from play), and to allow children space to process them, rather than intervening, can be difficult when policy agendas are focused on preparing young children for compulsory school education.

In contexts where the acquisition of cognitive skills – such as numeracy and literacy skills – is privileged over the more difficult to measure 'non-cognitive' dispositions and skills (Carr and Lee, 2012) such as kindness, compassion, empathy and curiosity, young children's spiritual voice can go unheard.

Questions for further thinking and reflection

1. How might greater awareness of spirituality as a dimension of all humanity influence your interactions with young children?
2. Reflect on observations you have made of young children's imaginative play. Were the children allowed space and time for inner reflection or to bring dimensions of their spirituality?

Further reading

Adams, K., Bull, R. and Maynes, M.L. (2015) Early childhood spirituality in education: Towards an understanding of the distinctive features of young children's spirituality, *European Early Childhood Education Research Journal*, *24*(5): 760–74.
Selbie, P. (2015) Spirituality and young children's wellbeing, in Parker-Rees, R. and Leeson, C. (eds) 4th edn, *Early Childhood Studies*. London: Sage.

References

Abbs, P. (2003) *Against the Flow: Education, the arts and postmodern culture*. London and New York: Routledge Falmer.
Adams, K., Bull, R. and Maynes, M.L. (2015) Early childhood spirituality in education: Towards an understanding of the distinctive features of young children's spirituality, *European Early Childhood Education Research Journal*, *24*(5): 760–74.
Adams, K., Hyde, B. and Woolley, R. (2008) *The Spiritual Dimension of Childhood*. London: Jessica Kingsley.
Beghetto, R.A. and Kaufman, J.C. (2007) Towards a broader conception of creativity: A case for "mini-c" creativity, *Psychology of Aesthetics, Creativity and the Arts*, *I*(2): 73–9.
Berryman, J. (1985) Children's spirituality and religious language, *British Journal of Religious Education*, 7(3): 120–27.

Best R. (ed.) (2000) *Education for Spiritual, Moral, Social and Cultural Development.* London: Continuum.

Bone, J. (2007) Everyday spirituality: Supporting the spiritual experience of young children in three early childhood educational settings (unpublished PhD thesis). Palmerston North, New Zealand: Massey University.

Bone, J. (2008) Creating relational spaces: everyday spirituality in early childhood settings. *European Early Childhood Research Journal, 16*(3): 343–356.

Bone, J., Cullen, J. and Loveridge J. (2007) Everyday spirituality: An aspect of the holistic curriculum in action, *Contemporary Issues in Early Childhood, 8*(4): 344–54.

Bronfenbrenner, U. (1979) *The Ecology of Human Development.* Cambridge, MA: Harvard University Press.

Brown, C. (2001) *The Death of Christian Britain.* London: Routledge.

Bruce, S. (2002) *God is Dead: Secularization in the West.* Oxford: Blackwell.

Bruce, T. (2004) *Developing Learning in Early Childhood.* London: Paul Chapman.

Bruner, J. (1996) *The Culture of Education.* Cambridge, MA: Harvard University Press.

Carr, M. and Lee, W. (2012) *Learning Stories, Constructing Learner Identities in Early Education.* London: Sage.

Champagne, E. (2001) Listening to . . . listening for . . . : A theological reflection on spirituality in early childhood, in Erricker, J., Ota, C. and Erricker, C. (eds) *Spiritual Education. Cultural, Religious and Social Difference: New perspectives for the 21st century,* pp. 76–87. Brighton: Sussex Academic.

Champagne, E. (2003) Being a child, a spiritual child, *International Journal of Children's Spirituality, 8*(1): 43–53.

Chappell, K. (2008) Towards Humanising Creativity. *UNESCO Observatory* E-Journal, Special Issue on *Creativity, Policy and Practice Discourses: Productive tensions in the new millennium, 1*(3).

Chappell, K., Craft, A., Burnard, P. and Cremin, T. (2008) Question-posing and question-responding: The heart of 'Possibility Thinking' in the early years, *Early Years, 28*(3): 267–86.

Claxton, G. (1997) *Hare Brain, Tortoise Mind: Why intelligence increases when you think less.* London: Fourth Estate.

Craft, A. (2002) Little c creativity, in Craft, A., Jeffrey, B. and Leibling, M. (eds) *Creativity in Early Years Education: A lifewide foundation,* London: Continuum.

Craft, A. (2008) Trusteeship, wisdom, and the creative future of education? *UNESCO Observatory* E-Journal, Special Issue on *Creativity, Policy and Practice Discourses: Productive tensions in the new millennium, 1*(3). www.abp.unimelb.edu.au/unesco/ejournal/vol-one-issue-three.html (accessed 17 March 2017).

Craft, A., Gardner, H. and Claxton, G. (eds) (2008) *Creativity, Wisdom and Trusteeship: Exploring the role of education.* London: Sage.

Crompton, M. (2009) Spiritual equality in the experience of Quaker children. *Friends Quarterly.* www.thefriend.co.uk/fq/027.pdf (accessed 20 October 2013).

Csikszentmihalyi, I. (1988) Flow in a historical context: The case of the Jesuits, in Csikszentmihalyi M. and Csikszentmihalyi, I. (eds) *Psychological Studies of Flow in Consciousness,* pp. 232–49. New York: Cambridge University Press.

Csikszentmihalyi, M. (1975) *Beyond Boredom and Anxiety* San Francisco, CA: Jossey-Bass.

David, T. (1998) Changing minds: young children and society, in Abbott, L. and Pugh, G. (eds) *Training to Work in the Early Years: Developing the climbing frame.* Buckingham: Open University Press.

Dowling, M. (2010) *Young Children's Personal, Social and Emotional Development*, 3rd edn. London: Paul Chapman.

Duffy, B. (2006) *Supporting Creativity and Imagination in the Early Years*, 2nd edn. Buckingham: Open University Press.

Duffy, B. (2010) Using creativity and creative learning to enrich the lives of young children at the Thomas Coram Centre, in Tims, C. (ed.) *Born Creative*. London: Demos. www. demos.co.uk/files/Born_Creative_-_web_-_final.pdf?1289392179 (accessed 12 November 2016).

Eaude, T. (2005) Strangely familiar? – Teachers making sense of young children's spiritual development *Early Years, 25*(3): 237–248.

Erikson, E.H. (1965) *Childhood and Society*. Harmondsworth: Penguin.

Fraser, D. and Grootenboer, P. (2004) Nurturing spirituality in secular classrooms, *International Journal of Children's Spirituality, 9*(3): 307–20.

Geertz, C. (1971) *Myth, Symbol, and Culture*. New York: Norton.

Goodliff, G. (2006) Spirituality and young children's learning: Evaluating the perspectives of early years practitioners (paper given at the European Early Childhood Education Research Association (EECERA) conference, Reykjavik, Iceland, 30 August–2 September 2006).

Goodliff, G. (2013a) Young Children's expressions of spirituality: An ethnographic case study (unpublished EdD thesis). Milton Keynes: The Open University.

Goodliff, G. (2013b) Spirituality expressed in creative learning: Young children's imagining play as space for mediating their spirituality. *Journal of Early Child Development and Care, 8*(2013): 1054–71.

Goodliff, G. (2016) Spirituality and early childhood education and care, in de Souza, M., Bone, J. and Watson, J. (eds) *Spirituality across Disciplines: Research and practice in education, health and social care, theology, business, sustainability and cultural studies*. Cham, Switzerland: Springer.

Hay, D. (2006) Children's spirituality – what we know already, in Hay, D. with Nye, R. (2006) *The Spirit of the Child* (rev. edn), pp. 49–62. London: Jessica Kingsley.

Hay, D. and Nye, R. (1998) *The Spirit of the Child*. London. Harper Collins.

Hyde, B. (2005) Beyond logic – entering the realm of mystery: Hermeneutic phenomenology as a tool for reflecting on children's spirituality, *International Journal of Children's Spirituality, 10*(1): 31–44.

King, U. (2009) *The Search for Spirituality: Our global quest for meaning and fulfilment*. Norwich: Canterbury Press.

McCreery, E. (1996) Talking to young children about things spiritual, in Best R. (ed.) *Education for Spiritual, Moral, Social and Cultural Development*, pp. 196–205. London: Continuum.

Myers, B.K. (1997) *Young Children and Spirituality*. London: Routledge.

National Curriculum Council (1993) *Spiritual and Moral Development: A discussion paper*, April (reprinted SCAA, 1995. York: NCC.

Paley, V.G. (2004) *A Child's Work: the Importance of Fantasy Play*. Chicago, IL: Chicago University Press.

Rosen, M. (2010) Foreword, in Tims, C. (ed.) *Born Creative*. London: Demos. www.demos.co.uk/files/Born_Creative_-_web_-_final.pdf?1289392179 (accessed 12 November 2016).

SCAA (School, Curriculum and Assessment Authority) (1995) *Spiritual and Moral Development*. SCAA Discussion Papers, No. 3. London: HM Stationery Office.

Trotman, D. (2006, 2 May) Evaluating the imaginative: Situated practice and the conditions for professional judgement in imaginative education. *International Journal of Education & the Arts*, 7(3). http://ijea.asu.edu/v7n3/ (accessed 8 August 2011).

Winnicott, D.W. (1971) *Playing and Reality*. London: Tavistock.

Wright, A. (2000) *Spirituality and Education*. London: Routledge Falmer.

Wright, S. (2002) Multi-modality in a new key: The significance of the arts in research and education (paper given at AARE (2002) Australian Association for Research in Education Researchers International Conference, Brisbane).

Wright, S. (2011) Meaning, mediation and mythology, in Faulkner, D. and Coates, E. (eds) (2011) *Exploring Children's Creative Narratives*. Oxford: Routledge.

Young, S. (2006) Seen but not heard: Young children, improvised singing and educational practice, *Contemporary Issues in Early Childhood*, 7(3).

Young, S. (2011) Children's creativity with time, space and intensity: foundations for the temporal arts, in Faulkner, D. and Coates, E. (eds) *Exploring Children's Creative Narratives*. Oxford: Routledge.

Chapter 7

5×5×5=creativity: principles, learning and our legacy

Penny Hay

Chapter introduction

The vision of 5×5×5=creativity, an arts-based action research organisation, includes giving children and adults the means to develop their creativity no matter what their background or circumstances. In this chapter, Penny Hay, an artist and educator, the director of research for 5×5×5=creativity and senior lecturer in education at Bath Spa University, outlines the core values and principles that underpin all their work. Highlighting the influence of the philosophy and pedagogy of Reggio Emilia, with its emphasis on listening, documentation and critical reflection, she draws on examples from research projects with young children to illustrate how participation in creative environments supports critical thinking and the wider well-being of children and adults.

5×5×5=creativity: principles, learning and our legacy

> 5×5×5=creativity is a visionary and ground-breaking research project which demonstrates the depth of learning fostered through exquisitely sensitive creative partnership. Children and adults involved in 5×5×5 are sowing seeds of systemic change in our education system, well beyond early years and primary, into secondary, further and higher education phases.
>
> (Dame Tamsyn Imison, Patron of 5×5×5=creativity, 2016)

This chapter attempts to capture the complexity of the process involved in 5 × 5 × 5: its structure, values, intellectual depth and aesthetic qualities. Artists, educational settings, cultural centres, arts organisations, families, local authorities and universities are all involved in this process. The chapter will explore the philosophical foundations of the approach that involves a fundamental shift in thinking about children, their learning and creativity. This philosophical framework is based on creativity as a democratic notion and valuing children as competent creative learners. 5×5×5 offers a strategic approach that is child-focused and long-term in contrast to much other practice. The chapter aims to share our practical and philosophical experience and to encourage more people to work in this creative way.

5×5×5=creativity is an independent, arts-based action research organisation with charitable status that supports children and young people in their exploration and expression of ideas, helping them develop creative skills for life. Groups of five artists, five educational settings and five cultural centres (galleries, theatres, music centres) work in dynamic, researchful partnership to collect evidence of children's creativity and how best to support it. Since 2000, 5×5×5 has worked with over 300 settings across ten local authorities mostly in the South West of England, although the research project is now influencing practice beyond, and is nationally recognised. Originally focused on early years children, the approach now extends to primary and secondary schools. Throughout the research, there has been a transformation of practice in classrooms and across whole schools (Bancroft et al. 2008; 5×5×5=creativity evaluation reports 2001–16).

5×5×5=creativity is influenced by the creative educational approach of early years settings in Reggio Emilia in Northern Italy, but has developed its own identity. Inspired by the approach in Reggio Emilia pre-schools, the co-construction of knowledge is a key feature of 5×5×5=creativity, in which teachers, parents and adults work together in documenting children's learning, 'researching children researching the world' (Bancroft et al. 2008: 2). The image of child (Edwards et al. 1998: 184), children and adults as co-researchers and meaning-makers (Craft 2008a: 14, 22); the role of creativity (Cremin et al. 2006: 110) and the need to explore and document pedagogies that build on these beliefs (Drummond 2005: 12) are key processes explored in this context. In Reggio Emilia, they refer to children, teachers and parents as 'protagonists' (Rinaldi 2006: 58). Pedagogy is built upon reciprocal relations, participation, exchange, dialogue and negotiation (ibid.: 186–187). The teachers' role is to help children discover their own problems and questions, to focus on a problem or difficultly and formulate hypotheses (Edwards et al. 1998: 185) in an enabling environment.

5×5×5 aims to inspire and transform learning. The vision of 5×5×5 is to develop creative reflective practice and influence systemic change. Multi-professional teams work in partnership to support children and young people in environments of enquiry, challenging orthodoxies and developing new ways of thinking. The mission of 5×5×5=creativity as a charity is the advancement of education and in particular:

- working in partnership with educators and artists, and with museums, galleries, theatres and other artistic and cultural settings to support children in their exploration, communication and expression of creative ideas;
- producing and disseminating research and guidance on creative values, relationships, dispositions and environments in order to help develop children as confident, creative thinkers;
- providing integrated training and mentoring for educators, artists and cultural centres.

The ambition of 5×5×5 is to change society's understanding of creativity and to centralise its place in learning and teaching. The vision is to give children and adults the means to develop their creativity, no matter what their background or circumstances. Through their involvement in creative research and activity, children are able to develop life-wide creative capacities (Craft 2000) and become confident, creative learners in every aspect throughout their lives. Craft (ibid.) highlights the notion of little 'c' creativity, that everyone has the capacity for creativity, it is not just the preserve of the genius. Our evidence in 5×5×5=creativity is that children spontaneously and creatively connect all forms of thinking and expressive representations.

5×5×5=creativity research is underpinned by the following set of creativity principles:

Everyone is born with potential

We are sociable, creative and curious about the world around us. The image of the child is rich in potential from the moment of birth (Edwards et al. 1998). Children are perceived as communicators from birth and as they develop in their early years, they discover many ways of representing their feelings, theories and imaginative ideas.

The hundred languages of children

The phrase, 'the hundred languages of children', comes from a poem by Loris Malaguzzi (founder of the Reggio Approach) (1996). Valuing children's expression through all forms – verbal, non-verbal, through movement, music, drawing, painting, constructing, using technical equipment such as cameras and computers – helps us grasp and respond to children's thinking. More than this, offering different forms of representation to children opens up learning opportunities for all. In Reggio Emilia, every class has its own *atelier* or workshop, a place to explore the 'hundred languages'. Our evidence is that children spontaneously and creatively connect all forms of thinking and expressive representation.

Child-focused processes (not necessarily products)

We are interested in how children are learning and how this informs their development. The whole process by which children explore, think, represent and discuss is the focus, not the final product. It is easy to be impressed by tangible objects constructed by children rather than the thought-processes that inform them. Too often, educational settings offer adult-directed activities with little thought or imagination expected from the child. In 5×5×5, creative interventions and provocations from the adults are catalysts for the children's own thinking and meaning making. When children have the opportunities to play with ideas in different contexts, they discover new connections and understanding.

A pedagogy of listening

Underpinning all the work in 5×5×5 is the 'pedagogy of listening' (Rinaldi 2006). Everyone's worth and their contributions are recognised; children's ideas are heard and supported. When children are listened to and offered a creative environment they 'take off', they experience a sense of ownership and satisfaction that is lasting. Careful listening, observations and reflection on children's learning give shape to pedagogical thought. In 5×5×5, the adults' role is to create a context in which the children's curiosity, theories and research can be legitimated and listened to, as this extract from a longer conversation between 3–4-year-olds illustrates. Here the children were creating ideas together about how the world works, exploring what it is and is not, to evolve an agreed theory. Questions follow the children's explorations and were genuine and open, resulting in a mixture of playful imagination and enquiry:

Lily: 'Outside is outside the door.'
Adult: *Can you see it?*
           'No'
           Can you feel it?
           'No it's too cold.'
           Can you hear the outside?

Tilly:	'You can hear the wind.'
Lily:	'You can hear the wind whistling in the trees.'
Jo:	'You can't hear the clouds.'
	How big is it?
	'It's this big.' [arms outstretched] 'it's much bigger.'
	How big?
	'They say it's as big as the room; it goes to the edge of Bath; it goes as far as London.'
	Is London outside?
	'Yes.'
Jo:	'The sky is much bigger than in here.'
Lily:	'The sky is as big as the whole world.'
	How are we going to get the outside inside?
Lily:	'You could put all of the things inside outside, and put all of the outside inside.'
Jo:	'You can't get the sky inside.'
Lily:	'A person could go up a very, very, very long ladder and get the sun and the sky and the birds and get them inside. If it's midnight, you could get the moon and the stars.'
Lily:	'We could break it and then it would fall into a box.'
Jo:	'You can't hold the sky because it's not made of metal.'
Thomas:	'If we open the window it could get in.'
	Lily 'If we open all of the windows all of the world outside would come in, and all the inside would go out.'

As adults, we listen to and place trust in children's and young people's ideas, their curiosity and questions; we nurture creative capacities – we encourage enquiring minds, independent thinking and reflection. Deep, probing enquiries challenging each other's perspectives open up the creative possibilities in children's learning.

Documentation, reflection and evaluation

Careful observations and documentation of children's words provide insight into their ideas and understandings. Documentation is a *reflective process* that makes flexible planning possible and modifies the teaching and learning relationship. It informs our way of being with children – how we 'see' them, respond and relate to them – and ensures children or childhood is not 'anonymous'. It improves our professional knowledge of how children think, feel and learn. It involves gathering and interpreting the children's learning experiences using all possible means, visual and written:

The room was darkened and the *eighteen* children (3–4 year olds) were constructing boats and houses from large cardboard boxes with torches as their light source. All manner of other decorative materials were available such as cardboard tubes, pipe-cleaner wires, feathers and beads. The children remained totally engaged for almost two hours. They were supported by several adults: the artist, a colleague from the cultural centre taking video and photographs, the educator and a parent both documenting the children's conversations.

Mary Fawcett, Trustee, 5×5×5=creativity

All the material documentation is examined through dialogue with colleagues, themes found and future possibilities developed. From the recorded sequences of learning, 'learning stories' (Carr 2001) are identified and displayed for children, parents and other colleagues to share, review and revisit.

The child at the heart of the process

Children will always come up with good ideas, with unexpected theories that are purposeful and imaginative. Careful observations of children provide an insight into their interests and preoccupations. The adults facilitate and support the children's depth of learning by respecting their individual interests and taking time to make connections with the children's thinking. The emphasis is on supporting children's developing ideas, thoughts and feelings. Children have opportunities for exploration, for response and contextualisation of their learning, using innovative and imaginative approaches that stimulate the imagination and encourage independent thought. If adults take children's ideas seriously, they can support children in the exploration and expression of their ideas in a 'hundred languages' (Edwards et al. 1998).

Respect for children's ideas

Relationships and a sense of active citizenship are central to effective educational experiences. All the adults, artists, educators and cultural colleagues have demonstrated their commitment in 5×5×5 to work based on a deep respect for children. The children see themselves as researchers, as protagonists in their own learning. Time, space and attention are given to supporting and developing children's hypotheses and theories about the world. Focusing on children's questions, schemas and learning dispositions allows us to negotiate the lines of enquiry. When children collaborate in small groups, this allows for more significant, powerful learning to take place alongside interested adults, to re-evaluate their thinking and theories through conversation and dialogue. Dialogue, negotiation and companionship arise out of relationships and are formative in children's and young people's learning and development.

A creative and reflective pedagogy

Critical reflective evaluation of action is at the heart of the 5×5×5 research. In 5×5×5, the quality of the work depends on a creative and reflective pedagogy. A continuous cycle maintains a rich level of thinking that keeps 'research as a habit of mind' (Moss 2003). We want to make explicit and transparent the values that underpin our research. Emphasis is placed on children taking responsibility alongside adults for their learning, asking good questions, making choices and being curious about the world. In 5×5×5, we are supporting children as independent, creative and reflective thinkers involved in rich and authentic learning. Our 5×5×5 research projects have not been pre-structured, but have emerged through close collaboration, dialogue and observation. They have developed as interactive experiences, the adults learning from and supporting the children in their development as makers and creators–adults observe and listen to children's interests, hypotheses and motivations. The approach also affords time, space

Figure 7.1 Pitton Pre-School

and attention to engaging in formative research that is illuminating and qualitative. In practical terms, 5×5×5 starts by observing and listening to the children, followed by a reconnaissance of the possibilities, experimenting with different approaches and ongoing evaluation as part of a creative and reflective cycle (Aguirre Jones and Elders 2009).

Continuous professional development

5×5×5=creativity has a dual focus on personal development: on the participating children and on the education and arts practitioners. All the participants (artists, educators and colleagues from the cultural centres) take part in continuous professional development, an integral part of the project – 'RED' days are identified for Reflection, Exchange and Dialogue. Colleagues present their research, learning stories and discuss challenges. Wider professional development continues throughout the research and also involves whole staff teams and the parents. The continuing professional development of 5×5×5 practitioners – both education and arts – is essential to effecting sustainable change in policy and practice: 'it's like putting on a pair of glasses and seeing everything much sharper and in focus' (Carrie Beckett, Pitton Pre-school).

Collaboration with parents and the community

Parents' and carers' involvement in 5×5×5 enriches the experience for everyone. As adults, it is our role to facilitate and support children's depth of learning: by respecting children and taking time to make observations and connections with the children's thinking, we can refine our own efforts in supporting their learning more effectively. 5×5×5 is focused on exploring children researching and representing the world together, with adults supporting them. Our main focus is adults' scaffolding of children's enquiries and hypotheses about the world through creative values, behaviours and environments. We value an active partnership with parents and carers, and the knowledge and experiences of families, as a critical part of a child's development.

Democracy and participation

Engagement with creative people with different skills and knowledge, e.g. artists, musicians, mathematicians, philosophers, etc., is an enriching experience for all. This research depends on the collaborative working at all levels: children together, professional colleagues (artists, educators and colleagues from cultural centres), parents and the community with each other and all these groups with the children. All are seen as co-learners and co-constructors of knowledge, forming creative, collaborative and reflective learning communities. All aspects of 5×5×5 are documented and thus made transparent and accessible to all participants: everyone's voice is heard. Key principles of access, democracy and participation have underpinned our collaborations. The willingness and open minds of the adults in the research has allowed us to take purposeful risks together. Uncertainty and mutual trust coexist:

> . . . to recognise doubt and uncertainty, to recognise your limits as a resource, as a place of encounter, as a quality. Which means that you accept that you are unfinished, in a state of permanent change, and your identity is in the dialogue.
>
> (Rinaldi 2006)

The four elements of our research in 5×5×5=creativity

From all the learning journeys over the last sixteen years, we have collected vast quantities of documentation at many levels. This storehouse of experience is only valuable if we can share it with others and if we can raise the understanding of creativity in education much more widely and contribute to the understanding of creativity in our culture. The research radiates from this central idea that we are 'researching ourselves, researching the children, researching the world'. Our research has evolved identifying four elements:

- *Creative values* – the competence and strength of the child, pedagogy of listening
- *Creative relationships* – attentive, respectful adults and children working collaboratively
- *Creative environments* – both physical and emotional
- *Creative behaviours and dispositions* – supporting creative thinking and learning dispositions; holistic learning.

The invisible framework

Using these four elements of research, 5×5×5=creativity are creating a new language to describe creativity – indeed, these definitions are not fixed. The respect for ideas and difference, the commitment to reflection, exchange and dialogue are central to this process. Participants are partners in critical and creative enquiry. The project offers a clear framework without prescription for these enquiries, with choice and control in a learning context. This 'invisible framework' is one of the key aspects and involves integrated professional development and peer mentoring support, as well as the supportive networks being created at different levels and the sharing and discussing of practice between individuals, schools, artists, parents and cultural centres.

5×5×5=creativity offers this invisible structure for teachers to work alongside artists and cultural centres to critically analyse, reflect on and appraise their values in relation to their pedagogical practice. Working in this way, and in the spirit of Reggio Emilia, teachers recognise that children can become active citizens as protagonists in their own learning and contribute to a negotiated curriculum. This means an education that belongs to them in a society with a vision of children who can act and think for themselves: '5×5×5=creativity helps improve the life chances of children by developing their confidence in themselves as creative learners, thinkers and problem solvers whilst inspiring higher levels of motivation and engagement in their learning' (Sally Jaeckle, Strategic Lead for Early Years, Bristol and 5×5×5=creativity Trustee).

Figure 7.2 Girls hammering

The significance of the arts

This research has opened new horizons for both artists and educators and highlighted the importance of self-reflection. Multi-sensory and multi-modal learning approaches have developed the notion of learning as a multi-dimensional concept: 'The arts raise the human condition and enrich personal experience, they give us a sense of identity, stretch our intellectual and emotional responses and help us become more flexible and creative in our attitudes' (Steers and Swift 1999).

The work of 5×5×5 has shown that the arts have the power to be transformational in our lives. Working alongside creative professional artists has been a privilege that all children and adults should have access to: to be able to learn together in ways which value our human capacities for being creative, for being artists. The arts are an important element of our lives; their role should be central and their contribution vital. The research has shown the exploration of big themes: identity, belonging, community, relationships, conflict, birth and death. Giving attention to different interpretations and fluid meanings in constructing knowledge has generated 'possibility thinking with wisdom': creative thinking and social responsibility (Craft 2008b: 10).

In Reggio Emilia, the comparable role of the artist is known as the *atelierista:*

> The *atelierista* is a studio worker, an artisan, a lender of tools, a partner in a quest or journey. In this way you are a maker, but maybe more richly you are an enabler, someone who will attend to others in their creation, their development and their communication of knowledge.
>
> (Vecchi, in Edwards et al. 1998: 139).

In Reggio Emilia, an *atelierista* will be someone with a teaching qualification specialising in art, who enables and facilitates the children. 5×5×5 extends that role by working with 'professional artists of outstanding calibre', whose aim is 'to enable, facilitate, collaborate and co-research with people – both children or adults' (Fawcett and Hay 2003: 12). Most are artists with an ongoing, professional, contemporary arts practice.

Creative and critical thinking

5×5×5=creativity is creating an environment where thinking processes are transparent, valued and shared, where adults are willing to observe, listen and work closely with children's ideas with endless curiosity. Exploring Craft's (2008b: 14) notion of 'possibility thinking', we identified strategies for supporting possibility thinking in learners as those that include 'standing back', 'profiling learner agency' and 'creating time and space':

> 'When young children are encouraged to think creatively by following their own lines of enquiry, establishing hypotheses about the world, exploring possibilities, making new connections and solving problems, they are developing the skills of life-long learning. When their ideas and feelings are sought and valued and they are encouraged to decide for themselves how they can best represent these ideas, through story making, painting, sculpture, dance, role play or music for example, they come to see themselves as citizens of the world who can make a positive contribution to their community.
>
> (Sally Jaeckle, Strategic Lead for Early Years, Bristol and 5×5×5=creativity Trustee)

Well-being and self-esteem

This way of working supports the emotional well-being and self-esteem of both adults and children. Individual creativity and possibilities for personalised learning have been enhanced. The personalised learning being developed reflects the learning styles, interests, preferences and needs of individual learners. It follows their individual learning journeys to support progression, instil confidence and encourage positive dispositions to learning. We have developed a culture of openness and enthusiasm, bringing together enquiring minds and a genuine desire to assist the children in their investigations. Children's choice is at the heart of all the work we do, as it informs a way forward and provides both children and adults with an open forum for discussion and debate. Without choice we would not be creating a culture of enquiry with opportunities for individual contributions and questions:

> We have noticed the children leading and facilitating other children's ideas. The children are highly imaginative and eager to embrace a collective idea. Their language skills and ability to focus and concentrate for extremely long periods of time have been astounding. The children show their playfulness and desire for invention as they bounce ideas to and fro amongst the group. They have true respect for each other's thoughts and ideas as they engage in discussion. At no time did we observe any disrespect. Their listening skills were exemplary and their thought processes both complex and philosophical.
>
> (Artists and educators in discussion at Freshford Primary School)

The close attention paid to detail and the valuing of individuals have been recurring themes. The increased freedom and responsibility enjoyed by the learning group is evident. Notions about what constitutes a 'rich and stimulating environment' have become much more sophisticated. Some of the richest learning has taken place with very modest resources.

Adults learning together

As researchers, we are constantly exploring new ways of learning. By valuing curiosity, ingenuity, playfulness, imagination and risk, as adults we have been able to immerse ourselves in complex ideas and in reflection distil the essence of these for our own and others' learning. Artists and cultural settings working in the context of education have helped to develop a creative ethos with the pleasure of collaboration and the support of an experienced team of mentors. 5×5×5=creativity has built a critical mass of creative reflective practitioners who have developed research as a habit of mind. Relationships built on trust, respect and responsibility are overarching features of the success of any partnership.

Transforming learning capacity

One of the imperatives of this work is to make a difference and transform learning capacity. We need to improve the life chances of children through developing their confidence in themselves as creative learners, thinkers and problem solvers with greater motivation and engagement in their learning. Supporting a 'learning to learn' agenda will help equip children with the skills to view learning as a purposeful pursuit and become independent, lifelong learners. An environment of enquiry and a culture of *sustained shared thinking* (Siraj-Blatchford et al. 2002) can be developed – open-ended conversations that are genuinely child-led, with adults scaffolding thinking by getting involved in the thinking process themselves. Sustained shared thinking builds on children's interests and understandings, making connections in learning in a shared enquiry where adults and children question, debate, hypothesise and reflect on their ideas together.

Conclusion

Creativity is an essential and attainable part of life-wide and lifelong learning. Our concept of creative learning has developed to encompass creative and reflective learning communities for teachers as well as children, parents and others interested in being involved in an inclusive democratic education.

Central to our work is a democratic notion of creativity: adults and children working together to seek new connections in a climate of creative enquiry. The 5×5×5 research has demonstrated that its activities raise achievement by developing a more creative pedagogy and by deepening and strengthening our understanding of children's learning. In line with best practice, it is supporting children's holistic development through learning experiences that foster both cognitive and affective aspects of learning, developing active citizens with rights and offering an entitlement to a creative education. Within 5×5×5's growing learning community of teachers and creative practitioners, we value idiosyncratic practice and diverse lines of enquiry in pursuit of creative values, dispositions, environments and relationships.

The 5×5×5 model is built on the principle of partnership: partnership between the educational and cultural settings, their staff, mentors, artists, the children and their parents and carers. 5×5×5 has a rich legacy of documentation that demonstrates how all those that have participated in the journey have been empowered and energised by the process. Perhaps more importantly, through researching ourselves researching children, researching the world, we are deepening and developing our understanding of creativity and through our own reflective practice are ensuring that the quality of every child's experience is strengthened and enhanced. The professional development is integrated into the research – the adults experience the work first hand and can analyse and articulate what is happening. As a result, they become ambassadors for the work in a wide variety of professional situations.

The project has established a strong research ethic and a rigorous intellectual and emotional integrity that we hope will inform future policy. The generation of a culture of openness and reflection goes beyond mechanistic solutions and demands political will for systemic change. We have seen a willingness to observe, listen and work closely with children's ideas – a community of adults who understand what it means to be creative, who are interested in how children learn and who model the creative process alongside children. Providing vital, rich and creative learning opportunities, with openness to possibility, has generated depth in collaborative learning. 5×5×5 now has a body of evidence to draw on that clearly links and influences practice both in individual settings and on a national level.

5×5×5 is a research process designed to deepen thinking, challenge perception and stimulate change. 5×5×5 explores exciting ways in which the creative and cultural community can be involved in meaningful learning with children and young people. The legacy of 5×5×5 is in its continuing research, developing creative, engaging and authentic learning and relationships in real contexts, and exploring connections between children, families, school and the community. We need to contribute to an international and critical debate about education in a social democracy in order to build a creative educational culture that can change lives:

> This exciting enterprise is as much about the transformation of teachers as it is about the transformation of children. The teachers involved now have an exceptional quality and rigour of educational thought. They are true 'lead learners': excited about and skilled, not only in their own learning, but in scaffolding the learning of others: children, parents, artists and members of the enlightened participating cultural communities.
>
> (Dame Tamsyn Imison, Patron of 5×5×5=creativity)

Questions for further thinking and reflection

1. What is your image of the child?
2. What is your experience of creative learning?

Originally published in Bancroft, S., Fawcett, M. and Hay, P. (2008) *Researching Children Researching the World: 5×5×5=creativity*. Stoke-on-Trent: Trentham Books. (Chapters 1 and 8 have been revised and updated.) Website: www.5×5×5creativity.org.uk (accessed 17 March 2017).

References

Aguirre Jones, D. and Elders, L. (2009) 'Reflecting on the reflective cycle', *ReFocus Journal* 9, pp. 12–13.

Bancroft, S., Fawcett, M. and Hay, P (2008) *Researching Children Researching the World: 5×5×5=creativity*. Stoke-on-Trent: Trentham Books.

Carr, M. (2001) *Assessment in Early Childhood Settings: Learning stories*. London: Paul Chapman.

Craft, A. (2000) *Creativity Across the Primary Curriculum: Framing and developing practice*. London: Routledge.

Craft, A, Cremin, T. and Burnard, P. (eds.) (2008a) *Creative Learning and How We Document It*. Stoke-on-Trent: Trentham Books.

Craft, A., Gardner, H. and Claxton, G. (eds.) (2008b) *Creativity, Wisdom and Trusteeship. Exploring the Role of Education*. Thousand Oaks, CA: Corwin Press.

Cremin, T., Burnard, P. and Craft, A. (2006) Pedagogy and possibility thinking in the early years, *Thinking Skills and Creativity* 1(2), pp. 108–119.

Drummond, M.J. (2005) *Learning Bulletin Number 2: Pioneers in Creative Learning: Challenge and change*. London: NESTA (National Endowment for Science, Technology and the Arts).

Edwards, C., Gandini, L. and Forman, G. (1998) *The Hundred Languages of Children – Advanced reflections*. Greenwich, CT: Ablex Publishing.

Fawcett, M and Hay, P. (2003) *5×5×5=creativity in the Early Years*. Bath and North East Somerset Council.

Malaguzzi, L. (1996) *The Hundred Languages of Children* (exhibition catalogue). Reggio Emilia: Reggio Children.

Moss, P. (2003) *Beyond Caring: The case for reforming the childcare and early years workforce*. London: Daycare Trust.

Moss, P. (2006) *Contesting Early Childhood . . . and Opening for Change*. Thomas Coram Research Unit. University of London, Institute of Education.

Rinaldi, C. (2006) *In Dialogue with Reggio: Listening, researching and learning*. Oxford: Routledge.

Siraj-Blatchford, I., Sylva, K., Muttock, S., Gilden, R. and Bell, D. (2002) *Effective Pedagogy in the Early Years: Researching effective pedagogy in the early years*. London: Department for Education and Skills Research Report 356.

Steers, J. and Swift, J. (1999) A manifesto for art in schools, directions, *International Journal of Art and Design Education* 18(1), pp. 7–13.

Chapter 8

Children at play: digital resources in home and school contexts

Lisa Kervin and Irina Verenikina

Chapter introduction

Lisa Kervin and Irina Verenikina are Associate Professors at the University of Wollongong, Australia. This chapter draws on their research exploring pre-school children's use of technology in their play and the seamless transition between on-screen and off-screen interaction. They explore shared meaning making between children as they play with digital resources and consider how technology can help children make connections within their play. They argue that technology can support children taking control of real world situations and experiment with possibilities, leading to sustained collaboration with other children.

Introduction

This chapter examines how children engage with play and digital resources in home and school contexts. The meaning-making opportunities children have in their early years, both in their homes and schools, and across these contexts, play an important part in the development of creativity and communicative competencies. Their participation in physical and virtual social relationships supports these meaning-making opportunities. In this chapter, we argue digital resources that encourage and support children to engage with activity and create, make connections and collaborate with others best support children at play.

Children and play

Play is an integral childhood activity. Article 31 of the United Nations Convention on the Rights of the Child (UNCRC) states 'that every child has the right to rest and leisure, to engage in play and recreational activities appropriate to the age of the child and to participate freely in cultural life and the arts' (United Nations, 1989). While there is no universal definition of play, it is typically characterised as a spontaneous, self-initiated and self-regulated activity for young children, which is relatively risk free and not necessarily goal-oriented (Verenikina & Kervin, 2011; Verenikina et al., 2010). Children are intrinsically motivated to play and they actively seek opportunities for play, as they create their play scenarios and take control, making play 'the very serious business of childhood' (Grieshaber, 2008:30).

The contexts within which children play are important. While play is acknowledged as an important contextual activity for children's development of communication and collaborative skills (Siraj–Blatchford, 2009), it is this notion of the *context for play* that provides an avenue to explore the ways that young children play for a range of purposes. A focus on play contexts enables us to examine the cultural meaning-making opportunities for children as they participate in social relationships (Wood, 2010). It is through play that children connect to the intricacies of their cultural settings (Vygotsky, 2004). While freely engaging in play, children acquire the foundations of self-reflection and abstract thinking, develop a range of complex verbal and non–verbal communication skills, learn to manage their emotions and explore the roles and rules of functioning in adult society.

Digital play

While not all children have access to digital technologies, for many children these resources are firmly instilled in their daily activities. The reality is that, increasingly, younger children have access to technology and are using it for leisure from a very young age. Spontaneously, children utilise digital technologies available to them in their play which allows researchers to talk about a new type of children's play, labelled 'digital play' (e.g. Verenikina & Kervin, 2011; Fleer, 2014). Digital play is conceptualised according to the ways children interact with technologies (e.g. Marsh, 2010), ways technologies are used in playful ways (e.g. Verenikina & Kervin, 2011), and the digitally mediated contexts within which children participate (e.g. Edwards, 2013). Participation in on–screen and off-screen spaces provides opportunities for children to communicate their ideas and understandings in new, interesting and different ways (Vasquez & Felderman, 2013). The convergence of play and technology has introduced very new activities for many children and requires 'an especially careful examination of its role in the lives of children' (Salonius–Pasternak & Gelfond, 2005:6).

Play in the digital world is complex. The playful activities children engage with creates synergies between online and offline and digital and non-digital play (Marsh & Bishop, 2014). Davies (2009:31) identified that 'many new technologies provide routes to playful activities.' Children's access to mobile media devices (such as iPads and other tablet technologies) continues to increase. As children negotiate digital play, they negotiate a range of technological literacies (e.g. the device and how to interact with it, what application or software program) and a range of content and activities (e.g. specific applications) that all compete for their attention.

Children and digital resources

Many young children interact with digital resources in their homes and often they engage with digital devices for play. For example, according to the Australian Bureau of Statistics, 88 per cent of 5–8-year-olds used the computer to play games while the use of a computer, the Internet and games consoles rose from 83 per cent in 2009 to 85 per cent in 2012 (ABS, 2012). This asks questions about the value of these devices and what they offer during the formative early years.

The emerging phenomenon of 'digital play' largely depends on (and is often restricted by) the actual design of the software and hardware. Staggering numbers of apps, self-contained programs or pieces of software, are available for tablet devices. Available apps grow exponentially each month as new products and revised versions enter the market. At the time of writing, the iTunes apps store featured 240 'popular' educational games, with more than half of those targeted at children under 8 years old. Interestingly, while children spontaneously engage with apps for recreation and leisure, their parents and educators access apps with the intention of engaging children with technology and in the process supporting them with their learning (Chiong & Shuler, 2010).

Over the past decade, we see the increased access that young children have to mobile devices across various contexts (such as tablets and iPads), and we need to continue to examine the role of digital play in the lives of young children. The data from which we draw in this chapter aims to explore the ways that young children's traditional, spontaneous imaginative play are affected and transformed when young children make use of modern digital technologies in a variety of contexts.

Our research project

In our research approach to digital play, we theorise digital resources as cultural tools or artefacts which are rapidly becoming part of our everyday life and therefore are utilised by members of society in a natural way, by embedding them in their various activities. The use of such digital resources can enhance or hinder such activities, and also transform them (Verenikina & Gould, 1998).

Using criteria that emerged from an extensive review of the literature and our previous and current research (Verenikina & Kervin, 2011), we have analysed the top-downloaded apps for preschoolers (as determined by iTunes). This criteria focuses our attention on design characteristics of the app such as:

- open-ended
- discovery oriented
- controlled by the child with opportunity for the user to take a non-linear path
- not limited in scope to 'teaching' particular skills, and
- provides opportunities for collaborative engagement.

From our analysis, we have been able to identify focus apps and load these onto devices for children to use. We have observed children using these apps in a pre-school, in a Digital Play playgroup hosted at the University of Wollongong (UOW) Early Start facility and families have recorded and shared with us app use in their homes. Our observations enabled us to identify a number of play effects that emerged when children engaged with purposefully selected apps based in our criteria. These effects include:

- children's engagement in creative imaginative play
- sustained interaction with peers and adults
- sustained motivation to continue the play, and
- movement between on-screen and off-screen activities.

In this chapter, we use vignettes to illustrate instances of play in home, school and across contexts.

Digital resources in home contexts

McPake and colleagues (2013:422) report on the growth of 'domestic digital technologies' and the effect this has had on children's lives. Technology use shapes children's communicative and creative practices as they are encouraged to engage with creative practices. For example, carefully selected digital resources offer opportunities for children to interact with familiar activities (e.g. going to the hairdresser and Toca Boca's *Hair Salon* apps), document their own experiences through image and video recordings, view material of interest (e.g. YouTube) and create their own texts (e.g. *PuppetPals*).

There is much to learn from the everyday, incidental and momentary encounters young children have with digital resources in their home contexts. In this vignette, we share a 3-year-old child's home-based play experience that is informed by his digital encounters.

Ronan

Ronan, a 3-year-old boy lives in the suburbs of Sydney and enjoys playing with his train set. Ronan takes times to set up and orchestrate some complex train manoeuvres. As Ronan plays, he talks about the trains and describes what his friends like to do with their train sets.

Later, when sharing observations about Ronan at play with his parents, the friends Ronan talks about come up in conversation. At the mention of these names, his dad began to laugh. Ronan's father shares how when they had first got the train set he was a little unsure about how to put it together. He Googled the name of the train set and was able to access a range of YouTube videos that showed what others had done with the equipment. Ronan viewed these clips with his father.

In the time that followed, Ronan asked to watch those clips again and again. Seeing how much Ronan enjoyed viewing these, his father subscribed to Really Simple Syndication (RSS) feeds so they were alerted when that person had added a new clip. It turned out the 'friends' that Ronan had talked about were indeed his virtual network that he had connected with through a shared artefact and play interest.

Ronan's father valued digital resources. Ronan's introduction to YouTube occurred through his father searching for information and YouTube was positioned as a knowledge source. The search results provided insights into the train set which both Ronan and his father viewed. It was for this purpose that the YouTube clips were initially accessed. Ronan and his father needed advice and recommendations of what to do with a physical train set. Viewing the YouTube clips provided concrete ideas for what to do, which resulted in action.

The initial viewing experiences of these YouTube clips were shared experiences. While the father accessed the content, both he and Ronan viewed the clips together. It appears this shared experience positioned the clips as being worthwhile viewing material. From this, Ronan's request to watch the clips again was met. Ronan's apparent enjoyment of this video content was recognised by his father and demonstrated through RSS feed sign-up so they were notified of new content from these sources. This again heightens the value of these resources within Ronan's home context.

The creators of the digital resource (those that uploaded videos to YouTube) became part of an important network for Ronan. His subsequent viewing of the clips transformed the relationship he had with the creators from being an initial access point for ideas to people whom he considered friends, others who were engaged in similar sorts of activities as he was.

Later, we observed Ronan playing as the *Toca Train* app which fascinated him. Assuming the role of 'train driver', he loaded the cargo, looked after the passengers and experimented with the sound of the horn and variation of train speed. The engagement with the train app added to his interest and knowledge about trains.

Digital resources in school contexts

While digital technologies are not yet fully implemented in early years contexts (Edwards, 2013), discussion has evolved from 'Should digital technologies be used in early childhood contexts?' to 'How might digital technologies be used effectively?' Many Early Childhood organisations now acknowledge that technology use among pre-school aged children is inevitable, and argue that *how* technology is used is critical to determining whether its benefits can be realised. In this vision of the role for technology, digital resources are viewed as another set of important tools for communication and learning. That is, when used properly, they can be useful for education and work. However, if used improperly, they can deliver a number of potentially negative side-effects. Our challenge is then to consider how we might use digital resources in ways that are most responsive to the needs of children.

Given previous argument about the importance of play in the lives of young children, it is reasonable to consider the role of play and digital resources in guiding policy and curricula for early childhood contexts. While curricula identify play as essential for children's learning (e.g. Australia's Early Years Learning Framework, DEEWR, 2009), technology is not considered part of descriptions of children's play (Edwards, 2013). The apparent disconnect between play and technology in guiding curriculum frameworks poses questions about the role of digital play in classroom contexts for educators. Digital play has the potential to offer valuable meaning-making opportunities for children in classroom contexts. Edwards and Bird (2015) call for educators to consider digital play and the opportunities it presents to support children's learning activities within a play-based framework.

Technologies are continually evolving, becoming more mobile, more compact, equipped with multiple functionalities, with many tools enabling collaboration. Technologies allow learners to engage in or capture learning outside the traditional classroom walls and school hours, such as out in the community, and in their homes. In doing so, learners gain greater perspectives as they share/validate their understandings with others as they draw upon their personal networks and experiences. Digital technologies also present significant learning opportunities for young children (Edwards & Bird, 2015). Children quickly adapt to digital technologies and are generally respectful of the devices. The enticing nature of, and often familiarity with, the device increases engagement. Using technologies, children can seamlessly engage with independent and collaborative learning approaches. In this next example, we share a 5-year-old child's transformation of some paper-based drawing he had done, as he used an app and his storytelling abilities.

Oliver

Five-year-old Oliver likes to draw. He attended pre-school two days per week and frequently spent time at the drawing table in his classroom. Oliver was involved in a research project where the talk that surrounded his drawings was recorded and a copy of his drawings captured (Kervin & Mantei, 2015).

A few months have passed and Oliver is now in his first year of formal school and he joins our research as a participant in the digital play group. We accessed his drawings and recordings that he has previously done and invited him to listen to the recordings of his talk on an iPad. Oliver accepted the invitation and as he listened to the recordings of his talk and looked carefully at the printed colour scans of his drawings, he identified that he enjoyed using the app Puppet Pals at home and that he enjoyed finding it on the iPad in his classroom. He suggested that he create a play using his drawings and some new story ideas he was thinking about.

Oliver took photographs of two of his drawings on an iPad in his classroom. He decided the picture he had drawn of the house was to be included as a backdrop and added it to the backdrops in Puppet Pals. He then selected another two backdrops from the archive available within the app. One backdrop was of a park scene, the other of a brick building. Then, using the picture he had drawn of his family, he created five characters as he traced around the outlines using his finger on the iPad screen to cut out each of the family members (mum and dad and three children). These were then added to the characters for his play.

Oliver began moving his characters across the screen, flipping through his three selected backdrops. While his lips were moving, there was no audible oral text heard. After about five minutes, he indicated that he was ready to record his Puppet Pals *play.* Figure 8.1 *presents an overview of Oliver's play – it comprised 168 words and the recording lasted 1 minute and 18 seconds. During the play, Oliver made twelve backdrop changes (including three errors which were quickly changed) and moved his characters a total of thirty-three times as he recorded the script. Interestingly, the mother and the middle child had the most movements (eight each), the father was moved seven times and the eldest and youngest children moved five times each. Oliver is the middle child in his family.*

Screen shots from Puppet Pals *play*	*Oliver's oral annotation*
	Once upon a time there was a family / who /who went for a walk . . . I mean . . .
	They went to a walk to a school with the mum and dad / they let the three boys go to school / and when they got to the school they said goodbye to their children and they went inside / they saw the teacher Mrs Click and then
	/ and then they walked all the way back home the parents /
	They went inside to have a cup of coffee and in the afternoon they came back
	/ they walked down the street

Screen shots from *Puppet Pals* play	*Oliver's oral annotation*
	and then they went back to the school
	and then they got their children back / and then they /
	then they walked back home together / the kids ran /
	and then when they got back home they went inside /
	and then, do you know what happened? / then, they all went to sleep.

Figure 8.1 Oliver's *Puppet Pals* play

Oliver's initial interactions at the drawing table in his pre-school enabled him time to explore topics that were important to him (the magical house, family and volcano). Interestingly, these topics that Oliver chose to draw upon were not all represented in the story created in the *Puppet Pals* play. Oliver reframed and manipulated his drawings to create a story about a new topic. The magical house became his family's home and his static picture of his family was dissected to create characters for his play. Through this recontextualisation, Oliver was able to draw, talk and create text about things that were important to him (his parents taking him and his siblings to school).

Oliver had knowledge of the *Puppet Pals* app from home and was able to play with this app in his classroom to tell a new story. Oliver demonstrated that his knowledge of digital resources was able to transfer across contexts and he was given permission to do so with the allocation of both time and resources. His experiences were valued in his classroom and given currency in the time to initially create his drawings and to then revisit these using digital resources (iPad and *Puppet Pals* app) to build upon and even transform his initial ideas. Oliver was able to communicate meanings through both his drawings and *Puppet Pals* play. Through his use of digital mediums, he was able to transform previous ideas into resources for a new text (backdrop and characters) and in the creation process tell an entirely new story. This provides an example of how children can use the same materials in different ways to serve different intentions.

Digital resources across contexts

While educators and parents often see school and home contexts as being separate, children operate across spaces (Hull & Schultz, 2002). Children actively construct their social world and their place within this (Corsaro, 2003). It therefore makes sense that children seek opportunities to use and network digital technologies across contexts, emphasising the value in home and school contexts working together. Out-of-school settings create spaces that lie between home and school contexts, where unique texts and practices are created (Pahl & Kelly, 2005). The ways that children interact and engage within these contexts provide new ways of understanding the ways children chose to use language and play within these spaces. Indeed, it is the ways that children choose to use language that define their activities within these contexts, which in turn defines the spaces themselves. In this next example, we consider the experience of two 7-year-old children as they share a networked digital play experience first in a shared context that then moves to their individual home settings.

Adam and Dane

Adam and Dane, both 7 years old, visit the University of Wollongong Early Start Facility to participate in the digital playgroup. The boys attend school together, their families are friends and they share an avid interest in the Minecraft *app. The boys bring their own individual iPads to the session and decide to work together to create a shared world. They network their devices to enable them to co-create the world. As they do this, they discuss, describe and debate the developments they make. The parents of these boys share that this work continues after this playgroup session. The boys continue to network their devices and work on their shared* Minecraft *world.*

The children drew from a friendship that originated in their school classroom. They were then able to share their own interests and expertise with *Minecraft* to follow their own play pathway in this new setting. As they integrated their own knowledge of the app, they also drew upon their passion and interests to create a shared world. The children created a shared *Minecraft* world across contexts. While the idea originated from a physically shared space, the children continued the collaboration virtually as they moved to operate in their own different home contexts. The opportunity to do this was supported in both the out-of-school space (the digital playgroup) and each of their home contexts. Initially, the children operated in the same physical and virtual contexts to begin the creation of their shared *Minecraft* world. These children cooperatively conceived an idea and then actively followed this together and separately, remaining connected through virtual affordances of the digital resources they were using. These opportunities for collaboration led to powerful opportunities for shared interactions.

Insights from our examination of digital resource across contexts

The digital resources that children in our research engaged with, both in their home and school settings, appear to have distinct properties. While we acknowledge the purposes of 'use' in these contexts may be different (e.g. considering the role of interests to learning goals to access that impact upon use within a context), however, what it is that children do with these resources is interesting. The examples in this chapter share children's uptake of digital resources and the differing purposes for their use. The digital resources that children selected enable them to actively engage with these resources; that is, *to do* something with them, not just observe or simply consume. The focus appears not to be on the content within the resource, but rather the way the resource helps them solve a problem or achieve a self-selected goal. Such problems or goals may include the ways to interact with a train set, or provide a way to tell a story. The process of creation may be on-screen (as in the case of *Minecraft*) or off-screen (as in the case of Ronan's train set).

Conclusion

Digital resources have the power to help children make connections to, and make sense of, their real world. Accessing digital resources may provide information or new understandings. Alternatively, the digital resource may provide opportunities for children to take control of real-world situations and explore and experiment with possibilities within this. Digital resources can lead to sustained collaboration with others. These collaborations may take the form of an ongoing collaboration (as demonstrated in the *Minecraft* example) or through the extension of one's network (as evidenced in Ronan's YouTube network of friends). Each of these uses enables the child user to take meaning but also make meaning (Gee, 2012). The more that children are encouraged to access quality digital resources in their home and school contexts, and make connections between activities in both contexts, the more meaning they will make from the interactions.

The digital skills and interests children develop at home are freely transferred to the school context and vice versa. Indeed, much has been written about the need for schools to be more connected to what children do outside of school (e.g. Burnett, 2014). What is critical, though, is that the contexts become intertwined and what is valued in one as meaningful activity is also acknowledged and appreciated in the other. This becomes possible when children use digital resources that enable them to engage with activity and create, make connections and collaborate with others in meaningful ways.

Questions for further thinking and reflection

1.   For what purposes do children you encounter use digital resources in their home and school contexts?
2.   How might children's knowledge and experiences of digital resources transfer across contexts?

Further reading

Kervin, L.,Verenikina, I. & Rivera, C. (2015) 'Onscreen and offscreen play: examining meaning-making complexities'. *Digital Culture and Education* 7(2). Accessed 14 March 2017 from: http://ro.uow.edu.au/cgi/viewcontent.cgi?article=2945&context=sspapers.
Verenikina, I. & Kervin, L. (2011). 'iPads, Digital Play and Pre-schoolers,' *He Kupu*, 2(5). Accessed 14 March 2017 from: https://scholars.uow.edu.au/display/publication49310.

Acknowledgement

This work was supported by the Australian Research Council under Discovery Grant DP140100328 (Conceptualising digital play: The role of tablet technologies in the development of imaginative play of young children) awarded to Irina Verenikina, Lisa Kervin and Collette Murphy.

References

ABS (Australian Bureau of Statistics) (2012). *Children's Participation in Cultural and Leisure Activities, Australia*. Canberra, Australia. Accessed 15 December 2015, from http://www.abs.gov.au/ausstats/abs@.nsf/mf/4901.0

Burnett, C. (2014). Investigating pupils' interactions around digital texts: A spatial perspective on the 'classroom-ness' of digital literacy practices in schools. *Educational Review, 66*(2), 192–209.

Chiong, C., & Shuler, C. (2010). Learning: Is there an app for that? In *Investigations of Young Children's Usage and Learning with Mobile Devices and Apps*. New York: The Joan Ganz Cooney Center at Sesame Workshop.

Corsaro, W. A. (2003). *We're Friends, Right?: Inside kids' culture*. Joseph Henry Press.

Davies, J. (2009). A space for play: Crossing boundaries and learning onscreen. In V. Carrington & M. Robinson (Eds). *Digital Literacies: Social learning and classroom practices* (pp. 27–42). Los Angeles: SAGE.

DEEWR (Department of Education, Employment and Workplace Relations) (2009). *Belonging, Being & Becoming: The Early Years Learning Framework for Australia*. Accessed 15 September 2009, from http://www.deewr.gov.au/EarlyChildhood/Policy_Agenda/Quality/Documents/Final%20EYLF%20Framework%20Report%20-%20WEB.pdf

Edwards, S. (2013). Digital play in the early years: A contextual response to the problem of integrating technologies and play-based pedagogies in the early childhood curriculum. *European Early Childhood Education Research Journal, 21*(2), 199–212.

Edwards, S. & Bird, J. (2015). Observing and assessing young children's digital play in the early years: Using the Digital Play Framework. *Journal of Early Childhood Research* 1–16.

Fleer, M. (2014). The demands and motives afforded through digital play in early childhood activity settings. *Learning, Culture and Social Interaction, 3*(3), 202–209.

Gee, P. J. (2012). The old and the new in the new digital literacies. *The Educational Forum, 76*, 418–420.

Grieshaber, S. (2008). Interrupting stereotypes: Teaching and the education of young children. *Early Education and Development, 19*(3), 505–518.

Hull, G. A., & Schultz, K. (Eds). (2002). *School's Out: Bridging out-of-school literacies with classroom practice*. Teachers College Press.

Kervin, L. & Mantei, J. (2015). Drawing + Talk = Powerful insights for teachers of writing. In J. Turbill, G. Barton & C. Brock (Eds.) *Teaching Writing in Today's Classrooms: Looking back to looking forward* (pp. 87–103). Norwood: Australian Literary Educators' Association.

Marsh, J., and Bishop, J. C. (2014). *Changing Play: Play, media and commercial culture from the 1950s to the present day*. Maidenhead: Open University Press/McGrawHill.

McPake, J., Plowman, L. & Stephen, C. (2013). Pre-school children creating and communicating with digital technologies in the home. *British Journal of Educational Technology, 44*(3), 421–431.

Pahl, K., & Kelly, S. (2005). Family literacy as a third space between home and school: Some case studies of practice. *Literacy, 39*(2), 91–96.

Salonius-Pasternak, D. E., & Gelfond, H. S. (2005). The next level of research on electronic play: Potential benefits and contextual influences for children and adolescents. *Human Technology: An interdisciplinary journal on humans in ICT environments, 1*(1), 5–22.

Siraj-Blatchford, I. (2009). Conceptualising progression in the pedagogy of play and sustained shared thinking in early childhood education: A Vygotskian perspective. *Educational and Child Psychology, 26*(2), 77–89.

UNICEF (1989). Convention on the Rights of the Child.

Vasquez, V. M. & Felderman, C. B. (2013). *Technology and Critical Literacy in Early Childhood*. New York: Routledge.

Verenikina, I. & Gould, E. (1998). Tool-based psychology as a philosophy of technology. *Australian Journal of Information Systems, 6*(1), 136–145.

Verenikina, I., Herrington, J., Peterson, R., & Mantei, J. (2010). Computers and play in early childhood: Affordances and limitations. *Journal of Interactive Learning Research, 21*(1), 139–159.

Verenikina, I. & Kervin, L. (2011). iPads, digital play and pre-schoolers, *He Kupu*, 2(5). Accessed 14 March 2017, from: http://www.hekupu.ac.nz/index.php?type=journal&issue=15&journal=262

Vygotsky, L. S. (2004) Imagination and creativity in childhood. *Journal of Russian and East European Psychology, 42*(1), 7–97 (English translation M.E. Sharpe, Inc.)

Wood, E. (2010). Reconceptualising the play-pedagogy relationship: From control to complexity. In L. Brooker and S. Edwards (Eds). *Engaging Play (11–25)*. Maidenhead: McGraw-Hill.

Chapter 9

Making connections: young children exploring early friendships through play

John Parry

Chapter introduction

In this chapter, John Parry from the Open University explores how playing with others creates opportunities for young children to initiate actions and interactions that can be recognised as social connections. Drawing on his research in early childhood settings, he focuses on the friendship experiences of two children in their nursery and what they tell us about providing support for peer relationships.

Each friend represents a world in us, a world not possibly born until they arrive, and it is only by this meeting that a new world is born.

(Anaïs Nin, in Staub 1998)

Introduction

It is widely accepted that young children's experiences at pre-school make a fundamental contribution to their social development, building their self-confidence as they realise that they can exercise some control in another environment beyond their home (Kington, Gates and Sammons 2013). Therefore early childhood settings could be viewed as 'socialisation agencies' (Monaco and Pontecorvo 2010:193), environments in which young children negotiate and learn more about the complexities and connections that make up relationships. During the nursery day, children can explore their interest in one another, learning how to respond to each other's idiosyncrasies whilst participating and collaborating during play. Significantly, by making such social connections with their peers, they are also likely to be tentatively weaving their first friendships and endeavouring to position themselves within their expanding social world.

This chapter sets out to look in more detail at how young children explore early friendships between themselves within a pre-school environment. Using vignettes focusing on two children's experiences in their nursery as a starting point, the aim is to illustrate the intricacies and subtleties involved as young people make relationships through playing and being together. These vignettes are taken from a research study into children's early friendships carried out by the author (Parry 2014) and the chapter as a whole revisits the key findings from this research and a subsequent extended study (Parry 2015). It covers how children experience the transition from being playmates to being friends and the ways that their actions support these transitions. Consideration is also given in the chapter to the role that adults can take in facilitating an environment where friendships can flourish.

Exploring early friendships: two children's stories

Both these vignettes are taken from a research study in a combined Children's Centre and Nursery School in an inner city, urban environment in England. The focus of the research was to investigate the nature of the social connections made between young children labelled with special educational needs and their peers. It used the 'In the picture' approach developed by Paige-Smith and Rix (2011) for their study of home-based early intervention programmes. This approach to gathering research data involves three key components: recording observations in the first person to reflect the child's perspective; taking photographs of the observed situations and sharing these photographs with the children and practitioners who have been observed.

The two children whose stories are featured in this chapter – Ray and Isaac – were based in different rooms in the nursery and attended for five sessions a week, Ray in the morning and Isaac in the afternoon. The setting had substantial outdoor play areas which all the children from different rooms could access freely at will. In fact, the children could use the facilities in any part of the nursery at any time with their designated room acting as a 'port of call' only at the beginning and end of sessions. Consequently, all the practitioners in the nursery engaged with a wider range of children than those allocated to their room group.

Ray's story

Ray was 4 years old and lived close to the nursery with his parents, two younger brothers and older sister. His family were of mixed-race heritage, with English being the main language spoken at home. Ray received support from a range of professionals including the Community Paediatrician and Educational Psychologist. As a young person with a hearing impairment, he had used Makaton sign language to assist his communication when he had started nursery, but now he communicated with a mixture of gesture and short spoken phrases. At the time of collecting his story, he was coming to the end of his attendance at the nursery and was due to move to the reception class in a local primary school the following term.

Ray had been with this room group for over a year and he had two particular friends, Hayley and Ely, with whom he often played both in the group room and outdoors. The lead teacher recalled that the group initially came together around a mutual interest and enjoyment of building with a 'marble run' construction toy. All the staff now recognised that the three children seemed to gravitate to each other almost instinctively and that they formed a tight group almost to the exclusion of others. When asked what they thought drew the group together, the practitioners felt that the three children having similar ways and means of communicating was one determinant. However, similarities in personality, sense of humour, age, temperament and play interests were also seen to be key foundations for the three children's friendship.

Ray was very proactive in gaining Hayley and Ely's attention, calling out their names when they were involved in other activities and of all the children in his group, these were the peers that he often sought for help. Ray was also more willing to try and initiate games with these two friends rather than other children, particularly with Ely. This often involved putting toys on Ely's head which would cause his friend to laugh and take notice of him; adding to the activity he was engaged in, such as placing another brick on his tower or picture on his lotto board, or pointing to pictures that Ely was looking at. Such 'intrusions' were usually well measured by Ray as they led to further play with Ely and suggested Ray's awareness of the boundaries of this established relationship.

Ray was also beginning to explore relationships with other children besides Ely and Hayley, albeit less frequently. He would make subtle, testing approaches towards other peers which involved copying their actions, choosing to stand or sit next to them, and deliberately moving toys towards them. He often frequented a particular climbing area in the nursery which included a tunnel and would wait for other children to crawl through this, waving to them as they passed by. Ray had also previously tended to push other children away if they approached him, but he was becoming more tolerant, allowing them to play alongside. He would still shout 'no' or 'stop' if he felt they were encroaching too closely onto his play, but this initial reaction could form the platform for a developing social exchange. This was particularly the case if other children persevered with a sociable gesture like bringing him a toy or showing him how to do something. In response to this action, Ray would often re-interpret the situation, engaging in further play, interaction and exploring a possible new relationship.

Isaac's story

The nursery was Isaac's first experience of attending group provision. He was 3½ years old and had been coming to the centre for six months with another year to go until he started infant school. Before coming to the nursery regularly, he had received educational support at home through an early intervention team. His family was of Black African heritage and he was an only child. He expressed himself in two- or three-word phrases and understood the communication from others best when it was provided in short spoken units with gestures.

Despite being more likely to be on the fringes of other children's activity, there were two children at nursery that Isaac played with more frequently, Saul and Lisa. The factors underpinning the development of these particular friendships seemed to be different. Staff recognised that Isaac's connection with Saul was based on their having similar communication styles and also play interests, which revolved around their shared enjoyment of physical activity. For both boys, the focus was on being active together rather than having a conversation. Isaac's relationship with Lisa was more complex. She had initially been part of a group of children who babied Isaac when he first started at the nursery, but their positive relationship had endured despite these difficult beginnings. As with his connection with Saul, Isaac was drawn to Lisa's preference for physical games, but he also identified her as being someone who would provide him with patient help, particularly on the climbing frame and outdoor apparatus.

Isaac's recurrent interactions during play with these two children also had their own individual characteristics. Isaac was often the follower when playing with Lisa, taking on her suggestions and responding to her requests. However, he was also confident enough to reject this at times, preferring to make his own choices and without fear that Lisa would not return to play with him at another time. When playing with Saul, it was evident that the two partners would often agree a shared goal and then work on this together, for example collecting specific props together before embarking on some shared role play.

Besides the more prolonged connections he made with Lisa and Saul, Isaac also gravitated towards activities where groups of other children congregated, particularly the snack bar area. His visits seemed to have a social motive as well as the attraction of the refreshments, because he would often attempt interactions with other children by pushing his bowl towards them, copying their actions, and calling out object names to his peers. He demonstrated similar intentions and confidence when joining other activities, often attempting to share with a peer even if there was plenty of equipment available for individual play. At times, this approach to making connections would involve Isaac in taking more risks, for example spoiling or disrupting other children's games or initiating chase by taking items away from a group. Less risky was his interest in children who were new to the group and his willingness to play with them as they got used to the sessions. In these situations, Isaac would often take the lead in making a social connection as confidently as with his more regular companions Lisa and Saul.

Seeking connections in pre-school

A recurrent theme in early childhood research into young children's social worlds has been the extent to which babies and toddlers will actively engage each other and show an inherent interest in making contact with their peers. Selby and Bradley (2003), and Zeedyk (2006) carried out detailed observations of the intensive imitative play amongst groups of babies and recognised that such engagement represented clear signs of mutual interest, co-operation, social interaction and connectedness. Consequently, the move into a pre-school environment, where young children encounter an increasing range and diversity of peers, represents a rich social arena in which they can explore their interest in relationships further.

When part of a pre-school group, young children often use similar approaches to seek out connections and develop relationships with others, strategies which often do not depend on verbal communication. These can include:

- greeting another child by smiling, laughing, waving, or hugging;
- inviting them to play by bringing them toys and persistently encouraging them to join in;
- using non-verbal communication, for example making eye-contact, touching, or smiling to keep interactions going; and
- deliberately and spontaneously offering help and assistance (Engdhal 2012).

Both Ray and Isaac's exploratory approaches to engage other children described in the vignettes illustrate the significance of such non-verbal gestures and actions. They favoured making invitations by offering toys, Isaac most noticeably at the snack table, but they also developed more passive strategies like copying others, standing close or playing alongside the child they were interested in. In these instances, Ray and Isaac were using their own preferred 'entry strategies' (Ramsey, cited in Bal and Radke 2013:23) which they had found worked for them when seeking to make social connections. For many young children, these strategies become part of their routine to broker social exchanges and were accepted by their peers as part of a ritual of gaining access to playing together (Corsaro 2015; Engdhal 2012).

In seeking to make social connections with other children, Ray and Isaac also recognised key areas in their nursery where such engagement would be more probable. Ray spent a lot of time around the play tunnel and Isaac often frequented the snack bar. This illustrates the social potential that children attach to using larger toys and joining in with communal activities, a potential that they are keen to exploit and explore (Bertran 2015). From their perspective, the pre-school environment is not only a space which provides physical activities and variety but also 'an important social space for participation and practicing interaction with other children' (Einarsdóttir 2011 p. 398). Furthermore, areas in the pre-school which offer the possibility of shared play also provide children with opportunities to collaborate with each other. From these collaborative activities emerges 'a sense of *we-ness* that, in glimpses, transforms the individuality of an activity and opens up the opportunity for children's formation of friendships' (Svinth 2012:1248).

Making connections in pre-school

As well as being a place where children test and explore social connections with their peers, the pre-school environment provides a platform upon which children can develop more exclusive relationships with each other. Amidst the constant tangle of interactions in which children could be seen to be almost indiscriminately involving themselves in each other's play, they are also inclined to be more selective and seek out specific peers to engage with (Engdhal 2012). The relationships that Ray and Isaac were developing with Hayley, Ely, Saul and Lisa are examples of such selectivity in action.

The reasons for the mutual attraction and the preferences shown for each other as playmates are inevitably personal and unique. Both Ray and Isaac were drawn to children who enjoyed similar interests and engaged in high-energy physical activities. However, for Ray a tolerant partner, like Ely, was particularly important, someone who would accommodate him breaking into his games. For Isaac, Saul's non-verbal style of communication and Lisa's helpful disposition were key components in their relationships. It is often assumed that factors such as age, stage of development, physique, personality or language levels are determinants that draw children to each other as they play (Skinner, Buysse and Bailey 2004; Hollingsworth and Buysse 2009). These aspects may have some influence but they represent a single dimension underpinning the development of relationships between children. Using such typologies to explain why children form the first bonds of friendship overlooks their standing as active decision makers, choice takers and interpreters of their own situations (Nind, Flewitt and Payler 2010). Children themselves contribute to the production of their surrounding culture and social worlds (Corsaro 2015) and as such their choice of playmates cannot be pre-determined.

Playmates or friends?

Many studies have shown that children actively develop friendships through their play during their pre-school years (Dunn 2004; Engdhal 2012; Corsaro 2015) and these relationships are qualitatively different to frequent interactions with a variety of playmates. Some of the key characteristics that have been identified as being central to toddler friendships include:

- voluntarily and regularly spending time together (Dunn 2004, Dietrich 2005)
- shared affection (Dunn 2004)
- reciprocal actions and collaboration (Odom et. al 2006, Bertran 2015)
- consistent positivity and mutual understanding (Sebanc et al. 2007, Hollingworth and Buysse 2009)
- recognising each other's needs and helping to meet them (Dietrich 2005, Rosetti 2011).

Ray's relationships with Hayley and Ely, and Isaac's with Saul and Lisa, can be seen to reflect these markers of friendship. Both boys would seek out and respond positively to being asked to play by these close companions. They collaborated on joint projects: Ray, Hayley and Ely on construction activities like the 'marble run', and Isaac and Saul on prop gathering for role play. Asking for and offering help was a feature that distinguished the relationships within these two established groups, suggesting a personal, exclusive and mutual understanding between friends (Rosetti 2011). Such understanding also involved tolerance and acceptance which sustained the positivity between the friends. Ely frequently allowed Ray to intrude on his games or put objects on his head, and Lisa recognised that Isaac would sometimes not want to hold hands or be hugged. In fact, the close relationships that Ely and

Isaac enjoyed with particular peers could be considered illustrative of being 'best' friends because of their exclusivity, stability and predictability (Sebanc et al. 2007).

However, Ray and Isaac's relationships with close peers did not mirror all the key elements of friendship groups. Ray rarely showed any physical affection to either Hayley or Ely. Isaac was frequently helped by Lisa but did not see himself as her helper. This illustrates the unique and individual nature of the more robust social connections that children make. As adults, we have relationships with friends that are very different and the same applies to young children. They too are 'continuously involved in shaping and reconstructing each other through the locally organised relations and practices of the social groups in which they participate' (Engdhal 2012 p. 87). Children are constantly making meaning of their own situations and are instrumental in fashioning their friendships in their own way.

Recognising children's agency and thinking about their relationships from this perspective also reveals a further dimension to understanding the nature of their friendships that they make. It is possible that Ray and Isaac opted for play with Hayley or Ely, Saul or Lisa more regularly because they were confident that they could exercise their agency with these peers more than in other social interactions (Konstantoni 2012). It may be that outside established peer groupings, children are much less certain about maintaining control and consequently the interaction with less familiar peers is more transitory. However, like Ray and Isaac, there will still be times when children are more proactive in seeking out others beyond their friendship group and when they will take risks in attempting to make social connections. Such variations highlight something of the fluidity of children's relationship building where being 'insiders and outsiders' are 'under constant negotiation' (Konstantoni 2012:344) and in which peer cultures are constantly shifting (Lofdhal 2007; Corsaro 2015).

Supporting children's social connections and friendships

The nursery staff in the research study that involved Ray and Isaac identified taking a facilitative rather than directive approach as being key to supporting children to develop their social connections with their peers (Parry 2014). A facilitative approach involves practitioners demonstrating possibilities without attempting to elicit a response from the children, for example modelling how to help or how to exchange toys. It can also be more passive, where the adult is present amongst a group but not directly engaging with the children. Such presence brings reassurance that support is available whenever a child looks for cues 'on how to interpret what is going on and how to respond to those interpretations' (Anning and Edwards 2010:10). Facilitating children's social exchanges also requires practitioners to stand back, acting as participants in play but observing the interactions between the children at the same time (Parry 2014). Such 'standing back' provides the opportunity to watch children engage in uninterrupted social exchanges and prompts deep reflection on what these mean in terms of developing relationships (Parry 2015).

As Ray and Isaac's friendship stories suggest, children set about making connections with peers in individual and idiosyncratic ways. The way that different children use specific toys, games and routines to engage with each other can be unorthodox and unexpected. For example, in the vignettes Ray would often treat the initial offer of other peers to play with him negatively, shouting 'no' or 'stop', and Isaac frequently tried to engage others by spoiling games or taking toys away from them. Ironically, adults often view part of their role in supporting children to make positive social connections as being that of mediator or negotiator, particularly when there are apparent disputes (Hollingsworth and Buysse 2009). Intervening to support negotiations or sharing represents a trigger for practitioners to move from 'standing back' to becoming more directly involved. However, although adult intervention into disagreements appears on one level to be justified and appropriate, there is also a potential for such precipitous action to stifle children's attempts to negotiate and connect with each other (Broadhead 2009).

Similarly, it is often noticeable that children who are friends can exclude other peers who attempt to be part of their group (Lofdhal 2006). The 'outsider's' suggestions and ideas can be ignored however attractive they might be. The close-knit group formed by Ray, Hayley and Ely often acted in this way, prompting the practitioners in their nursery to intuitively encourage the three children to allow others to join in with them. Yet should such exclusion be seen as a primarily negative aspect of group play that requires adult support and guidance? Or could it be viewed in more positive terms as a powerful way in which children are able to: protect their developing friendships, retain control of their play space and resources, experience both the positives and negatives of relationships, and explore their shifting status within a group (Corsaro 2015). From this perspective, it is again clear that the adult's role in supporting the development of early friendships is a complex and nuanced activity (Meyer 2001).

An area where practitioners can make a more definitive contribution to supporting children's relationships is in creating a physical environment that sustains the constant flow of social connections. This environment is recognised as being an 'intricate interaction of spaces, resources, values and patterns of expected behaviour' which early educators play a key role in shaping and controlling (Annings and Edwards 2010:10). In Ray and Isaac's friendship stories, the provision of apparatus and areas where children could mingle and engage with each other as large and small groups was a crucial part of the social landscape of the nursery. Practitioners therefore need to ensure that the environment supports the pursuit of communal and collaborative activities which encourage children to explore and build on their relationships (Bertran 2015; Svinth 2012).

Conversely, children also need access to small private or hidden spaces where they can withdraw and take more control of their interactions with their friends, away from the adult gaze. In fact, if such spaces are not immediately available to children in their setting, they will set about creating their own often in 'forbidden' areas such as the toilets or behind structures in the outdoor area. Such strong motivation for children to seek out and fashion their own spaces in an environment is driven by more than a desire to avoid adult supervision. It is often in these private places that they build collaborative partnerships, develop their own friendships and form their own peer cultures (Corsaro 2015; Skanfors, Lofdahl and Hagglund 2009; Svinth 2012).

A final area for practitioners to consider when supporting children to make social connections and friendships is the degree of control the adults exert within the setting through organisational factors. For example, who decides on how children are grouped, both formally and informally, for activities? Do their friendships and relationships have any bearing on such decisions? Does the routine of the setting drive events and create discontinuity for the children by frequently moving them onto the next planned event, interrupting not only their play but also their relationship building (de Groot Kim 2010)? What demands are placed on children in terms of a focus on individual skills, developmental progress and attainment? Practitioners may be working under institutional pressure which values 'end product and individual work over collaborative work' so pushing children's collaboration to 'the outskirts of paedagogical activity' (Svinth 2012:13). In such an environment, opportunities are inevitably lost for children to freely explore social connections through the play partnerships and alliances they are creating for themselves. Consequently, practitioners need to re-evaluate the impact of their routines and the way they organise the environment and be prepared to 'approach children's perspectives and open up practice for children's collaborative encounters' (Svinth 2012:13). This seems a fundamental starting point to valuing, understanding and supporting children as they negotiate their expanding social world.

Conclusion

This chapter has explored the complexities of relationship building between young children in their pre-school settings. It emphasised the personal and individual approaches that children use to seek out and make social connections with each other, strategies which become mutually accepted between peers. The importance of an environment which invites collaborative activity and group play was highlighted as an essential platform for children to explore social exchanges and develop friendships.

Significantly in the chapter, children's early peer connections were celebrated as friendships with all the qualities of affection, reciprocity, positivity, support and mutual understanding that we as adults recognise as defining such relationships. However, recognition of the fluidity and transitory nature of young children's friendships was acknowledged along with their position as capable choice makers who fashion their own peer cultures.

Against this backdrop, the adult's role in supporting young children to make social connections is necessarily subtle and nuanced. A facilitative approach is required, built around modelling rather than prompting, watching rather than directing. Such an approach adds to the complexities of the adult's role within the children's social arena. Tensions are created between 'standing back' and the natural, and sometimes necessary, inclination to intervene in disputes and disagreements, tensions which need to be discussed and resolved by practitioners. In addition, the adult's role needs to be developed from a perspective of recognising children's agency and acknowledging their capacity to understand and influence their own world (Waller 2010). This is because 'without a focus on children's agency, there is a risk of underestimating what happens in the social situations and the power that lies within peer culture in real life situations' (Engdhal 2012 p. 87). As Ray and Isaac's friendship stories show, children's facility to make their own decisions and choices about relationships needs to be at the forefront of any consideration of their social world.

Questions for further thinking and reflection

1. It is often assumed that 'buddy' schemes, where practitioners pair children together, can help those who are less confident or who find it difficult to make connections, by introducing them to more socially outgoing peers. What assumptions are being made about children's relationships in such an approach?

2.   Reflect on where you stand on the suggestion that children should be trusted to negotiate and find their own solution to disputes?

Further reading

Corsaro, W. (2015) *The sociology of childhood* 4th Edition London: Sage
Engdhal, I. (2012) 'Doing friendship during the second year of life in a Swedish preschool', *European Early Childhood Education Research Journal*, 20 (1): 83–98.
Dunn, J. (2004) *Children's Friendships: The Beginnings of Intimacy*, Oxford: Blackwell.

References

Anning, A. and Edwards, A. 2010. 'Young Children as Learners', in Miller, L., Cable, C. and Goodliff, G. (eds) *Supporting Children's Learning in the Early Years*. Abingdon: Routledge.
Bal, A., and T. E. Radke. 2013. 'Diverse Perspectives on Social Interactional Strengths in Children with Disabilities: A Socio-ecological Study'. *International Journal of Early Childhood Special Education* 5 (1): 15–29.
Bertran, M. 2015. 'Factors That Influence Friendship Choices in Children under 3 in Two Schools: An Approach towards Child Culture in Formal Settings in Barcelona'. *Childhood* 22 (2): 187– 200. doi:10.1177/0907568214528224 (accessed 17 March 2017).
Broadhead, P. 2009. 'Conflict Resolution and Children's Behaviour: Observing and Understanding Social and Cooperative Play in Early Years Educational Settings'. *Early Years* 29 (2): 105–118. doi:10.1080/09575140902864446 (accessed 17 March 2017).
Corsaro, W. 2015. *The Sociology of Childhood* 4th Edition. London: Sage
de Groot Kim, S. 2010. '"There's Elly, It Must be Tuesday": Discontinuity in Child Care Programs and Its Impact on the Development of Peer Relationships in Young Children.' *Early Childhood Education Journal* 38: 153–164.
Dietrich, S. L. 2005. 'A Look at Friendships between Pre-school Aged Children with and without Disabilities in Two Inclusive Classrooms'. *Journal of Early Childhood Research* 3 (2): 193–215. doi:10.1177/1476718X05053933 (accessed 17 March 2017).
Dunn, J. 2004. *Children's Friendships: The Beginnings of Intimacy*. Oxford: Blackwell.
Einarsdóttir, J. 2011. 'Reconstructing Playschool Experiences'. *European Early Childhood Education Research Journal* 19 (3): 387–402.
Engdhal, I. 2012. 'Doing Friendship During the Second Year of Life in a Swedish Preschool'. *European Early Childhood Education Research Journal* 20 (1): 83–98.
Hollingsworth, H., and V. Buysse. 2009. 'Establishing Friendships in Early Childhood Inclusive Settings: What Role Do Parents and Teachers Play?' *Journal of Early Intervention* 31 (4): 287–307. doi:10.1177/1053815109352659 (accessed 17 March 2017).
Kington, A., P. Gates and P. Sammons. 2013. 'Development of Social Relationships, Interactions and Behaviours in Early Education Settings'. *Journal of Early Childhood Research* 11 (3):292–311. doi:10.1177/1476718X13492936 (accessed 17 March 2017).
Konstantoni, K. 2012. 'Children's Peer Relationships and Social Identities: Exploring Cases of Young Children's Agency and Complex Interdependencies from the Minority World'. *Children's Geographies* 10 (3): 337–346. doi:10.1080/14733285.2012.693382 (accessed 17 March 2017).

Lofdahl, A. 2006. 'Grounds for Values and Attitudes: Children's Play and Peer-cultures in Pre-school'. *Journal of Early Childhood Research* 4 (1): 77–88. doi:10.1177/ 1476718X06059791 (accessed 17 March 2017).

Meyer, L. H. 2001. 'The Impact of Inclusion on Children's Lives: Multiple Outcomes, and Friendship in Particular'. *International Journal of Disability, Development and Education* 48 (1): 9–31. doi:10.1080/10349120120036288 (accessed 17 March 2017).

Monaco, C., and C. Pontecorvo. 2010. 'The Interaction between Young Toddlers: Constructing and Organising Participation Frameworks'. *European Early Childhood Education Research Journal* 18 (3): 191–221. doi:10.1080/1350293X.2010.500075 (accessed 17 March 2017).

Nind, M., R. Flewitt, and J. Payler. 2010. 'The Social Experience of Early Childhood for Children with Learning Disabilities: Inclusion, Competence and Agency'. *British Journal of Sociology of Education* 31 (6): 653–670. doi:10.1080/01425692.2010.515113 (accessed 17 March 2017).

Odom, L., C. Zercher, L. Shouming, J. Marquart, S. Sandall, and W. Brown. 2006. 'Social Acceptance and Rejection of Preschool Children with Disabilities: A Mixed Method Analysis'. *Journal of Educational Psychology* 98 (4): 807–823. doi:10.1037/0022-0663.98.4.807 (accessed 17 March 2017).

Paige-Smith, A., and J. Rix. 2011. 'Researching Early Intervention and Young Children's Perspectives – Developing and Using a "Listening to Children Approach"'. *British Journal of Special Education* 38 (1): 28–36. doi:10.1111/j.1467-8578.2011.00494.x (accessed 17 March 2017).

Parry, J. 2014. 'Making Connections and Making Friends: Social Interactions between Two Children Labelled with Special Educational Needs and their Peers in a Nursery Setting'. *Early Years: An International Research Journal* 34 (3): 301–314. doi:10.1080/09575146.2013 .878317 (accessed 17 March 2017).

Parry, J. 2015. 'Exploring the Social Connections in Preschool Settings Between Children Labelled with Special Educational Needs and Their Peers, *International Journal of Early Years Education* 23 (4): 352–364. doi:10.1080/09669760.2015.1046158 (accessed 17 March 2017).

Rossetti, Z. S. 2011. '"That's How We Do It": Friendship Work between High School Students with and without Autism or Developmental Delay'. *Research & Practice for Persons with Severe Disabilities* 36 (1–2): 23–33.

Sebanc, A., K. Kearns, M. Hernandez and K. Galvin. 2007. 'Predicting Having a Best Friend in Young Children: Individual Characteristics and Friendship Features'. *Journal of Genetic Psychology* 168 (1): 81–95.

Selby, J.M. and Bradley, B.S. 2003. 'Infants in Groups: A Paradigm for the Study of Early Social Experience'. *Human Development*, 46: 197–221.

Skanfors, L., Lofdhal, A., and Hagglund, S. 2009. 'Hidden Spaces and Places in the Preschool: Withdrawal Strategies in Preschool Children's Peer Cultures'. *Journal of Early Childhood Research* 7: 94–109.

Skinner, M., V. Buysse, and D. B. Bailey. 2004. 'Effects of Age and Developmental Status of Partners on Play of Preschoolers with Disabilities'. *Journal of Early Intervention* 26 (3):194–203. doi:10.1177/105381510402600303 (accessed 17 March 2017).

Staub, D. 1998. *Delicate Threads – Friendships between Children with and without Special Needs in Inclusive Settings.* Bethesda, MD: Woodbine House.

Svinth, L. 2012. 'Children's Collaborative Encounters in Pre-school'. *Early Child Development and Care* 1–16.

Waller, T. 2010. 'Modern Childhood', in Cable, C., Miller, L. and Goodliff, G. (eds) *Working with Children in the Early Years*. Abingdon: Routledge.

Zeedyk, M. S. 2006. 'From Intersubjectivity to Subjectivity: The Transformative Roles of Emotional Intimacy and Imitation'. *Infant and Child Development*, 15 (3): 321–344.

Chapter 10

Playful meaning making in music with young children and parents

Alison Street

Chapter introduction

In this chapter, Alison Street, a specialist in music in Early Childhood, an Associate Lecturer in Early Childhood Studies at Oxford Brookes University, and a member of the review panel for Music Educators and Researchers of Young Children (MERYC) Eunet, discusses a range of theoretical perspectives that have informed research related to babies and young children's musicality. Drawing on case studies from her own and others' research and practice, Alison explores young children's varied musical experiences and how adults can support children's musical meaning making.

Introduction

> The essence of communication is mutual creativity. It is from creativity in communication that we inherit creativity in personal action.
>
> (Fogel, 1993:41)

This chapter is about playful musicality in young children and explores ways that those living and working with them might understand and support this play. So why start with Alan Fogel's words? His words put the ways we communicate with each other at the heart of creative action. In this chapter, I will emphasise how important early social interactions are as foundations for what it means to be musically expressive both as an individual and with others. We have only to think about a young child banging with a spoon on a bowl, or a baby blowing raspberries as she forces her breath between vibrating lips, a grandparent bouncing a 1-year-old on his knee as he chants a playful rhyme, or a 2-year-old shaking her head and arms to recorded music on the TV to realise how children both respond to, and create meanings from, the sounds and gestures they have learned from their situations and relationships. Fogel's words emphasise that creativity emerges both as personal action and through our understanding of each other's expressions.

This then becomes key to how we think about the nature and role of music in early childhood, both as a self-initiated activity gaining its meaningfulness from the interaction of an individual with things around him and also as part of social play with others.

I begin by exploring the musical nature of children's play and how we think of the role of music in early childhood. Then I outline some of the theoretical perspectives that have informed research on babies' and young children's musicality. While these theories originate mainly in developmental social psychology, I draw attention to the voices of parents and carers whose accounts complement the psychological research in showing how they support their children's expressiveness and reveal qualities of their own emotions in the process. I have learned so much from watching adults interacting with their children over the last twenty years, especially through my involvement in the charity Peeple (www.Peeple. org.uk). This work was the background to my own research on maternal singing (Street, 2006) and to the development of helpful strategies using music in practice that aims to empower parents in their role (Street, 2009). The second part of the chapter takes a slightly different perspective, using a sociocultural lens to interpret playful meaning making in music. It explores the relevance of researchers such as Vygotsky and Bronfenbrenner to interpret how adults may approach decisions on what and how to provide musical activities with young children and their families in educational contexts that are increasingly culturally diverse.

The musical nature of play

Children enjoy playing with sounds, both in those they make themselves through vocalising and using their bodies as resonators – clapping and slapping – and also with things around them, as in using sticks, stones, kitchen utensils, musical instruments, and digital devices in applications on mobile phones, tablets, and toys. This play is often interpreted as just exploratory or having fun, but if we look carefully at how it evolves it becomes clear that young children play with sounds that intrigue them, and that this play is rarely trivial: it has its own purposes for the players. It is meaningful in a broader sense too, in that it reflects the impact of children's everyday social and cultural situations as the following vignettes illustrate.

The first describes Lily at an electronic keyboard.

Three-year-old Lily in her front room in a small town in the UK explores a keyboard, switching the power on and off and pressing different buttons that cause a range of samples with their inherent rhythmic backing to tunes. Sometimes she stops and listens to one particular mode, with her head on one side, then nodding in response to the given beat. She finally makes her choice, the 'piano', which is touch sensitive. First with spread fingers making spidery shapes, and then with flat palms, she moves her hands up and down the keyboard, her upper body swaying from side to side following each hand. As she lifts and lets her hands fall onto the keys she chants, 'I'm the big goat, big goat' as she alternately hits the black keys strongly.

The second was observed at a family outing:

On a wooden boardwalk over tidal wetlands in Queensland, Australia, two 4-year-old boys run along the straight section, their feet making a hollow sound that resonates through the structure. When they get to the corner they stop, look at each other and pound the boardwalk with their feet enjoying the resonance and the flexibility of the wood underneath them. They kick, stamp, and jump, sometimes together, sometimes separately. They stop, wait, and then carry on again, repeating and extending the patterns they make as they fling their legs wide in star jumps, each trying to outdo the other in the height and energy of their leaps. A shoe falls into the mud and the adults with them become absorbed in finding a long stick with which to retrieve it.

What is of interest in these two examples is that the children are individually experimenting with the sounds in their environment, experiencing the changes in pitch or quality of tone they create. In the first, Lily is absorbed in her experimenting but then finds that by trying different ways of playing with weight and force she is associating this with a story she already knows about the Billy Goats Gruff. The meanings for her expressive gestures and drumming of the keys come from her relationship with the keyboard and in how her own actions remind her of a story character she knows.

In the second example, the boys respond to the innate resonance of the structure as they test it out. Through their joint energies and timing, they produce something that is enhanced and sustained by their togetherness – until it is abruptly brought to an end as the shoe flies off. These two examples show playful musicality as drawing its meaning from the situation, where the children build on what they already know and explore sound qualities in relation to their actions 'in the moment' or with each other. The moment may be fleeting but the experience is meaningful and very present to them.

How is music perceived here? Susan Young (2005), writing on musical communication in early childhood, suggested that instead of considering music as the outcome of individual thinking, as for example the result of

composing a piece on the piano or writing a song, we might in the context
of young children's play turn to writers such as Blacking. He explored the
social and cultural nature and functions of music through his studies in
ethnomusicology (Blacking, 1987). To him, the meaningfulness of music
comes from the contexts in which it arises and through the processes and
interactions of those who make it. Young suggests that when viewed this
way it is 'music-as-action, constituted in and gaining meaningfulness from
"extra-musical" processes' (Young, 2005:282). In the examples above,
through looking carefully at how the children behave musically – how they
move and match gesture, weight, time, and energy to suit their purpose – we
can conceive of music as a process actively constructed and created by players
in relation to each other and their environment.

In early childhood education, there is sometimes a tension between
perceptions of music as a sophisticated art form, in which musical elements
are thought to be important to be taught in isolation (pulse, tempo, phrasing,
for example) and those views which may seem to be more about forms of
playfulness. Yet playfulness need not reflect a lack of sophistication in terms
of young children's perceptual powers of musical dimensions. We know
from experiments in acoustic laboratory studies such as those by Sandra
Trehub in Canada, that even at 6 months old, babies are very good at
detecting differences in conventional musical phrases, melodies, and rhythmic
patterns (Trehub, 2011). If given opportunities to experience music playfully
and meaningfully in educational and home contexts, they can develop into
young children who discern what it means to be musically expressive. This
leads to questions such as 'What do we mean by musicality?' and 'How do
young children use music to express what they mean?' Through answering
these, we might then be able to apply this knowledge to provide the
opportunities for ongoing musical learning. These questions will be answered
in part by looking first into studies that have explored musicality in infancy,
to understand how playful interactions with babies and young children are
both musically expressive and meaningful. Understanding the relevance of
these can inform what and how and why we choose what to do in practice.

Musicality in talking with babies

For the last fifty years, Western developmental psychology has been very
influential in how we think of infant development – of what happens when,
and how the roles of adults relate. While it is important to consider how
research in this field has been driven predominantly by Euro-American
studies that often neglect the diverse social and cultural contexts of families,

nevertheless the closely observed, acoustically measured nuances in adult-child interactions have been invaluable in providing rich data about the musicality of early communication.

Mechthild Papoušek, working in Munich spent much of her life researching young children's play, creativity, and parent-child relationships. In her research of infant-directed (ID) speech (1996), she shows how caregivers alter the tone, pitch, and timing of their voices when they interact with babies in normal day-to-day caring routines. She and her husband Hanuš drew attention to the importance of the lively stimulation that parents intuitively give their babies in the earliest years through their rocking, cuddling, and bouncing, and they particularly focused on the way parents use their voice. Through research methods that included sonographic and digital acoustic analyses of timing, frequency, and amplitude, they opened up a world of evidence of the way babies and their close adults signal their emotions, give non-verbal messages, and play creatively with their voices. So, in intuitive healthy parenting, they identified distinctive melodies – or contours – which have meanings for babies, much in the same way that musical tunes can arouse or soothe us or keep our attention. The human voice has endless ways of appearing exciting and interesting, and although as adults we might think repetitive imitating of coos or babbles could be boring, it is hardly ever boring to the baby with whom we pass time. Thus they found that when mothers responded to their babies' cues, they would alter their utterances intuitively to regulate their babies' state; if the baby seemed passive or inattentive, their voices would rise in pitch with increasing rate and intensity, and if the babies appeared to need soothing, their vocal melodies became longer, flatter, and lower. Through imitating young babies' non-crying vocal sounds, parents are also matching and modelling how speech works. In joining with playful babble, raspberries, and bubbling, they are encouraging creative use of the voice through vocal play. Babies appear to use their soft palettes and vocal tract as an inexhaustible toy, as they practise and extend, even in the absence of their parents, the sounds they know from their surroundings.

Singing to babies

What is interesting about the musical stimulation that both mothers and fathers give their young babies through their vocal play is that it is almost always done unconsciously. Numerous interview studies including Street (2006) and Custodero and colleagues (2002) have revealed that parents do not consider their singing as intentionally musical; parents are usually extremely modest and self-conscious about how they use their voices in these intimate situations. Sandra Trehub studied the acoustic properties of mothers' and fathers' singing to babies in her work at the University of Toronto. From her laboratory experiments, she observed that parents alter the tone of their voice when in the presence of a baby (Trehub et al., 1997). She and her colleagues found that adults tend to make their voices higher in pitch, slower in pace, more airy and warm in tone, and often leave pauses between phrases. They took these experiments into naturalistic conditions, that is, at home, where, from testing samples of a baby's saliva, they found the level of the hormone cortisol changes according to the emotional state of the baby. Singing to babies in response to their mood had measurable effects seen in the level of cortisol to either rouse and excite or soothe and relax babies (Shenfield, Trehub, & Nakata, 2003).

In my own research, singing to babies was found to be a very fluid activity where parents draw on sound effects from toys, other relations' tone of voice, TV programmes, their own favourite downloadable tunes or soundtracks (Street, 2006). My study used video playback with fifteen mothers as they spent time (three-minute episodes) talking, playing, and singing with their babies who were between 4 and 11 months old. In response to seeing the recordings of themselves with their babies, their interpretations of their singing were not about a known repertoire of conventional nursery songs or rhymes, but rather their own intentions towards their babies and the emotional effect the act of singing had on themselves: *how* they sang was important to them. Below are some snapshots of their accounts after seeing themselves on video:

Lucy had an invented song she always uses for washing [baby] Izzy's face in the morning. Clare said her 8-month-old daughter recognised nursery tunes whistled rather than sung, as she could never remember the correct words. Six mothers said they sang 'absolute rubbish', making up strange noises, or copying the musical toys their children have, the utterances their babies make, mimicking other family members' singing and making things up 'on the spur of the moment'. Bea and Barbara spoke about singing as being about using different facial expressions: 'You do silly expressions with your eyes wide and your mouth wide.'

Vocal play was evident in the stream of sound effects that emerged in how mothers imitated their babies. Young (2005) suggests how imitation by both partners is a primary communicative strategy that establishes turn taking and is successful where it links rhythmically and synchronously in well-timed exchanges. In my study, the repetitive nature of the imitative behaviour by the mothers helped them to build up a repertoire of known and shared expressions derived from and associated with familiar contexts and playthings. A mother's imitative sequences served to show her baby not only that through copying his sounds, she recognised them as being important expressions with his own meanings, but also that they made sense to both of them in their own ongoing narrative. Ian Cross (2005) argues how these non-verbal ways of communicating are *helpfully ambiguous* – so they can have many meanings – but are also key elements in how we think of the origins of music itself, and therefore essential to our understanding of what it means to be musically expressive.

Why has this chapter focused so much on interactions with babies? Because I am agreeing with Cross in suggesting these early interactions embody powerful sources on which later models of expressiveness and creativity are founded.

Tuning in with movement and gesture

We know from studies in ethnomusicology that music is generally made with and for other people, and that it is a way of bringing people together, of experiencing 'the moment' together, as in feeling the beat or the emotional power of melodies and repeated rhythmic patterns. Whether we think of a pop concert, a disco, or a singing game in a circle of children, an important element is that it hardly ever happens without physical movement. In one mother's account above, the singing 'is the movement'. In many cultures, dance often occurs with singing. In Western early childhood education settings, by contrast, there is a tendency to separate out the singing times from the dancing times and we can learn much about the importance of movement in children's musical expressiveness from the way adults tune in to babies' moods and feelings.

Daniel Stern studied mother-infant interactions and was struck by the different modes they used to show their feelings – a sensitive parent responds to a child's crying by joining in or matching the 'affect' or feeling in the child through her gestures or tone of voice or facial expressions, in a way that is 'multi-modal'. His term 'affect attunement' (Stern, 2000) was developed from studying numerous recordings and video playback to the parents, in which they explained how they acted as they did in order to 'join in' and 'be with' their babies. This went beyond imitating. The mothers did not perceive their behaviours to have specific functions, as in regulating mood or entertaining the infants; they were rather sharing the mood or pulse or intensity of a mutual experience. 'How' the mothers joined in with their infants' expressions, rather than 'what' they did, Stern described as 'vitality affects'. Vitality, he asserted, is continuously present, though also changing, throughout all behaviour, and it is to do with qualities of intensity and time. So we might, for example, see these 'vitality affects' in the *way* that a mother changes her baby's nappy, lifts her out of a cot, or offers the bottle that immerses the baby in feelings of vitality. Stern drew on the examples of abstract dance and music to illustrate the expressiveness of 'vitality affects' as being *ways of feeling* rather than explicit *content of feeling*. Joining in with ways of feeling through affectionate and loving interactions has been seen to be key not only to social and emotional development and, as is argued here, to creative and artistic expressiveness, but also to general cognitive growth (Gerhardt, 2004).

These patterns of tuning in with each other form a stream of communication in which one party does not necessarily wait for the other to respond. The interactions often overlap flexibly, evolving through continuous communication (Fogel, 1993), where one expression may lead to another in fluid interdependence. We only have to think of two people sharing a series of stories or a joke on which they elaborate, adding asides, nuances, and innuendo to make each other laugh. Except that here the medium is mostly pre-verbal; the play is with sounds, gestures, or facial and body expressions which share or extend one another's sense of vitality. We are reminded of those two 4-year-olds on the boardwalk jumping, kicking and shaking their limbs, giggling, and playfully drumming with their feet in overlapping patterns that both imitate and elaborate.

Fogel's research (1993) has focused on how children develop essentially through their relationships with others. He suggests that carer and baby co-regulate each other's behaviour through shared meanings that are repeatedly explored and varied and extended. A good example is the game of 'peep-bo' where a parent may, over and over, go through this intimate game of hiding and surprising. This game both confirms the infant as an important partner in the interaction, as in 'I can see that this works and goes on working', and also provides anticipation of predictable structural patterns, building up a repertoire of remembered experiences. Similarly, singing the same song repeatedly performs both these functions. Wherever a carer is sensitive enough to prolong a musical phrase, in response to their baby's attentiveness, or to alter the timing of a climactic moment for dramatic effect, like a tickle at the end of the nursery rhyme, 'Round and round the garden', then baby and carer are co-creating a rich environment and exploring new meanings. (In my own research I found that parents would often play or sing this rhyme and instinctively wait and cause a surprise, but they would not admit to singing in any other context, nor consider what they did to be particularly musical!)

Another psychologist who has spent much of his life researching and interpreting the science of musicality in communication between parents and their very young babies from birth is Colwyn Trevarthen. With colleague Stephen Malloch, he formulated the theory of Communicative Musicality (Malloch & Trevarthen, 2009) based on research involving repeated listening and interpreting audio-recordings of mothers chatting with their babies. Within the fluid communicative give and take, Malloch could discern three dimensions: *pulse*, that defined regular successive events in the interaction; *quality,* that refers to how expressive the event is – in terms of the vocal contour like a swooping, or vitality of the gesture – as in a wave of the hand; and thirdly, the *narrative* or rather how moments in both pulse and quality are strung together in a continuum of expression and intention. When a playmate or companion joins – or tunes in with a baby or toddler in a game or song or dance-like stream of communication, Trevarthen interprets this as living out a general human capacity to be communicative 'in the polyrhythmic, stepping, swinging, dancing and melodic way human bodies move to celebrate and share' (Trevarthen & Malloch, 2002:12).

From the research explored so far, playful meaning making has been seen to emerge both as the process of individual self-initiated exploration and also to evolve from the social interactions and situations in which young children find themselves. The musical nature of this play has been described both as a kind of continuous stream of expressiveness and also as a sharing of vitality affects. Terms such as patterning, imitating, tuning in, and timing all have musical meanings themselves and refer to the qualities of the interactions observed by researchers and by parents alike.

In the next section, I explore music as it is used as a means of sharing cultural knowledge. Questions arise about what kinds of music might be meaningful in practice for families with young children.

How do adults support children's musical meaning making?

In the changing world of human endeavour research does not relate to practice as a template for application because in the changing world of human endeavour application always requires interpretation, imagination and creativity.

(Bowman, 2009:5)

These words deliver a challenge to those of us who aim to provide meaningful activities in music for young children and their families. They warn against lifting bits from research and translating directly into practice without taking into account the contexts and situations of those with whom we work. In this second part of the chapter, I move aside from developmental psychological perspectives to focus on sociocultural views of development. These have been influential in early childhood settings in the UK since the 1990s, and much of this thinking was informed by the work of Lev Vygotsky (1978). He emphasised the important role of the adult, or more competent learner, to support children's cognitive development. This is done by watching and understanding what children can already do and, through conversation that overtly expresses new ideas or perspectives on old knowledge, reinforces and supports a child's internalised mental representations. In this way, an adult or more sophisticated other mediates between the child and different forms of knowledge within the 'zone of proximal development'. These forms of knowledge are socially and culturally defined. Vygotsky argued that in play children re-enact situations, experimenting with rules and conventions they are familiar with from a range of influences. For example, in their socio–dramatic play they might use language quite unlike their normal interactions, adopting slogans, chants, or particular tones of voice as they 'become' super-heroes, or play at 'schools' or 'coffee shops', or imitate adults disciplining their siblings. In this way children's social and cultural knowledge is explored, shared and transmitted through play. We might think of examples of how they use forms or styles of music known to them too, as in the three short vignettes below:

A 6-year-old girl sings a song from the Disney's film Frozen *on her older sibling's karaoke machine in her bedroom at home. With one hand she clasps the microphone to her mouth while she stretches out the other arm with extended fingers as she sings, eyes shut, holding the final note strongly in the musical phrase, 'Let it goooooo'.*

Two 4-year-olds in the nursery playground using plastic tennis rackets as guitars, adopt the poses and movements of rock performers, and sing with gusto, watching each other, copying, and competing for the attention of the children playing near them.

Two-year-old Anusha holds a small cylindrical drum. She paces up and down her living room singing and playing the drum with a white plastic spoon. Occasionally she stops and her father encourages her by chanting, 'Dai, dai, dai, dai'. She stops, drops the drum, but as he continues, she picks it up again, nodding her head in time with her pacing and her playing.

What kinds of cultural knowledge are being explored in these examples? What kinds of meanings are children exchanging about musical style and performance? As adults witnessing these, do we encourage or do we inhibit? Are there some styles of music that we feel to be more appropriate than others for young children to experience?

It is worth pausing and asking what the children in each case are learning from their play and what meanings they might be building. In the first two vignettes, the children draw on their memory of Disney and their knowledge of rock musicians – picked up either from live artists or the media. In the third, Anusha's father recognises how she wants to play in the same way as she may have seen her mother and family friends from Pakistan using a 'dholak', a long round drum, played with hands and small spoons, and often seen at weddings.

These genres of musical meaning making are each embedded within the social and cultural, local and international networks in which family life proceeds and through which children build up knowledge of what is meaningful to them. They illustrate Bronfenbrenner's ecological model (1979) for children's development. This conceives of the child within their immediate family participating in their surrounding social and physical environments. His research portrayed the child as being 'nested' at the centre of concentric spheres of influence, as if in the middle of a set of Russian dolls, where the closest layer contains the family and the outer layer the politics and dominant beliefs and culture.

Barbara Rogoff (2003) in her studies of the cultural nature of human development proposed that these concentric circles should be seen as porous and interactive with one another, emphasising the dynamic interdependence of the individual using cultural tools, such as ways of singing or moving, or playing an instrument, in a way that can develop or transform those tools. In this way, culture does not sit only in the outside layer, but becomes significantly active – like Anusha playing her mini-dholak – as a physical means of playful meaning making between the child and her parent.

A second view of how to approach answers to the questions above is to consider how the three vignettes reflect the culturally diverse influences on young children and their families. Thinking of the 6-year-old singing Elsa's song from *Frozen* and the boys with their plastic guitars, reminds us of the dominance of Western media and how, for example, Disney films are part and parcel of many households with pre-school children in the UK. Arjun Appadurai, an anthropologist, developed the idea of 'scapes' or 'landscapes' as environmental influences on families (1996). His notion of 'mediascapes' is relevant here – that is, the way our realities and imagined worlds are shaped by the electronic distribution of information and opinion, for example through TV, games, and film. He also coined the term 'ethnoscapes' to refer to the migration of people across borders, including refugees, tourists and workers. We might here consider how Anusha came to be playing her drum. She had made it in a parent and child 'drop in' session at the local children's centre, where a number of South Asian mothers would gather to share experiences in common about adapting to life in the UK, to remind each other of stories they heard from their own parents and to discuss ways to support their children.

Conclusion

Across the world, families are on the move because of conflict, fluctuating patterns of work, changing climatic conditions, and aspirations for education and a better standard of living. This is leading to increasing cultural, social, economic, and linguistic diversity in early childhood settings across Europe, especially in urban areas. These conditions call for educational practice to be responsive and open to the opportunities this diversity affords. This chapter began by exploring the communicative power of musical meaning making and ends with questions about how music is used in practice to provide relevant meanings for young children and their parents. The answers may be found through asking what we learn about ourselves and our own expressiveness by watching and listening to young children playing, moving, and interacting, and through inquiring and reflecting on parents' perspectives of what is musically meaningful in their lives.

Questions for further thinking and reflection

1.   Think of a young child you know under 4 years old: how do they respond to music around them?
2.   What sorts of music do you consider are helpful for young children's development and why?

Further reading

Shehan Campbell, P. (2011) Musical enculturation: Sociocultural influences and meanings of children's experiences in and through music. In M. Barrett (Ed.) *A Cultural Psychology of Music Education*. Oxford: Oxford University Press.
Trevarthen, C., & Malloch, S. (2002). Musicality and music before three: Human vitality and invention shared with pride. *Zero to Three*, September, Vol. 23, No. 1, 10–18.
Young, S. (2003) *Music with the Under-fours*. London & New York: RoutledgeFalmer.

References

Appadurai, A. (1996) *Modernity at Large: Cultural dimensions of globalization.* Minneapolis, MN: University of Minnesota Press.

Blacking, J. (1987) *A Common-sense View of All Music.* Cambridge: Cambridge University Press.

Bowman, W. D. (2009) Professional knowledge: Imagining the obvious as if it weren't. *Action, Cricitsm & Theory for Music Education.* Vol. 8, No. 1. Available at http://act. maydaygroup.org (accessed 17 March 2017).

Bronfenbrenner, U. (1979) *The Ecology of Human Development: Experiments by nature and design.* Cambridge, MA: Harvard University Press.

Cross, I. (2005) Music and meaning, ambiguity and evolution. In D. Miell, R. MacDonald, & D. J. Hargreaves (Eds). *Musical Communication* Oxford & New York: Oxford University Press.

Custodero, L. A., Britto, P. R., & Xin, T. (2002) From Mozart to Motown, lullabies to love songs: A preliminary report on the parents' use of music with infants survey (PUMIS). *Zero to Three,* Vol. 23, No. 1, 41–46.

Fogel, A. (1993) *Developing Through Relationships. Origins of communication, self and culture.* Hertfordshire, UK: Harvester Wheatsheaf.

Gerhardt, S. (2004) *Why Love Matters: How affection shapes a baby's brain.* Hove & New York: Brunner-Routledge.

Malloch, S. & Trevarthen, C. (2009) *Communicative Musicality: Exploring the basis of human companionship.* Oxford & New York: Oxford University Press

Papoušek, M. (1996) Intuitive parenting: A hidden source of musical stimulation in infancy. In I. Deliège and J. Sloboda (Eds) (1996) *Musical Beginnings.* Oxford: Oxford University Press.

Rogoff, B. (2003). *The Cultural Nature of Human Development.* Oxford & New York: Oxford University Press.

Shenfield, T., Trehub, S. E., & Nekata, T. (2003) Maternal singing modulates infant arousal. *Psychology of Music (SEMPRE),* Vol. 31, No. 4, pp. 365–375.

Stern, D. N. (2000) Introduction. In *The Interpersonal World of the Infant: A view from psychoanalysis and developmental psychology,* 2nd edn. New York: Basic Books.

Street, A. M. (2006) The role of singing within mother–infant interactions. Unpublished PhD Thesis, University of Roehampton, London.

Street, A. M. (2009) Empowering parents through 'Learning Together': The Peep model. In J. Barlow & P.O. Svanberg (Eds) *Keeping the Baby in Mind: Infant mental health in practice.* London: Routledge.

Trehub, S. (2011) Music lessons from infants. In S. Hallam, I. Cross and M. Thaut (Eds). *The Oxford Handbook of Music Psychology.* Oxford & New York: Oxford University Press.

Trehub, S. E., Unyk, A. M., Kamenetsky, S. B., Hill, D. S., Trainor, L. J., Henderson, J. L. & Saraza, M. (1997). Mothers' and fathers' singing to infants. *Developmental Psychology,* Vol. 33, pp. 500–507.

Trevarthen, C. & Malloch, S. (2002) Musicality and music before three: Human vitality and invention shared with pride. *Zero to Three,* September, Vol. 23, No. 1.

Vygotsky, L. S. (1978) *Mind in Society: The development of higher mental processes.* Cambridge, MA: Harvard University Press. www.peeple.org.uk (accessed 17 March 2017).

Young, S. (2005) Musical communication between adults and young children. In D. Miell, R. MacDonald & D. J. Hargreaves (Eds). *Musical Communication.* Oxford & New York: Oxford University Press.

Chapter 11

Voices in the park: researching the participation of young children in outdoor play in early years settings

Tim Waller

Chapter introduction

In this chapter Tim Waller, Professor of Child and Family Studies at Anglia Ruskin University, Cambridge, looks back at the shifts and developments in an outdoor learning project with a nursery school in England over a ten-year period. He discusses the many influences that have impacted on the children's levels of participation during the lifetime of the project including changes to the physical environment and also the emerging focus on 'school readiness'.

Introduction

The project, which started in 2004, is ongoing and is based at a nursery school in England. The aims of the research are to elicit children's perspectives of their outdoor experiences and to investigate the relationship between outdoor environments and pedagogy in early childhood. The article analyses the research findings from a sociocultural perspective focusing on transformations of participation.

After 10 years of the Outdoor Learning Project (OLP), I wanted to take the opportunity to stand back and reflect on what we have learned from the project about outdoor play and learning, participatory research with young children and the relationship between pedagogy and research in early years settings. In particular, this article critically discusses recent changes within the project impacting on staffing, resources and location, and frames these within the wider context to identify a number of the implications arising from the research for leadership and management in early childhood settings.

Background

In the wider context, early years education in England is enacted within a background of the 'school readiness agenda' and a placeless curriculum

(Waller and Davis, 2014). Further, since 2009 there have been significant changes to the wider social and economic context impacting on young children and their families on a global scale, particularly in relation to 'austerity cuts' and reductions to the public funding of early childhood education and care (ECEC).

In addition, whilst there has also been an increasing trend in both public policy and practice towards fostering children's participation and voice, as Bae (2010) acknowledges, current neo-liberal or new management discourses have led to policies in many countries that have impacted on early years education to reduce children's participation to tokenistic routines regulated from an adult perspective.

Conceptual underpinning

The article draws upon the sociocultural perspective as a conceptual tool (Lave, 1988; Rogoff, 1990) in order to acknowledge and investigate the shared construction and distribution of knowledge in ECEC.

From a sociocultural perspective, drawing on Stephen (2010), this article focuses on the two forms of guided participation which Rogoff (2003) identifies as central to learning: (i) 'the mutual bridging of meaning' (which is the mutual understanding that develops between children and adults through interaction); and (ii) 'the mutual structuring of opportunities' (where children and adults together determine the range of activities and participatory approaches in the setting).

In her article on pedagogy, Stephen (2010) identifies two types of guided interaction:

a   distal – which is indirect action such as monitoring, planning and providing resources;
b   proximal – which concerns the direct action of adults, such as demonstrating, enjoying, sharing, instructing, providing feedback and supporting.

These two types of interaction are used as a lens to understand and critique the pedagogy within the OLP, which in turn impacts on the approach to participation.

Context

The OLP started in January 2004 and involves children, staff, parents and students at a state-maintained nursery school in England. Children aged

3–4 years are given regular opportunities to play and learn in natural, 'wild' environments, such as woodland and river-banks, accompanied by adults. The children normally attend the nursery for 1 year on a part-time basis (40 children in the morning and 40 in the afternoon) and then transfer to the reception class of local primary schools. Staff originally comprised a head teacher, class teacher, three nursery nurses and three learning support assistants. There is a base ratio of one practitioner to ten children, and the children are organized into 'key groups' of around 14.

Two different locations have been used so far for the project, and visits are undertaken on one day per week (morning and afternoon), whatever the weather. From 2004 to 2012 a local country park (Location A) was visited. The country park has elements of a 'natural, wild environment' and is built around an Edwardian reservoir and arboretum. The children were transported by bus to the park, with the journey lasting approximately 15 minutes in each direction. A number of adults accompanied the children, including practitioners, parents and students, allowing for a one-to-one or one-to-two adult–child ratio. However, during 2012 a severe storm devastated a large area of woodland in the country park and many of the trees that did not fall were also cut down by the Park Rangers, for safety reasons. The Rangers then installed a range of purpose-built play equipment, such as a slide, and the area completely lost its natural feel. As a result the practitioners decided to re-locate the OLP to Location B.

Location B is a small wooded copse within the grounds of an adjacent primary school (children aged 4–11 years). The children start the visit in the nursery by putting on their outdoor waterproof suit and Wellington boots. They are then invited to hold onto a rope so that they can walk together across the grass playing field behind the nursery to the wooded copse. Supporting resources, drinks, fruit and first aid equipment are transported in a hand-pulled trolley. The routine also usually involves stopping at the top of a small hill before the copse for a practitioner-led dialogue about a range of natural events and animals, such as what the children can see, shadows, sunlight and mini-beasts, depending on the season.

Methods

The OLP study draws on the 'Mosaic' approach for listening to young children as described by Clark and Moss (2001, 2005, 2011). The method uses both the traditional tools of observing children at play and a variety of 'participatory tools' with children. These include taking photographs, book-making, tours of the outdoor area and map-making. Also, part of the Mosaic approach is to involve adults in gathering information in addition to gaining perspectives from the children, such as observations, reflective discussion, focus groups and interviews with practitioners and focus groups, and surveys with parents (for further discussion of this process, see Waller and Bitou, 2011).

A particular feature of the research methods used by the OLP has been digital cameras, which are operated by children, staff and the researcher to record and document features of outdoor play. As the project developed in Location A, we evolved a 'reactive', method (Corsaro, 2005; Emond, 2005) where the children could decide to carry on playing, or to record an aspect of their play or space with the camera, or ask an adult to record it for them. The images recorded through this method were then used to document and reflect on the learning and experiences in the outdoor environment, and some are also published as learning stories (see Waller and Bitou, 2011).

Findings and discussion

For the first nine years of the project both the staffing and location for visits remained stable. However, during 2012 the staffing changed because of retirement and was further reduced by government-led cutbacks. These events also coincided with a change in location of the OLP to a local wooded copse. In addition, at the same time, a revised curriculum (DfE, 2012) was introduced with increased emphasis on 'school readiness' (Bingham and Whitbread, 2012).

The changes to the OLP over the past 10 years, involving people, space and curriculum, are significant in terms of pedagogy and the impact on participation within the project. The article now focuses on how outdoor pedagogy is enacted in two different spaces – Location A (the country park) and Location B (the wooded copse) – in order to discern how the pedagogy may have been influenced by the changes.

How does space and place influence pedagogy, participation and research?

In Location A the coach journey provided a regular opportunity for one-to-one dialogue between adults and children. The high staff-child ratio and the wide and varied space also afforded greater opportunity for child-led initiatives resulting from shared dialogue, which led to the construction of shared narratives around special places (see Waller, 2006, 2007).

In the quarterly research reviews from 2004 to 2011, practitioners consistently noted that they had 'more quality time with children, uninterrupted communication and time for response' in the OLP. Significantly, staff also acknowledged that in the country park the children had learned to wait for an adult response because they knew staff had time to give one. For example, individual practitioner comments documented at the reviews included:

> We are more relaxed about letting go and not having a set activity . . . tuned into children's ideas more. Changed the way we do planning – more flexibility. (EY practitioner, 27 years' experience)
>   Our whole attitude to children's learning changed – we started to trust that we could follow the children's learning . . . we changed our practice and planning. Staff have gained expertise and become more confident. Children have become more confident to communicate because of the individual attention. (EY practitioner, 24 years' experience)

In July 2011, practitioners reflected on the changes to the country park, noting that they had impacted on both children and staff, as follows:

> Recently S . . . (country park) itself has changed – the new play park has become the focus . . . children lost exploration and problem solving opportunities. (EY practitioner, 27 years' experience)
>   When the environment changed [at the country park] we became less enthusiastic about the visits because the children didn't get so much imaginative play. (EY practitioner, 16 years' experience)

Subsequent to the change in 2012 to Location B, research data revealed a much more routinized and practitioner-led approach. Once in the copse the staff and children have established a base on a circle of logs and use the base for discussion, planning and snacks. Sometimes a practitioner will lead an interactive activity such as dramatizing a story, collecting, observing and recording the natural environment, and sometimes the children engage in free play investigating the woods, climbing trees or collecting natural material to play with. A number of routines influenced by staff participation in Forest School training have also been incorporated into the organization of visits to Location B, such as the use of 'One, two, three, where are you?' to bring the children back together.

An analysis of video data (Miles and Huberman, 1994) from the project visits reveals distinct differences between the two outdoor environments in terms of both distal and proximal guided interaction. Following

Stephen (2010), Tables 11.1 and 11.2 give examples to illustrate the variation in pedagogy and practice.

Table 11.1 shows a comparison between the two OLP locations in terms of distal guided interaction. Here there are clear variations in the monitoring, planning and provision of resources that show that in Location B the approach is much more adult-led and is arguably less conducive to fostering the participation of the children. For example, planning in Location A involved regular opportunities for children to develop and extend narratives around special places through shared engagement with adults. In Location B practice observed so far has tended to focus on adult-led initiatives around storytelling and mini-beast hunts, for example.

The examples of proximal guided interaction shown in Table 11.2 also demonstrate a variation in practice. In particular, as could be expected, the lower adult-child staff ratio in Location B appears to have had the consequence of decreasing both the proximal guided interaction and the number of occurrences. Activities in the wooded copse are much more adult-directed and routinized. For instance, a significant change is the limited use of digital cameras by both children and staff, resulting in far less child-led pedagogical documentation. In the nursery, staff had to make a conscious decision to change practice because of a reduction in staffing levels brought about by local and national policy in ECEC.

Table 11.1 Distal guided interaction

Form of guided interaction	Location A – country park	Location B – wooded copse
Monitoring	Organizing children in pairs or one-to-one with an adult	Establishment of rules and routines such as holding onto the rope on journey to woods and 'One, two, three, where are you?' in the woods
Planning	Child-led – such as den building, supporting and developing narratives around special places. Informed by children's previous experiences, ongoing narratives and reflection on documentation	Planning activities related to the season – such as collecting, documenting and drawing natural objects in the autumn. Adult-led activities such as dramatic stories and mini-beast hunts
Providing resources	Digital cameras, small rucksacks to carry tools. Documenting learning (children and adults) through digital images.	Tools for digging, drawing and documenting. Affording equal distribution of resources. Artefacts to enhance storytelling, such as a 'Gingerbread Man' placed on the branch of a tree.

Table 11.2 Proximal guided interaction

Form of guided interaction	Location A – country park	Location B – wooded copse
Demonstrating	How to use a tool for den construction	How to use a magnifying glass to closely observe a mini-beast
Enjoying	Sharing a narrative around a special place. Acting as a character in the narrative, for example – the 'Goblin's Den'	Sharing the excitement of finding a worm
Instructing	How to climb a slippery slope	Playing out the story of 'Jack and the Beanstalk'. Group instruction on collecting mini-beasts
Providing feedback	Commenting on a child's picture, photo, map. Developing learning stories from the OLP documentation	Giving encouragement to a child to explore the mud! Highlighting the damage of hitting trees with sticks
Supporting	Tree-climbing – supporting a developing child initiated narrative about the 'Goblin's Den' by taking on a role of a character in the story.	Tree-climbing – giving a child physical and emotional encouragement to climb in a tree.

One significant consequence of this change was the reduction in staff time for documentation and reflection (practitioner review, July 2013), thus also limiting opportunities for shared dialogue between staff and parents about the OLP and impacting on the reification of the project.

Conclusion: Implications for leadership and management

In this chapter I have sought to understand the connection between pedagogy, participation and research in ECEC, and argued that the complex relationship between the wider context and local practice needs to be carefully considered. Through adopting a sociocultural perspective to analyse changes in an outdoor learning project I have aimed to make the links between the distal and proximal guided interaction of children and practitioners more visible, thus also identifying processes of participation. As the OLP evolved in the first few years, a participatory approach to research was adopted to match the pedagogy. However, following a number of significant changes to staffing, location, resources and policy, the OLP has changed and a more pragmatic and adult–led approach became evident. Reflecting on these changes, implications arising from the OLP research for management and leadership in early childhood settings are discerned below.

As with Theobald and Kultti (2012), this chapter has identified a number of dilemmas for practitioners as they try to balance an intended participatory pedagogy with institutional and policy expectations. In particular, the chapter has considered the impact of the wider context and the drive to cut resources, along with the 'school readiness' agenda and how this has impacted on a long-established pedagogy and participation in the OLP.

The empowering and limiting aspects of participation within the OLP are summarized as follows:

> empowering–style of adult–child engagement and interaction, space, number of adults;

> limiting – reduction to staffing and resources, limitations to time and space.

Consequently, the implications for leadership and management in ECEC are that careful consideration needs to be given to the following:

1. allocation of the appropriate of resources to support learning in outdoor spaces;
2. sufficient staff time for documentation and reflection on pedagogy and practice;
3. staff development programmes to support the development of guided interaction and participatory processes with young children;
4. the need for senior staff to be strong advocates for ECEC and engage with policy-makers at local and national level.

Questions for further thinking and reflection

1. In outdoor play activities, what do you think is the connection between adults tending to lead and their attitude to risk?
2. Why do you think that a participatory approach where the emphasis is on listening to children can be difficult for practitioners to sustain?

References

Bae B (2010) Realizing children's right to participation in early childhood settings: Some critical issues in a Norwegian context. *Early Years* 30(3): 205–218.

Bingham S and Whitebread D (2012) *School Readiness: A critical review of perspectives and evidence.* Croome D'Abitot, Worcs, UK: TACTYC.

Clark A and Moss P (2001) *Listening to Young Children: The Mosaic approach.* London: National Children's Bureau.

Clark A and Moss P (2005) *Spaces to Play: More listening to young children using the Mosaic approach*. London: National Children's Bureau.

Clark A and Moss P (2011) *Listening to Young Children* (2nd edn). London: National Children's Bureau.

Corsaro W (2005) *The Sociology of Childhood* (2nd edn). Thousand Oaks, CA: Pine Forge Press.

DfE (Department for Education) (2012) *The Early Years Foundation Stage* (EYFS). Available at: www.education.gov.uk/schools/teachingandlearning/curriculum/a0068102/early-years-foundation-stage-eyfs (accessed October 2013).

Emond R (2005) Ethnographic research methods with children and young people. In: Greene S and Hogan D (eds) *Researching Children's Experience: Approaches and methods*. London: SAGE, 123–140.

Lave J (1988) *Cognition in Practice*. Cambridge: Cambridge University Press.

Miles MB and Huberman AM (1994) *Qualitative Data Analysis: An expanded sourcebook* (2nd edn). Thousand Oaks, CA: SAGE.

Rogoff B (1990) *Apprenticeship in Thinking: Cognitive development in social context*. New York: Plenum Press.

Rogoff B (2003) *The Cultural Nature of Human Development*. Oxford: Oxford University Press.

Stephen S (2010) Pedagogy: The silent partner in early years learning. *Early Years: An International Journal of Research and Development* 30(1): 15–28.

Theobald M and Kultti A (2012) Investigating child participation in the everyday talk of a teacher and children in a preparatory year. *Contemporary Issues in Early Childhood* 13(3): 210–225.

Waller T (2006) 'Don't come too close to my Octopus Tree': Recording and evaluating young children's perspectives on outdoor learning. *Children, Youth and Environments* 16(2): 75–104.

Waller T (2007) The trampoline tree and the swamp monster with 18 heads: Outdoor play in the foundation stage and foundation phase. *Education 3–13* 35(4): 393–407.

Waller T and Bitou A (2011) Research with children: Three challenges for participatory research in early childhood. *European Early Childhood Education Research Association Journal* 19(1): 129–147.

Waller T and Davis G (eds) (2014) *An Introduction to Early Childhood: A Multi-disciplinary Approach* (3rd edn). London: SAGE.

Author biography

Tim Waller is Professor of Child and Family Studies in the Faculty of Health, Social Care and Education at Anglia Ruskin University. Tim is a Convener of the Outdoor Learning SIG in the European Early Childhood Education Research Association (EECERA). He has worked in higher education for over 20 years. Previously he taught in nursery, infant and primary schools in London and has also worked in the USA. His research interests include well-being, outdoor learning, pedagogy and social justice in early childhood. Tim is leading the UK research contributing to the SUPREME project

(Suicide Prevention by Internet and Media Based Mental Health Promotion), aimed at developing an internet-based mental health promotion and suicide prevention programme, targeting young people aged 14–24. Anglia Ruskin has joined academic institutions in Sweden, Estonia, Hungary, Italy, Lithuania and Spain to carry out the study. Tim was Co-Director of the Longitudinal Evaluation of the Role and Impact of Early Years Professionals (in England), commissioned by the Children's Workforce Development Council (2009–12). Since September 2003 he has been coordinating an ongoing research project designed to investigate children's perspectives of their outdoor play. This project has involved developing and using a range of 'participatory' methods for research with young children. Recently, he has edited a Special Edition of the *European Early Childhood Education Association Journal* on Outdoor Play and Learning and, with Deborah Harcourt and Bob Perry, *Researching Young Children's Perspectives: Debating the Ethics and Dilemmas of Educational Research with Children* (published by Routledge in March 2011). The third edition of *An Introduction to Early Childhood: A Multidisciplinaiy Approach,* edited by Tim Waller and Gerry Davis, was published in April 2014.

Chapter 12

Listening to young children: multiple voices, meanings and understandings

Elizabeth Wood

Chapter introduction

In this chapter, Elizabeth Wood, a leading academic in the field of early childhood education, extends our thinking about observing and listening skills, emphasizing that they are integral to being attentive to children's voices and perspectives. Furthermore, the author argues that reflective practice founded on tuning in to what children are saying through their play and activity, inspires practitioners to change and transform their provision. They can shift from being facilitators of learning experiences to being 'activist educators'.

Introduction

In this chapter, I argue that effective educators need to be good researchers, by developing inquiry-based approaches to their practice. Inquiry then becomes the basis for critical reflection through dialogue and knowledge exchange, leading to professional development. Rinaldi proposes that early childhood education should be based on a 'pedagogy of listening', which encompasses ethical and political commitments to children, families and communities, and involves:

> . . . listening to thought – the ideas and theories, questions and answers of children and adults; it means treating thought seriously and with respect; it means struggling to make meaning from what is said, without preconceived ideas of what is correct or appropriate.
>
> (Rinaldi 2006: 15)

For Rinaldi, a pedagogy of listening 'challenges the whole scene of pedagogy' because it demands that we see schools as places of ethical and political practice. This approach requires close attention to children's voices, in ways that pay attention to, and respect, their multiple ways of constructing meanings and conveying their understanding.

Consequently, I will go on to suggest that the skills of observing and listening are integral to repertoires of professional practice, as a means of being attentive to children's voices. Reflective practice can thereby extend into critical engagement with policy, theory and practice, from which new possibilities for action can be generated. Reflective educators can become change agents and 'activist educators', who have the ability to transform, rather than merely implement, policy frameworks (MacNaughton 2005).

In the first section, I examine the implications of developing inquiry-based approaches in the context of contemporary policy frameworks. In the second section, I discuss children's agency and voices, and how these can inform practice through observing and listening. The third section looks at these ideas in the context of assessment practices, based on the attributes of effective educators identified by Fisher (2015). Vignettes from research studies are used to provoke reflective consideration of children's voices, meanings and perspectives, and how these can be used to develop ethical practices.

Policy directions

Contemporary developments in early childhood provision and services are taking place within a dynamic framework of policy and research in national (UK) and international contexts. Policy frameworks for Early Childhood Education can be interpreted narrowly to promote a culture of conformity to technical practices, 'outcomes' and 'standards', or more broadly to promote a culture of entitlement, empowerment and inclusion. Personalized learning and services, assessment for learning, children's well-being, the voices and rights of the child, are policy aspirations that are shared across integrated service providers – education, health, law, social care and playwork. Such aspirations must also respect cultural and social diversity, and promote social justice by incorporating equal opportunities and equal access to provision and services. The implications of these policy aspirations are far-reaching: all practitioners need to develop the skills for active listening and observing, along with a language of critique and reflexivity. From this perspective, reflective practice becomes a means for moving from policy rhetoric to ethical practices and relationships, informed by children's voices and perspectives.

So why do we need to remind ourselves that listening to young children is essential to ethical practice? Fisher points out that much communication in early years classrooms is asymmetrical in terms of who has control of the right to speak:

> While teachers have the right to speak at any time and to any
> person – to fill the silence; to interrupt any speaker; to speak across
> one child to another; to speak at any volume or using any tone of
> voice – the child does not have the same rights. Indeed, in most
> classrooms children would be chastised for any attempt to behave
> in such ways.
>
> (Fisher 2015: 172)

Fisher discusses the importance of reciprocity in addressing this asymmetrical
communication, highlighting the concepts of equal contribution of
both parties to an interaction, as well as their mutual involvement, joint
engagement and satisfaction: 'So, it can be seen that reciprocity lies heavily
in the hands of the practitioner and their willingness to engage in interactions
that have meaning, purpose and relevance for the child as well as for
themselves' (Fisher 2015: 171–172).

A focus on reciprocity also involves understanding how children
experience and interpret their social worlds, and their relationships with
other people. Research in Icelandic preschools (Einarsdóttir, 2014;
Pálmadóttir and Einarsdóttir, 2015) focused on children's perceptions of the
role of their preschool teachers, and indicates that children are aware of the
different aspects of those roles (such as playing, caregiving, supporting their
learning), different types of interaction, and what children do and do not
like. In terms of power relationships, the children reported their awareness of
teachers' responsibilities for making rules, and distinguished between adults'
and children's cultures. Their research highlights that children are good
observers and listeners, and should not be seen as passive participants in these
complex spaces.

Young children's voices and perspectives in research

Recent developments in research ethics reflect a willingness to involve young
people as research participants, and to access their voices and perspectives
(Flewitt, 2005; Maybin 2013). These developments are supported by
postmodern and emancipatory theories and methodologies, which recognize
children's rights, agency and competences (Smith, 2011). Children are seen
as expert informers and witnesses, enabling researchers and practitioners
to take account of their experiences, choices and perspectives. The role of
practitioners as researchers is to understand children's ways of representing
and voicing their perspectives, by following their trails of thinking and

meaning making. From this perspective, 'voices' incorporate multi-modal communicative practices such as body language, movements, gestures, facial expressions, symbolic actions, and vocalizations such as gurgling, laughing, singing, chanting and crying.

Drawing on their work in the field of special educational needs, Norwich and Kelly (2004) argue that eliciting children's perspectives is not just a technical matter, it also involves complex ethical considerations and contextual factors, including:

1. the child's and young person's competences and characteristics,
2. the questioner's competences and characteristics,
3. the purpose and use made of eliciting child and young person's views,
4. the setting and context: power, relationships and emotional factors,
5. ethical and human rights considerations.

(Norwich and Kelly 2004: 45)

Participatory approaches to research thus raise methodological and ethical issues (Wood 2015a), not least because children are capable of challenging and resisting dominant discourses and power relations in classroom and research contexts. Researchers need to incorporate respectful views about young people, and sensitive approaches to eliciting their voices and perspectives about issues that are of direct concern in their lives, such as their health, welfare, play, education and legal rights. Those concerns are situated in networks of influence, such as home and community cultures, practices and discourses. Therefore, whilst participatory approaches to research and practice claim to 'empower' children, for this rhetoric of empowerment to be embedded in children's lived experiences, a broad definition of voices needs to be adopted. In relation to issues of power, Silin (2005) argues that a concern with children's voices should include a concern with silence and silences, and whether those silences are self-chosen or imposed by others.

Accessing children's thinking and understanding is also challenging because adults' perceptions of intent and meaning are only ever partial. What we see and hear is influenced by the lenses that we adopt: interpretations of child- and adult-initiated activities may also be partial where defined learning goals and curriculum content are the main lenses through which children are viewed and assessed via indicators of progress and achievement. Children are also adept at reading the cultural 'scripts' of the setting. Fisher talks about the importance of practitioners being genuine in their communications, because:

. . . when children sense that a practitioner's response is not genuine then they come to believe that any contribution on their part of some sort of game, rather than a genuine dialogue. They come to believe that they are taking part in an interaction which is being manipulated by the practitioner and, therefore, that they are expected to respond in the way the practitioner expects, rather than in the way they might choose.

(Fisher 2015: 169)

This important point highlights the problems that all practitioners face when policy frameworks are interpreted in ways that foreground specific goals and learning outcomes. A counterbalance to this position comes from the work of Reifel (2007), who argues for hermeneutic approaches to data collection and analysis, with researchers 'placing texts within multiple narratives, reflecting the multiple perspectives of participants' (2007: 26). In hermeneutic enquiry, '*texts* can be used to describe any number of productions: written words, oral discourses (a conversation, an interview), performances (staged, informal, impromptu), and works of art (language based or otherwise)' (Reifel 2007: 28). Texts can also include assessment information such as learning stories, photographs, children's art works and written observations of children in different contexts. Therefore, textual analysis in early childhood settings can capture complex and multiple meanings, taking into account the contexts in which these are produced and negotiated. Such approaches are relevant to researchers and educators for exploring meanings and actions, for individuals and for groups of children. Researchers (and practitioners as researchers) can go beyond the boundaries of policy frameworks, because observations and interactions can be used as texts for analysis, not merely as evidence of developmental milestones and learning outcomes.

Many contemporary theorists (Dahlberg and Moss 2005; Ryan and Grieshaber 2005; Yelland 2005; Fleer 2006) contest established normative interpretations of children's learning and development that have been reified through child development theories. Normative interpretations create expectations of what can be expected of the 'normally' or 'typically' developing child, and are used to inform how curriculum goals and objectives are defined in policy frameworks. Normative understandings of children also serve to regulate their development and progress, thereby defining what is considered valuable in terms of their learning outcomes, behaviours and competences (Wood 2015b). Other characteristics and dispositions may receive less attention so that children may be silenced by the conformity that is required to achieve what is valued, which is typically what can be measured.

In contrast, contemporary theoretical perspectives view learning and development as socially and culturally situated within complex cultural practices, belief systems, and relationships between the child, the home, early childhood institutions and wider society (Fleer 2006). Moreover, individually centred notions of child development are no longer acceptable within culturally diverse communities, because these notions reflect predominantly western values. Guttiérez and Rogoff (2003) argue that, by understanding cultural ways of learning, educators can move beyond theories that see learning as being influenced predominantly by individual traits, dispositions and learning styles. They propose that people develop repertoires for participating in a range of practices: they engage in activities according to how they have observed and interacted with other people in different communities (for example, home, playgroup, school, workplaces). Socio-cultural theories emphasize children's motivations to exercise agency and mastery in their social and cultural worlds. Therefore, rather than waiting for developmental readiness, culturally situated teaching and learning processes help children to participate with increasing competence in the activities of their communities, whether these are classified as work, leisure, play or formal education.

In socio–cultural theories of learning, the challenge for children (indeed for all learners) is how they move between different communities and practices, and how they choose from their personal and cultural repertoires of practice in order to participate in different activities. As demonstrated by Einarsdóttir (2014) and Pálmadóttir and Einarsdóttir (2015), children have to be good listeners and observers in order to negotiate their ways into different contexts, spaces and practices, to understand rules, roles, rituals and expectations. By observing and listening to children, educators can go beyond narrowly conceived performance on individual tasks to understand their repertoires of participation across a wide range of activities. There is a world of difference between seeing a child's performance in an activity as a 'unit of assessment' and understanding that performance within a broader pattern of shared interests, meaning making, choices and representations.

From active listening to ethical practices

The processes of active listening, observing, reflecting, arguing, discussing and interpreting all contribute to ethical practices. Fisher (2015) illustrates these principles in a four-year collaborative study of

professional development with early years practitioners, called the Adult–
Child Interaction (ACI) project. Fisher and her team of practitioners were
interested in exploring the attributes of effective practitioners, particularly the
ways in which they supported children's thinking through their interactions
and conversations. Fisher identified seven attributes of effective practitioners:

- being attentive
- being sensitive
- being responsive
- being respectful
- being genuine
- being a good role model
- being at ease in the company of children.

(Fisher 2015: 164)

On the surface, these attributes may seem to be 'common sense', but Fisher goes
on to describe what is involved in each of the attributes and how these need
to be orchestrated and adapted according to different children and different
contexts. A key issue that emerged through reflective dialogues between the
team members was interacting but not interfering, which means that not
interacting may be the right pedagogical decision at a particular moment, but
some input may be appropriate at another point in time. Fisher also talks about
the importance of 'tuning in', for example to children's body language, moods
and behaviour, as a means of practitioners tuning their comments, interactions
and roles. So the apparent 'common sense' of the seven attributes belies a great
deal of complexity in how practitioners develop their interactions in ways that
engage, support, challenge and extend children's thinking.

Practitioners also need to develop a critical understanding of play, and the
efficacy of play-based learning. Ryan (2005) has argued that the commitment
to free play can sustain inequitable practices, and may privilege certain
groups of children who are confident with exercising choice and know
how to benefit from such freedoms. The choices made by individuals or
groups of children may be biased in terms of culture, social class, gender,
sexuality, ability/disability, which may result in unequal power relations
and create detrimental dynamics within free choice. Children's choices and
meanings are often imbued with their cultural knowledge, their interests and
their desires to act more knowledgeably, more skilfully and with a sense of
agency. Their interests and preoccupations range across sharks and monsters,
domestic practices and routines, ghosts and zombies, popular culture, magical
and superhero powers, and may include the big existential questions of

life, death, justice, power and ethics. They need to play with power, and play at being powerful in order to experience the emotions, actions and consequences that occur. Research on play has also revealed children's interpretation of the forms of power that are enacted by adults, and the forms of resistance that are possible (particularly in education settings). During observations of children's free play choices, Wood (2014) documented the ways in which this resistance was expressed: children used visual cues to protect their play from the researcher's gaze, which included freezing play, turning away from the researcher and becoming silent.

It may be uncomfortable for early childhood professionals to confront cherished beliefs about free choice and free play, and to reflect critically on the power effects of children's choices. However, a pedagogy of listening and observing can enable practitioners to contest their assumptions, and to challenge stereotypical and discriminatory practices.

Using a pedagogy of listening to inform assessment

Detailed knowledge of children is developed when adults take time for observing, listening to and interacting with them, across a range of contexts and activities. The processes of reflection involve mapping evidence of children's activities across child-initiated and adult-initiated contexts. Educators can then take pedagogical decisions on the basis of informed insights into children's competences, perspectives and meanings, and their unique interpretations of their social and cultural worlds. Pedagogical documentation (such as recorded observations, examples of children's representations and communications, video and still images) creates an evidence base that informs interpretive discussions between team members. As Fisher (2015) demonstrated in the ACI project, reflective professional conversations can ensure that decision making takes place within and beyond curriculum frameworks, and that children's perspectives, knowledge and competences are acknowledged.

These processes are exemplified in the following vignettes, which were recorded in a Foundation Phase setting in a primary school in Wales (the Wales Foundation Phase includes children from age 3 to age 7). Around 87 per cent of children in the school were from minority ethnic groups, with around 26 languages spoken in the school. The whole school team was involved in an action research project to improve the quality of teaching and learning through play, with each year group team choosing its own focus. The Foundation Phase team focused on improving the quality of language in imaginative play activities with the children age 3–4. Episodes of play were videotaped for around ten minutes, and provided data for professional discussion and reflection. In the first episode, a teaching assistant (TA) is playing with the children in an outdoor role-play area, based on the story of 'Little Red Riding Hood'. The TA is supporting language development by playing alongside them. This vignette shows what happened when the TA's interactions did not flow with the children's play:

TA to Majida: Hello Little Red Riding Hood. Who are you going to visit today – to see today? Are you going to see grandma? What are you going to take her?

Majida to TA: Buns.

TA to Majida: Have you? Look at all that lovely food for grandma. That is super.

Majida to TA: Grandma not in there, not in there.

TA to Majida: Pardon? Grandma not in there? OK. It should be the wolf. Who's the wolf?

Rajiv to TA: He's already in the bed.

TA to Rajiv: But he needs someone to talk. Can you talk and be the wolf?

Rajiv to TA: It's not easy. I don't know what to think.

Rajiv leaves the area and the play finishes.

This episode provided much interesting evidence for reflection, focusing on whether the adult really listened to the children's meanings and understood the flow of the play. The team realized that they tended to slip into question–and–answer mode when trying to understand what was happening, especially if they had not observed the beginning and the development of the episode. When adults were present (in this and other episodes), children tended to say very little, and relied on the adult to take the lead (even where the bilingual support assistants were involved). Rajiv's final comment – 'It's not easy. I don't know what to think' – indicated that he did not know what was expected of him by the adult, and perhaps did not have sufficient knowledge to further develop the role of the wolf. Rajiv was beginning to understand what it means to play in role, but needed to do this in his own way. His play skills were demonstrated in a subsequent observation of an episode of outdoor play, where he leads two friends in a 'Spider-Man' game.

Rajiv to TA: Mrs L. I am Spider-Man. There are two Spider-Men and more Spider-Men.

He climbs the climbing frame, then gets a scooter and demonstrates jumping off the scooter while it is moving.

Rajiv to Jamil: Come on Jamil, we are Spider-Men. Spider-Man can do this. You do it Jamil.

This activity continues for a few minutes before the boys stop and run away.

Observing and listening to Rajiv showed the team that he could lead imaginative play with friends of his choice, and that he was willing to talk about his game and demonstrate his competence to an adult. Play provides many opportunities for 'out-loud thinking', as children reveal the purposes and direction of the action, and the imaginative context of their activities. By playing with meanings, they can also reveal quite sophisticated levels of understanding of their social and cultural worlds.

In a subsequent episode, listening to children involved observing their body language, facial expressions and symbolic activities, and, as Silin (2005) argues, listening to children's silences. Mohammed, a shy child, was reluctant to speak to peers and adults. It was difficult for team members to know how much he understood of spoken English, and how much he was able to communicate in his home and additional language. In the nursery, there was a 'three-way' puppet that was used to tell the story of 'Little Red Riding Hood' (the puppet could be transformed into the wolf, the grandmother and Red Riding Hood, to show each character). Mohammed approached the TA with the puppet, and she engaged him in the story. As she told the story, he revealed his understanding by showing each different character at the correct cue. After much encouragement, he did respond verbally (but in a very quiet voice), using individual words. His facial expressions and body language conveyed enjoyment and engagement with the adult. He was happy to participate on his own terms and was under no pressure to communicate verbally. The TA understood Mohammed's intentions and meanings through respecting his silence, then tuning in to his communicative competence.

This study had some valuable outcomes for the Foundation Phase team, particularly in informing how they could accurately read and interpret play activities. Interrogating these play texts, and reflecting on their own assumptions and beliefs, helped them to develop a collaborative pedagogy of listening and observing, and enhanced their understanding of children's interests and capabilities. Their assessment practices became located within a process of understanding children as learners and players, based on sharing and building knowledge. The study also demonstrated how analysis of classroom texts captures complex and multiple meanings, and the contexts in which these are produced and negotiated (Reifel 2007).

These vignettes exemplify how young children are not passive recipients of knowledge but are 'epistemologists' in their own right: they actively seek new knowledge and understanding, and engage with peers and adults to support those processes. Therefore, a pedagogy of listening and observing respects children's understanding of their identity and individuality, and helps educators to understand the influences of wider social systems such as class, culture, ethnicity, gender and sexuality. A pedagogy of listening and observing also ensures that multi-modal forms of communication are recognized and valued, and that children are not silenced by their inability to communicate in a dominant language, or within a dominant culture.

From reflective to activist educators

Contemporary researchers and theorists have extended the concept of 'reflective practitioners' to 'activist educators', who see their practice as inherently ethical and political. A pedagogy of reflexivity incorporates listening, observing and critical engagement. These developments are essential as educators work in increasingly complex contexts, with diverse communities and within challenging policy frameworks. Activist educators can transform, rather than merely implement, policies: they go beyond the platitudes of 'facilitating' and 'enabling' children's development. Instead, they work towards greater equity and social justice, and become co-constructors of vibrant communities of practice, which draw on the perspectives, meanings and resourcefulness of all members. They are prepared to act as researchers, to generate knowledge, to engage critically in their practice and to sustain collaborative professional development. These approaches will always provoke more questions than answers. However, activist educators will welcome such questions in order to sustain their commitment to children's well-being, and to processes of educational change and transformation.

Questions for further thinking and reflection

1.   Look at Julie Fisher's seven characteristics of effective practitioners. How might you use these to reflect on your interactions with children, to support their creativity and playfulness?
2.   When you are observing children at play, what forms of multi-modal communication do they use to support interactions?

Wood, E. (originally published 2007) 'Listening to young children: multiple voices, meanings and understandings', in Paige-Smith, A. and Craft, A. (eds) *Developing Reflective Practice in the Early Years*, Maidenhead: Open University Press. (This chapter has been revised and updated by the author.)

Further reading

Fisher, J. (2015) *Interacting or Interfering? Improving the quality of interactions in the early years.* Maidenhead: Open University Press.

Hedges, H. (2015) Sophia's funds of knowledge; theoretical and pedagogical insights, possibilities and dilemmas. *International Journal of Early Years Education,* 2015, 21(2): 83–96. doi:10.1080/09669760.2014.976609 (accessed 16 March 2017).

Yahya, R. and Wood, E. (2016) Play as third space: bridging cultural discourses between home and school, *Journal of Early Childhood Research,* 9(2): 137–149. doi:10.1177/1476718X15616833 (accessed 16 March 2017).

References

Dahlberg, G. and Moss, P. (2005) *Ethics and Politics in Early Childhood Education.* London: RoutledgeFalmer.

Einarsdóttir, J. (2014) Children's perspectives on the role of preschool teachers, *European Early Childhood Education Research Journal,* 22(5): 679–697. doi:10.1080/13502 93X.2014.969087 (accessed 16 March 2017).

Fleer, M. (2006) The cultural construction of child development: creating institutional and cultural intersubjectivity, *International Journal of Early Years Education,* 14(2): 127–140.

Fisher, J. (2015) *Interacting or Interfering? Improving the quality of interactions in the early years.* Maidenhead: Open University Press.

Flewitt, R. (2005). Conducting research with young children: some ethical considerations. *Early Child Development and Care,* 175(6): 553–565.

Guttiérez, K.D. and Rogoff, B. (2003) Cultural ways of learning: individual traits or repertoires of practice, *Educational Researcher,* 32(5): 19–25.

MacNaughton, G. (2005) *Doing Foucault in Early Childhood Studies. Applying Poststructural Ideas.* London: Routledge.

Maybin, J. (2013) Towards a sociocultural understanding of children's voice. *Language and Education,* 27(5): 383–397.

Norwich, B. and Kelly, N. (2004) Pupils' views on inclusion: moderate learning difficulties and bullying in mainstream and special schools. *British Educational Research Journal,* 30(1): 43–65.

Pálmadóttir, H. and Einarsdóttir, J. (2015) Young children's views of the role of preschool educators. *Early Child Development and Care,* 185(9): 1480–1494.

Reifel, S. (2007) Hermeneutic text analysis of play: exploring meaningful early childhood classroom events, in J.A. Hatch (ed.) *Early Childhood Qualitative Research.* London: Routledge: 25–42.

Rinaldi, C. (2006) *In Dialogue with Reggio Emilia: Listening, researching and learning.* London: Routledge.

Ryan, S. (2005) Freedom to choose: Examining children's experiences in choice time, in N. Yelland (ed.) *Critical Issues in Early Childhood.* Maidenhead: Open University Press: 99–114.

Ryan, S. and Grieshaber, S. (2005) Shifting from developmental to postmodern practices in early childhood teacher education, *Journal of Teacher Education,* 56(1), January/February: 34–45.

Silin, J.G. (2005) Who can speak? Silence, voice and pedagogy, in N. Yelland (ed.) *Critical Issues in Early Childhood Education.* Maidenhead: Open University Press: 81–95.

Smith, A.B. (2011) Respecting children's rights and agency: theoretical insights into ethical procedures, in D. Harcourt, B. Perry and T. Waller (eds) *Researching Young Children's Perspectives.* London: Routledge: 11–26.

Wood, E. (2014) Free choice and free play in early childhood education – troubling the discourse. *International Journal of Early Years Education,* 22(1): 4–18. doi:10.1080/09669760.2013.830562 (accessed 16 March 2017).

Wood, E. (2015a) Interpretivist research in play: The illumination of complexity, in S. Farrell, S.L. Kagan, and E.K.M. Tisdall (eds) *The Sage Handbook of Early Childhood Research,* London:Sage: 291–303.

Wood. E. (2015b) The capture of play within policy discourses: A critical analysis of the UK frameworks for early childhood education, in J.L. Roopnarine, M. Patte, J.E. Johnson and D. Kuschner (Eeds) *International Perspectives on Children's Play.* Maidenhead: Open University Press.

Yelland, N. (ed.) (2005) *Critical Issues in Early Childhood Education.* Maidenhead: Open University Press.

Part II

Practitioners responding to young children's play and creativity

Chapter 13

Equality inclusion and the Persona Doll approach

Babette Brown

Chapter introduction

In this chapter, Babette Brown outlines how and why the Persona Doll approach provides an effective, stimulating and non-threatening way to combat discrimination, empower young children and promote social justice. The author explores how Persona Dolls and their stories can sensitively and effectively challenge children's assumptions, misconceptions, stereotypical thinking and feelings of superiority. Attention is also drawn to the fact that children need to be able to build a deep sense of self-worth and clarity in their cultural identities in order to be proud of where they come from.

Introduction

The Persona Doll approach is an interactive learning approach designed to develop communication, listening and critical thinking skills. Educators bring the dolls to life by giving each one its own persona, i.e. a name, gender, age, family, personal likes and dislikes. The appearance of the dolls, and the fact that their imaginary lives and experiences reflect those of the children, contributes to this transformation. The children and the dolls become friends and the educators treat the dolls as children.

The educator Paulo Freire (1972) argued that all education has social and political consequences, and that as educators we have a moral, social and political responsibility to be involved in education for social transformation. For him, collaboration between educators and children develops through confronting real problems. He called this a 'problem-posing' approach and contrasted it with traditional education which he described as 'banking'— teachers make the deposits which the children receive, memorise and repeat. Problem-posing educators reflect critically on the social consequences of what they teach; they work against the existing inequalities and injustices children face in their daily lives and towards empowerment. This gives the less powerful greater ability to control and participate in decisions about their lives. I suspect that had Freire encountered the Persona Doll approach, he would have approved of it.

The approach is also underpinned by the principles of children's rights. Article 29 of the UN Convention on the Rights of the Child (1989) states that education shall be directed to:

- giving the pupil the possibility to develop in his or her own way and according to his or her ability
- teaching a respect for human rights and freedoms
- developing respect for the pupil's cultural identity, language and values, and for cultures different from his or her own, and
- preparing the pupil for a responsible life as an adult in a free society in a spirit of understanding, peace, tolerance, equality of the sexes and friendship among all peoples.

In addition, Article 24 of The UN Convention on the Rights of People with Disabilities (2006) requires countries to ensure that children with disabilities 'can access an inclusive, quality, primary and secondary education on an equal basis with others in the communities in which they live.'

For children knowing that they have the right to be heard boosts not only their sense of security but also their self-confidence. Adults are encouraged to work with children in an inclusive way to ensure their views are heard and valued. There is recognition of the emerging capacities of children to play an increasingly informed and active role.

What is learned can be unlearned

The dolls and the stories they 'tell' offer a stimulating and fun way to raise equality issues without preaching or pointing fingers. They encourage children to unlearn the stereotypes and prejudices they might have already picked up. These include attitudes and behaviour that give them permission to dislike those who are different from themselves, leading them to physically abuse others, exclude them from play, tease, harass and call them hurtful names. The saying that 'Sticks and stones will hurt my bones, but names will never harm me' is simply not true – names can break children's hearts.

Even young children understand the concept of 'fairness' – you've probably heard them or remember yourself shouting, 'It's not fair.' Developing their understanding of fairness and unfairness can help them appreciate that treating other people unfairly causes pain and unhappiness, comparable to hitting, kicking and other physical responses. Through

Figure 13.1 Standing up for rights

listening to Persona Doll stories, they get an idea of how it feels to be treated unfairly and are less likely to feel superior or inferior to others.

Creating personas

Before introducing the dolls into a setting, in-depth staff discussions ensure that everyone understands and is committed to the Persona Doll approach. The personas they then create are likely to reflect a range of cultural backgrounds, types of families, abilities and disabilities. Consulting parents, libraries, resource centres, embassies and the Web can be helpful. Having more than one Persona Doll encourages children to value shades of skin colour, various facial features and hair textures.

The process of giving the dolls their own unique identity, appropriate name, age, gender, cultural and family background, transforms them from being inanimate objects into 'people' – members of the group. Details help to bring the dolls to life, details such as where they live and sleep; who they live with; the language(s) they speak; the things they enjoy doing and the things they can't manage (perhaps they're not old enough or they have a disability); their food preferences; the things that make them happy and those that upset, frighten or worry them; anything that has happened in their lives or will soon happen that the children should know about. These basic details remain constant in their created identities though circumstances may change, e.g. a new baby, or moving house.

Children know they are dolls and that dolls cannot talk, but they suspend disbelief. They accept that the dolls 'tell' the educator about their thoughts and feelings and talk about the things that have happened to them. The stories they 'tell' help children understand that being different is not something to tease, name call, or hassle each other about.

Persona Doll story-telling sessions

These sessions give young children a voice – an opportunity to express their ideas opinions and feelings, talk about their own experiences, learn from each other, gain approval and acceptance, and experience a sense of belonging and achievement. In this safe and supportive environment, they share common experiences and feelings with the other children who may look different from them and speak different languages. Listening to a doll 'telling' a story about being excluded and the pain she/he felt, can help children appreciate that picking on others because they are different is unkind and unfair.

In their everyday speaking voice, educators tell the children what the doll has come to tell them about. The doll usually sits on the educator's lap and communicates by 'whispering' in her/his ear. The educator then tells the children what the doll 'said' and encourages them to respond accordingly. The children are helped to think critically and outside the box, as well as develop their communication and listening skills. Crucially, everyone is given time to respond. Educators ensure that every child feels comfortable in the group, that their contributions are acknowledged and valued, and that the voices of the more articulate and self-assured don't drown the less assertive, or those not fluent in the dominant language. Self-esteem and confidence are boosted and the ability of those who speak more than one language is acknowledged and praised. Suggesting solutions to the dolls' problems can be empowering and although not all problems are solvable, children see that talking about them with friends can be helpful.

Many Persona Doll stories are about everyday experiences like going to the park; others deal with exclusion, name calling, teasing or physical confrontation. They may relate to an incident that occurred in the setting or one created by the practitioner to raise the children's understanding and awareness of an issue. The stories can help children appreciate that they are not alone – that others are in the same or similar situation, experiencing the same or similar painful feelings. Telling stories that reflect the lifestyle, traditions and culture of a wide range of communities also helps foster the general knowledge, imagination and self-esteem of every child. If children or their families are discriminated against because of their skin colour, ethnicity, culture, religion, gender, disabilities, additional needs or economic position, they are unlikely to feel good about themselves.

Thandanani: a doll with a story to 'tell'

The following story told to a reception class illustrates the impact a doll and her story can have when used by a sensitive and empathetic educator.

The children expressed their delight at seeing one of their Persona Dolls sitting on the teacher's lap and the story telling session began.

Teacher: 'I wonder if anyone remembers who this is?'
Children instantly responded: 'Thandanani.'

The teacher then gave the children an opportunity to individually greet Thandanani by passing her around the circle. From the caring way they hugged and spoke to her, they had obviously identified and bonded with her – she was their friend.

Teacher: Do you remember how Thandanani was feeling when she visited us last time?

After a moment's hesitation, there were shouts of: Happy.

Teacher: And do you know why she was happy?'
Children: 'Cos she went for a picnic with her mum and dad.
             And her little brother William.
             And her Grandma.
             We went for a picnic. We had crisps and marmite sandwiches.
             I don't like marmite.
             We had boiled eggs and tomatoes.
             So did we!

To bring their attention back to the story, the teacher asked: 'Do you think Thandanani is feeling happy today?' The children shook their heads.

Teacher:	How do you know?
Children:	She's not looking at us.
	Why doesn't she want to talk to us?
	She's too sad.
	Doll whispers in the teacher's ear.
Teacher:	Thandanani told me that Olivia, Emily and Saskia were playing in the hospital area at her school yesterday. Because Thandanani's, mum and her dad are doctors, she knows all about hospitals. She's been to their hospital loads of times so she asked if she could join in their game.
	Then something horrible happened. Emily shouted at her 'No you can't. My dad says I mustn't play with brown girls like you.' And Saskia shouted 'Go away. We don't want you in our game.'

The children gasped.

The teacher maximised their input by asking: 'Have you ever felt like that?' and to extend their vocabularies asked if they had ever been excluded and explained what the word meant.

Children:	My brother always does that to me. He says, 'No girls!'
	My cousin told me that nobody wants to play with her at her school. They say she's too fat.
	That's not fair.
Teacher:	You're right, it isn't fair to exclude children – to make them feel miserable and left out.

Doll whispers in the teacher's ear.

Teacher:	Thandanani said she was so upset she went and sat all by herself in a corner. She didn't feel like talking to anyone. She made herself as small as she could. She hid her face so nobody could see she was crying.

The children's faces reflected their concern and distress.

Doll whispers in the teacher's ear.

Teacher:	She said she's really worried about tomorrow. What if they say nasty things and don't want to play with her?
	What do you think she should do if that happens?

Children: She could tell them to stop being so horrid and unkind.
          She could find somebody else to play with.
          How about telling her teacher?
          When her Gran comes to fetch her, she could tell her.
          She could also tell her mum or dad.
          They could hug her. It's what my mum does when I'm sad.
          Doll whispers in the teacher's ear.

Teacher: Thandanani said she's going to do all the things you suggested.
          She's feeling happier now. She likes talking to you.

Thandanani was then sat on the special chair so she could be cuddled and
talked to particularly by children who had been in a similar situation.

Persona Doll research

Research around the Persona Doll approach has revealed that educators
who think critically about their own attitudes, beliefs, actions and practice
are key to implementing the Persona Doll approach appropriately and
effectively. Without the necessary knowledge, experience and skill, they might
inadvertently pass on their own negative stereotypes and prejudices to the
children. The following are two interesting examples from research studies.

University of Maine (2011)

An innovative three-year Persona Doll project was set up at the University of
Maine, in the US, to promote diversity awareness by Mary Ellin Logue, V.
Susan Bennett-Armistead and SooJoung Kim (2011). When asked, all sixty-
three students in the sample had replied that after graduating, they intended
teaching young children from a similar upbringing and culture as themselves.
Although all of them had had some personal exposure to children with
disabilities, only two had an ongoing friendship with a person from a
different racial or linguistic background.

Each student was given a Persona Doll and a brief description of its
background and circumstances, different in each case from the student's.
Their task was to research as much as they could about their doll's imagined
life in and out of school, and to then create and tell the rest of the class
authentic Persona Doll stories centred on their doll. As they became more
knowledgeable about their dolls, they also became more aware of the
similarities and differences between their own childhood experiences and
those of the dolls. Their eyes were opened to the diversity around them.

Australian primary schools (2015)

Australian researchers (Srinivasana and Cruza 2015) used Persona Dolls to question 6- and 7-year-olds about 'race' and colour differences from their everyday school experiences. The children expressed the view that having friends was a major factor enabling the dolls to be happy at school. When asked what would make them sad, they said that the dolls with the darker skin colour would be teased. They believed that the dolls with the lighter skins would have the most friends and be invited to birthday parties and sleepovers. The children were then asked to respond to the following scenario: one of the dolls has been told that they have 'yucky black skin' by another child in their class. The doll is hurt and sad and does not know what to do.

The solution that most proposed was that the darker-skinned dolls should walk away and ignore what was said. The researchers concluded that both the children who had experienced racism and those who were onlookers had learnt to 'silence' such events. They suggested that this 'silencing' allowed racism to continue. Contrary to the children's awareness that the darker-skinned dolls experienced racism, teachers often failed to acknowledge or respond to children's complaints.

Conclusion

From early childhood, we begin absorbing many of the prejudices and much of the stereotypical thinking so deeply rooted in Britain's history. As adults, we have the capacity to reflect on our attitudes and a responsibility to counter the detrimental effects of prejudice and discrimination on children's lives. We need to know not only about which groups in our society are the targets of prejudice and discrimination, but also to appreciate the extent to which the lives and education of children are affected by racism and other oppressions. Hopefully, the seeds planted in children's hearts and minds by Persona Doll stories will take root so that as adults they will work with others to create a more equal and just society.

Questions for further thinking and reflection

1. Think back as far as you can to when you were a child. Did the schools you attended help you feel good about yourself?
2. What strategies are used in your work place to promote equality and anti-discrimination?

Further reading

Brown, B. (2008) *Equality in Action: a way forward with Persona Dolls*. Staffordshire: Trentham Books.

Derman-Sparks, L., Ramsey, P. G. and Edwards, J. O. (2006) *What if All the Kids are White? Anti-bias multicultural education with young children and families*. New York: Teachers College Press.

Srinivasana, P. and Cruza, M. (2015) Children colouring: speaking 'colour difference' with Diversity dolls *Pedagogy, Culture & Society* Volume 23, Issue 1, pp. 21–43.

References

Freire, P. (1972) *Pedagogy of the Oppressed* (Myra Bergman Ramos, Trans.). Middlesex: Penguin Books.

Logue, M. E., Bennett-Armistead, V. S., and Kim, S. (2011). The Persona Doll Project: promoting diversity awareness among preservice teachers through Storytelling. Child Development and Family Relations Faculty Scholarship, University of Maine.

Srinivasana, P. and Cruza, M. (2015) Children colouring: speaking 'colour difference' with Diversity dolls *Pedagogy, Culture & Society* Volume 23, Issue 1, pp. 21–43.

United Nations (1989) *Convention on the Rights of the Child*, UN General Assembly Document A/RES/44/2, New York, NY, United Nations.

United Nations (2006) Convention on the rights of persons with disabilities. Available at: www.un.org/disabilities/documents/convention/convention_accessible_pdf.pdf (accessed 17 March 2017).

Chapter 14

Taking the initiative: creative collaborations for family literacy

Tara Copard with Roger Hancock

Chapter introduction

Tara Copard is a family outreach worker, supporting parents and their children. In this chapter, Tara looks back on the way in which she established cross-agency, family-focused practices in her setting in order to support parent understanding and enhance young children's language and literacy learning. Her story also focuses on the collaborative nature of multi-agency working, an approach which needs to maintain parents and children at the centre.

My pathway to my current role

When at school I wanted to work with children, but was persuaded by my family to opt for something else. At age 15, I therefore secured my first job as a clerk/typist and worked my way through the various office-based roles over six years. I then had my two boys and did part-time work around them before finding Kestrels. At the time, I was looking after my mother-in-law who had terminal cancer and she encouraged me to apply for a playworker job. I started work with Kestrels Daycare in October 2004, supporting children's play, planning and facilitating activities for and with them, helping with homework and generally interacting with them. It was not long before I increased my hours by working mornings. In between the two roles, I popped back to take care of my mum. I had no childcare qualifications and so my training began. My first course was a National Vocational Qualification, Level 3, in Playwork. Within the setting, I was able to take on training and workshops, and developed an interest in children's special educational needs and child protection. These training environments are a great way to meet with others in similar roles in order to network and generally share effective practice.

Approximately two years into my work at Kestrels I felt sufficiently confident to take on the role of morning supervisor for the 3–4-year-olds room. At this point, I was also attending child protection meetings and case conferences when the nursery manager wasn't able to.

Around April 2009, Kestrels Daycare expanded to also become a children's centre. My training background, my experience of hands-on work with the children and relationships with parents and families gave me the foundations needed to take on the outreach worker position. Additional qualifications were needed and so I embarked on a City and Guilds Level 3 Working with Parents award, equipping me further to better support the needs of our families.

Caterham Children's Centre is situated within the grounds of Marden Lodge, a one-form entry primary school in Caterham, Surrey. We are in an area classified as semi-rural, although we are based within a residential community. The Children's Centre is open from 8 am to 4 pm for fifty weeks a year and there are currently seven members of staff employed to facilitate sessions and services within the remit and 'core purposes' of:

- child development and school readiness
- parenting aspirations and parenting skills, and
- child and family health and life chances.

(DfE, 2013, p.7)

In September 2014, Kestrels Children's Centre and Daycare merged with Hillcroft Children's Centre, and this soon became Kestrels Daycare and Caterham Children's Centre. Kestrels Daycare was taken over by the school and since September 2015 is now known as Marden Lodge Nursery; the Children's Centre, although it is linked to the school via the overseeing Glyn Learning Foundation,[1] is a separate entity.

My outreach role is to support parents and families. This requires me to facilitate parent group sessions, carry out home visits, role model play and offer helpful strategies for a variety of issues. I work alongside a whole host of other professionals and agencies, and very closely with the staff from local nurseries and daycare settings, health visitors, midwives, police and social workers. I am also parent support advisor for the nearby school for ten hours a week, which is, in effect, similar to my outreach work. Some of the families have linked siblings and so my work benefits in that it can be holistic across families.

New initiatives

Over the years, we have become very aware of the number of children attending the Centre who appear to have some form of speech and language difficulty. We have also heard concern expressed about the literacy abilities presented within the nearby school. It was my attendance and participation at a National Professional Qualification in Integrated Centre Leadership (NPQICL) course at the Institute of Education, London that made me think more deeply about this issue. I was able to use and explore this issue to my advantage in my second assignment and I wanted to make it a multi-agency piece of work.

On 17 March 2014, I attended a presentation by Book Trust about the use of Bookstart packs[2] across the age-groups. The presentation's primary purpose was to promote the pack for 2-year-olds, which was a brand new resource. However, before this event, my colleagues and I were only aware of the green universal Bookstart Corner packs. Upon returning to the office, I was able to discuss how each pack could be integrated into the work that we do. Thus, there would be a black-and-white book for new borns, a purple pack for under-1-year-olds, a red bag for 2-year-olds (with fifteen hours of 'free early education') and a green universal bag for Bookstart Corner sessions, aimed at families of children with speech and language needs. Ideally, Bookstart packs should be available throughout primary school and so this was an idea also put to the lead person in charge of literacy in the office. Special educational needs packs were to be used at the 'one-step-at-a-time' group in neighbouring Hamsey Green Children's Centre.

Research

To help the development of our practice, I felt there was a need to know more about parents' perceptions of their children's early literacy, so I compiled a short questionnaire to be distributed to a number of our parents. It contained questions on books and reading to children at home, and asked parents if they would like to attend forthcoming sessions about using rhyme and sharing books at the Children's Centre. From our point of view, this would be a pilot initiative. I had read a lot about closer multi-agency working, including its effectiveness for 'school readiness' in the United States (Head Start, 2015), so thought it important to reach out to our existing services. I therefore invited representatives from a number of known services for a focus group meeting. Including Kestrels staff, twenty-four individuals were invited and eighteen were able to come. I was disappointed that no one was available to come from the speech and language service, but I know they are very thin on the ground. A range of early reading books was displayed, Bookstart packs were laid out, agendas were placed on each seat and refreshments were provided. I gave an enthusiastic presentation about Kestrels' literacy work with families, and the reasons why more needed to be done to support young children's language and literacy learning. Then, using a discussion method called 'turning the curve',[3] I asked small groups to consider three questions, all related to how we might work together to offer more to families:

- Is there anything else you could offer to this initiative?
- How will we know if it is working?
- Are there any gaps, and what have we missed?

The participants' responses and ideas were noted on Post-its. The room buzzed with conversation. After a while, I brought everyone back together and each group shared their thoughts. The box below gives responses to the three questions and the agreed action points.

Responses arising from group discussions

Is there anything else you could offer to this initiative?

- 0 to 19 – will share the information with their nursery nurses and ask for their input.
- Book Co. – offer parents a variety of children's books through children's centres at £2.50 each.
- Early Years Child Care Service – invite outreach to childcare meetings.
- SENCo and outreach – family story-telling event during the day as well as evening.
- SENCo and outreach – monthly book-reading sessions with parents in the nursery.
- SENCo and outreach – parent area in nursery to be based around Bookstart.
- Library – personally bring a child's Pebble Penguin membership card to them at the centre.

How will we know if it is working?

- Evaluations from attending parents
- Feedback from children
- Facilitator evaluations
- The families continue the process, follow the programme all the way through to Reception age
- Greater attendance at local library
- Greater parental involvement in child's ongoing learning

(continued)

(continued)

- Parents enrolment in adult learning literacy sessions
- Parents enrolment in a variety of adult learning sessions.

Are there any gaps, and what have we missed?

- How to reach those parents/children who do not attend health follow-ups
- Ways to reach the more vulnerable families
- Home visits for 'hard-to-reach' families
- Visit local mother and toddler groups to share the initiative.

Action points

- Following the pilot, roll out the parent initiative to the rest of Caterham, make it universal
- Involve Speech and Language Service
- Dads to be involved as facilitators
- Community tent at street party/carnival event
- Give parents ideas of further activities to do at home with their children.

To an extent, the 'Any gaps' list above resonates throughout all agencies but in respect of my pilot, referrals from health, midwifery and children's services would be an ideal starting point.

Two days after my presentation, I emailed everyone who attended to ask if they could give an informal evaluation of the morning and if they had, since then, had any further ideas. The responses were very encouraging to me personally, confirming the reasons for coming together, and in agreement that we need to work more closely together for families. Kestrels is now taking a leading role in strengthening multi-agency links. I think that our developments, and our sincere wish to collaborate with other agencies, link well with the Government's original ideas for children's centres when they were first set up.

Paralleling these developments, having registered for the NPQICL, I needed to carry out a piece of practitioner research. For this assessed assignment, I looked back on the family-focused developments I initiated at Kestrel, wrote up an account and evaluation of the above meeting and further developments, and analysed the results of my parent questionnaire.

These results can be summarised as follows. The majority (thirteen) of the fifteen parents felt that birth to six months is the best time to introduce books to young children; some, however, thought it should be later. Eleven parents felt bedtime is the most popular time to share books with children. Library membership was very patchy, with only four families where both child and adult were members. There was interest in attending adult literacy and/or school readiness sessions from eight parents. Nine parents indicated that they would like to come to the proposed 'Creative Little Characters' – a group session for parents and children providing sensory experiences relevant to the content of a chosen story book. For instance, with *Big Red Bath* by Julia Jarman, there would be areas devoted to water play, bubble snakes, shaving foam and hand/finger painting with red paint. My small-scale questionnaire study was enough to confirm to me that some parents were already sharing books with their children, but with further support, they could be more knowledgeable and feel more effective.

Finally . . .

Eighteen months on, Creative Little Characters is going from strength to strength. It's proved to be a very popular programme that families themselves enquire about when they hear about it via word of mouth. Also, other professionals regularly refer families to these sessions, especially the health team when children are found to have a speech and language concern.

Without having studied for a leadership qualification and the insights and confidence that the course gave me, I would not have thought of embarking on such an extensive and lasting workplace project. However, what we have achieved to date is very much the beginning. I do aim to work more closely with the speech and language service and also with midwifery. I continue to strongly believe that multi-agency partnerships can make a great difference to families. Already, we are putting together a follow-up programme, which will involve different ways of storytelling together for both parent and child. This will involve different ways of storytelling together for both parent and child.

Questions for further thinking and reflection

1. If you work with parents, to what extent do you feel you enable them to bring their knowledge and experience into a collaboration? What approaches have worked for you and why are these more successful?
2. What steps would you take to make multi-professional working even more effective in a setting?

Notes

1 The Glynn Learning Foundation is a Multi-Academy Trust with fifteen primary, one special and two secondary (community) schools.
2 Book Trust, a reading charity, has developed free resource packs for families (containing storybooks, songs and games) that can be used to promote children's early reading and language development.
3 This is a 'talk-to-action' approach for meetings, originally developed by Mark Friedland, whereby people start with the ends they want and then work backwards to establish the means to achieve these outcomes. See, for instance, DCSF, 2008.

Further reading

Burgess, S.R. (2011) Home literacy environments (HLEs) provided to very young children, *Early Child Development and Care*, 181 (4), pp. 445–462.
Kennedy, A. (2010) Family support for early literacy and numeracy: examining events in the home and community, *The Early Childhood Leaders' Magazine*, 191, pp. 18–21.
Rix, J., Parry, J., Drury, R., Mercer, D. and Hancock, R. (2015) *The Family Experience of Bookstart Corner*, BookTrust, Wandsworth.

References

DCSF (Department for Children, Schools and Families) (2008) Turning the curve stories, DCSF, London. Online: http://webarchive.nationalarchives.gov.uk/20130401151715/ http://www.education.gov.uk/publications/eOrderingDownload/00523-2008DOM-EN.pdf (accessed 17 March 2017).
DfE (Department for Education) (2013) Sure Start children's centres statutory guidance, (DFE-00314-2013), Online: https://www.gov.uk/government/organisations/ department-for-education (accessed 17 March 2017).
Head Start (2015) http://eclkc.ohs.acf.hhs.gov/hslc (accessed 17 March 2017).

Chapter 15

The role of environments and spaces in the pedagogy of Pistoia

Donatella Giovannini, with introduction by Myra Barrs

Chapter introduction

In this chapter, Donatella Giovannini, one of two co-ordinators leading the advisory team responsible for early years practice in the city of Pistoia, Italy, reflects on the role of environments and spaces in the education of young children in Pistoia's early years centres.

By way of introduction, Myra Barrs, an Honorary Senior Research Associate at The London Institute of Education, UCL and with a long-term association with the early years services in Pistoia, sets the scene for Donatella's discussion, providing a background to the city of Pistoia and the underpinning philosophies of its pioneering system of early childhood education.

Introduction

In this chapter, Donatella Giovannini reflects on the role of environments and spaces in the education of young children in Pistoia's early years centres.

Pistoia is a city which, along with some other cities in Italy, has pioneered a system of early childhood education that has become known worldwide. It is recognised as a centre of excellence for its 'nidi d'infanzia' (for children from 3 months to 3 years old) and 'scuole d'infanzia' (for children from 3 to 6 years old). These schools are run by the city, the 'Commune'. There are no head teachers in this system – all administration is the responsibility of the Commune.

The advisory team responsible for the 'pedagogic coordination' of early years practice in all the city's 'nidi' and 'scuole d'infanzia' is led by two coordinators, one of whom is Donatella Giovannini, who has been working in the system since its inception. This approach to organisation has led to the establishment of a clear 'Pistoia style' across all the early childhood centres. They are marked by a strong common philosophy of children's learning. Relationships with homes and families are viewed as fundamental to the work.

The visitor to Pistoia is initially struck by the sheer beauty of these early childhood centres; they are striking for the studio-like quality of their generous, uncluttered spaces, which are designed with plenty of natural light. The architecture and the planning of the spaces also allows for peaceful small corners, and for settings that encourage dramatic play. There are rich displays everywhere, and there is a strong emphasis on documentation, featuring large photographic wall displays, with commentaries on children's activities and on recent projects.

The reasons for a choice

In Pistoia, our reflections about the environment of the preschool have been part of more general reflections about the value of space in any educational project designed for children. A close attention to the value of space has always been a major aspect of education services in Pistoia, from 'nido' to nursery school, from studios and workshops to children's specialist 'centres'. This focus has created a culture and a model for places designed for children to live and play in. The development of this shared vision has been a long and complex process, the result of a common project that has been tenaciously and passionately supported by all those involved in founding and directing these early childhood services.

The aim of the project has to been to make these environments beautiful places, capable of responding to children's developmental needs, but also of communicating the value of childhood and reflecting the community life of children, educators and parents. Attention to space has been the result of a creative approach, which has integrated several disciplines, from architecture and design to developmental psychology and pedagogy. Such a project has required the sensitive interpretation of children's needs and the elaboration of educational programmes closely related to what these places were intended to express. The environment is not considered as a mere container but as an integral part of education, which is not only rooted in it, but also represented by it. So an educational environment is not a shapeless shell for experiences but a context, which can enable or prevent, encourage or discourage attitudes and activities. Spaces can suggest a uniform and conventional atmosphere, or favour a climate of general well-being. Environments can be places of emotional attachment and well-being, or discouraging places that do not value individuals. So in Pistoia preschools, efforts have been made to develop in children, but also in adults, what is defined as the 'sense of place',

Figure 15.1 Gabri lago m – Gabri at Lago Mago Nursery

i.e. the perception of belonging to an environment. This is a fundamental feeling which promotes participatory and responsible attitudes towards the host context.

The global quality of space

We have focused on the global quality of space, without limiting our research only to the classrooms, but through planning a 'soft complexity', to create an ecosystem which shapes all the many areas of a preschool. As a consequence, each room and each area of the preschool has been designed and organised with the same care. The places where children eat, sleep or get changed are just as important as the ones where they draw or build something: all the rooms are well-designed; they all speak to the children's minds and souls of their own potential and skills.

Even the transit areas – the corridors and halls – have a special character; they have been transformed into big 'piazzas', or long 'boulevards', where there are a lot of possibilities for play and for meeting other children and adults. This is because education does not reside only in classrooms, but also in the spaces connecting them. These spaces, normally considered marginal, can actually broaden and enlarge the area of the preschool, if they are given a living character and if more activities are possible there. Besides, children themselves show us their natural disposition to create new places, not originally envisaged by designers, and to use space in an unconventional manner. The floor, the steps, the thresholds between one room and another, the edges of spaces, can open up new possibilities and become malleable, transformable areas for working or meeting.

The construction process

The 'character' of Pistoia's preschools can be defined through some keywords, which were the basis of some precise and coherent guidelines within the early years service. These words are: identity, relationship, knowledge, aesthetic quality and memory.

These values became the basis for the creation of nurseries and nursery schools which are pleasant places, which generate emotional attachment and where a process of identification takes place. These are places capable of protecting and caring for children so that new possibilities can open up in their lives.

Identity of places, identity of individuals, spaces for relationships

Preschools in Pistoia have been planned and designed over time as special places, with their own features and identities, resulting from the original choice of furniture, equipment and displays, and the presence in each of unique features capable of creating emotion and surprise. Even if the fundamental choices are the same, every education centre is different from the others, because, like a home, it reflects the taste and habits of the people who live in it: children, educators and families. Preschool educators have broadened and enriched these spaces with their own planning, passion and practical skills. This has prevented the spaces from falling into the twofold risk which often characterises early childhood services: on the one hand, the risk of an excessive institutionalisation, due to fossilisation – i.e. everything remains the same over time – or, on the other hand, the risk of being regularly reset to zero, because the places are characterless and people do not feel sufficiently attached to them.

In our work, we have tried to communicate a sense of safety and welcome to the children, in which their own subjectivity is recognised and supported. This means that every child can find within the preschool particular items – pictures, photos and other clues – that refer to them; they can find evidence of their history, which can help them to remember events. In this framework, the classroom is the natural container of individual stories, which are preserved and which confirm the unique experience of each child and enrich their inner life. Starting from this recognition, it is possible to create a rich, positive web of relationships between children, adults and these spaces.

Indeed, space organises and reflects the social structure of the relationships existing between adults and children, and the different ways in which adults establish relations with children. This is the reason why the areas within the preschool have been organised so as to allow for different social situations: there are places for being alone, being in pairs, in small and large groups – and for doing things and having parties all together.

A dimension which has been particularly safeguarded is privacy. This has been achieved through the creation of private areas where children are free to play on their own or with another. They are small, safe places, where the

Figure 15.2 Piccoli grillo – little ones at Il Grillo Nursery

intensity of the relationship and of the communication cements a sense of sharing with peers. This in turn helps children to understand each other and play better together. Small homely corners, dens, rugs, huts, boxes, big cars, have all become containers for relationships and opportunities for cognitive and social learning, and for play – which from individual play becomes small-group play, and vice versa. These are spaces where children are tempted to get down on the floor, because 'only those who get down on the floor can live in an imaginary place with intensity.'

A space to learn

Preschools are environments for growth – and for learning, thanks to the establishing of educational contexts that encourage children to develop competent behaviours through activities which engage them. There is an organic relationship between the organisation of space and the quality of learning: in order to learn, children need a context which promotes curiosity and exploration, and which supports motivation and the acquisition of knowledge.

For these reasons, educational activities are organised in a predictable and accessible way within the premises. The areas to promote learning are well-defined, rich, concrete and attractive; through the quality and nature of materials and equipment provided, they can suggest models and ideas for play and exploration.

These are areas dedicated to 'doing' something, which are sometimes created within classrooms, but just as often in other functionally designed spaces. Often these are spaces which enable children to carry out specific activities, and which are specially designed to allow children to take part *together* in an activity. These are spaces which help children develop the ability to organise play and other activities which show how pleasant it can be to learn with others. For instance, a large walk-in cupboard can become a science laboratory, a restaurant kitchen or a dress-up centre resourced to enable children to act out particular stories.

All the areas are equipped with a lot of both natural and synthetic materials, which can be manipulated, transformed and used, thus leading to discoveries, shared activities and tactile, visual and acoustic explorations. The materials are always arranged in a clear and organised way, so as to be easily visible and accessible on open shelves or in attractive containers. For instance, an area might feature a small exhibition where teachers and children have arranged, carefully categorised and displayed in small baskets, the dead leaves, seed-heads, dry flowers, berries, nuts and bits of bark that they have found on an autumn walk.

Figure 15.3 Lavagna luminosa – light box

Aesthetic quality

Space is an evocative element that can arouse emotions. This is why we have tried to use our emotions in order to reconcile the functional aspects of the preschool's space and its emotional sphere. Preschools are to some extent seductive; they are places where unexpected events occur. Above all, they stimulate senses and emotions, and they are places where children's surprise is welcomed – the surprise which opens their minds, makes them curious and stimulates learning, because there is no conflict between learning and feeling. The pedagogical approach in Pistoia's preschools is characterised by the attention to aesthetic qualities: the general idea is that one of the rights that children have during development is the right to beauty. People are happy to stay in a beautiful place, where they feel well and at ease; in these conditions, they are also more willing to establish relations and to explore. The task of education is to awaken children's sense of curiosity and to discover the soul of things through an awareness of beauty.

Memory: spaces of documentation

The rooms in preschools have a strong communicative value, which makes them familiar and warm, thanks to the careful use of meaningful photos, images, words, drawings and works of children. The rooms contain the accounts of the experiences made with the children, souvenirs of projects and important moments in their social life. These objects and signs help children feel the space as their own. Over the years, a new approach has emerged, which may be called 'the architecture of documentation and of its languages'. This architecture has transformed the walls of preschool into large open books; it has increased the volumes of the preschool with panels full of pictures and words, and it has created new spaces – not envisaged by designers – through creative solutions which make the most of particular corners and edges.

Through documentation, the spaces in the preschool bear witness to children's intelligence, skills, ability to learn, curiosity and cooperative spirit. These spaces speak to parents and help them to form a community of friends, to establish relations, to establish a collective memory and to learn together.

Developmental psychology has underlined that the child's emotional attachment to the places where he/she made new experiences becomes, over time, an important aspect of his/her identity, establishing a continuity with the affection felt for people. This is why over the years we have tried to give children the possibility of growing up in spaces which have become their own, to which they are attached and which, once adults, will be part of their childhood memories. We as human beings are defined by the places where we grew up, which will always remain a point of reference inside us.

Questions for further thinking and reflection

1. What key messages do you take away from your reading about early childhood centres in Pistoia?
2. How do the fundamental characteristics of the pedagogical approach in Pistoia connect with your own work with young children?

Further reading

Galardini, A., & Giovannini, D. (2001) Pistoia: Creating a Dynamic, Open System to Serve Children, Families and Community. In Gandini, L. & Edwards, C.P. (eds.) *Bambini*. New York: Teachers College Press.

Mantovani, S. (2001) Infant-Toddler Centers in Italy Today: Tradition and Innovation. In Gandini, L. & Edwards, C.P. (eds.) *Bambini*. New York: Teachers College Press.

Musatti, T. & Mayer, S. (2011) Sharing attention and activities among toddlers: the spatial dimension of the setting and the educator's role. In *European Early Childhood Education Research Journal*, Vol. 19, No. 2, June 2011, 207–221.

Picchio, M., Giovannini, D., Mayer, S. & Musatti, T. (2012) Sharing reflection on children's experience among ECE practitioners. In *Early Years: An International Journal of Research and Development*, Vol. 32, no. 2, pp. 159–170.

Chapter 16

Mud, glorious mud! Mud kitchens and more

Menna Godfrey

Chapter introduction

Menna Godfrey is an early years trainer and Nursery Manager from York. In this chapter, she draws on observations of children in her setting to discuss the rich experiences the 'Mud Kitchen' and playing with mud offers. Menna considers the wider benefits and opportunities of mud play in early years contexts, and concludes with some practical considerations for the provision of mud play.

Introduction

> . . . we play in sand, each covering his neighbour up; and times
> we make mud pastry — oh, the lovely mud, it hath not its like for
> delightfulness in all the world. We do fairly wallow in the mud . . . .
> (Mark Twain, *The Prince and the Pauper*, 1882)

In this chapter, I draw upon my experience as an early years practitioner and trainer, to describe and reflect on the opportunities that mud play presents for children. I consider some of the benefits of mud play for children's learning and development, the ways in which practitioners can offer meaningful opportunities for children to engage in mud play, and how they can support parents in understanding the possibilities of mud play. Some common concerns of staff and parents in relation to mud will also be considered, and suggestions offered to enable practitioners to reassure colleagues and parents that wallowing in mud is not only delightful for young children, but offers opportunities that support children's holistic learning and development.

A visiting parent looked at our Mud Kitchen and commented that she could not think of anything worse — yet when her son looks at the Mud Kitchen, he sees a myriad of opportunities. Throughout this chapter I consider what it is about mud that provides such rich learning opportunities for young children, and I suggest some types of exploration and play that children may engage in given such an enabling environment.

The garden, a good place for learning

My own childhood involved plenty of opportunities to explore the soil in our family garden as well on our allotment. I have happy memories of making mud pies, digging and planting my own seedbed, with one or other of my parents supporting my play and my developing understanding of the natural world. As I recollect these experiences, it seems to me that it was the combination of being known and being in relationship with these knowledgeable adults, along with the flexible nature of the environment, that enabled me to wallow in the experience so deeply. In England, the four themes of the Early Years Foundation Stage (EYFS) Statutory Framework remind practitioners to consider how the 'unique child' supported in 'positive relationships' by their key person, provided with an 'enabling environment' will 'learn and develop' (DfE 2014:5).

Experiences such as those described above may be the root of my love of the garden and of my conviction that gardens are a good place for children to play and learn, yet many of the children you meet or work with, may not have similar opportunities. They may live in homes with no garden spaces, or their gardens may be so designed that there is no place for them to dig and explore. As a provider of learning experiences for young children, I argue that practitioners should consider how access to mud and water might be provided to ensure that children have opportunity to experience this type of sensory play using the elements of earth and water.

Voices from the past

The provision of mud in spaces for young children is not a twenty-first century idea.

The Early Childhood pioneer Friedrich Froebel (1782–1852), who recognised the benefits of outdoor play, chose to call his nursery a *Kindergarten* (children's garden). He interprets his observation of a child playing with the water and soil in the nursery garden as follows:

> ... he (the child) is fond of busying himself with plastic substances (sand, clay), which to him are, as it were, a life-element. For he seeks now, impelled by the previously acquired sense of his power, to master the material, to control it. Everything must submit to his formative instinct . . . .
> (Froebel 2013:106)

Margaret McMillan (1860–1931) and Maria Montessori (1870–1952) both advocated the provision of gardens where children could explore earth and water for themselves (McMillan 1919; Montessori 1988). The American horticulturalist Luther Burbank (1849–1926) includes mud pies in his list of things that every child should experience, stating, 'any child who has been deprived of these has been deprived of the best part of education' (Burbank 1922:91), and *Peanuts* comic strip creator Charles Schulz's characters make reference to mud play. In the cartoon entitled 'Dirt, marvelous dirt' (1953), one character, Patty, explains to Violet, 'It's our duty to revive fully the lost art of mud pie making' (Peanutsroasted.blogspot.co.uk 2016).

Can you imagine what your 4-year-old self would say about mud play? What might this mean for you as you spend time with children?

Play in the nursery garden

As I write this chapter, we are experiencing one of the wettest winters in recent history in the UK. This has created enormous opportunities for mud and water play in my setting. Children have provided us with numerous cups of coffee and bowls of soup made in the Mud Kitchen (White and Godfrey, 2015), which is rich in opportunities for children to use their imagination and develop symbolic understanding as well as exploring mathematical and scientific concepts.

The physical skills employed by the children as they collect water and pour from one container to another, add mud and sand to their mixture, and stir well are reminiscent of those required in a domestic kitchen. Opportunities to count and measure are in abundance; children begin to develop an embodied understanding of 'heavy' as they carry bowls of muddy ingredients. In the Mud Kitchen, children set themselves physical and scientific challenges, as they transform watery mud to muddy water (adjusting the viscosity by adding more water) and then transferring the resultant liquid from bowls to bottles. As they do so, they discover the advantages of using a funnel to aid pouring into narrow-necked containers. They feel a sense of their own ability to bring about change, that is, their agency. They test out colanders and discover that they are not an effective way of transferring water; the less experienced children look quizzically at the holes as water flows out, and check inside to see whether any water remains. As adults, we can find it hard to resist the temptation to intervene and explain why this is not an effective tool for their purpose or, worse still, to tell the child their idea will not work and they need to use, for example, a saucepan. On each occasion that I have managed to remain silent, I have observed children reach the conclusion themselves by trial and error. The case study (of the missing trowel) below contains one such example.

One hole, three case studies

The following case studies are drawn from observations in my playgroup setting, where an area of ground is set aside where children can dig without restriction.

Digging to Australia

On a hot summer's day, I observed Joe (3½ years) and Sam (4 years) kneeling on the hard earth with trowels in hand. They were stabbing at the dry soil, and as I approached, I could hear them discussing the fact that they were going to dig a deep hole; they looked at me and commented, 'We're digging to Australia!'

These two boys continued to dig this hole, enlarging it as they worked, for the next few days.

We're digging for treasure

Later the same month I noticed that the hole was surrounded by a group of girls and boys (2–4 years old); it was hot and they were digging lazily at the hole. 'We're searching for treasure', they explained to a practitioner who was standing close by, as though that gave their gathering a purpose acceptable to the adult. The chat, however, was about roles in a very different role play: who was the mummy, who was the daddy, and who was the dog. The play continued for some time, the digging became less of a feature as the conversation developed. Children left the circle to get drinks of water and returned to continue with the play.

The missing trowel

Later in the term, on a dry day when the hole was still full of water from an overnight downpour, I noticed a lot of activity around the deep puddle. Four or five 3–4-year-olds were in deep discussion and were clearly trying to solve a problem. As I watched, they appeared to be trying to extract something from the depth of the puddle. It was too deep to reach by hand. One child employed a stick to try to remove the object, but to no avail. I watched as a third collected a colander and tried to remove water from the puddle, whilst another child used a bucket to add water to the puddle (apparently in

Figure 16.1 Boys playing with a tyre

a attempt to float the object out). Tempted as I was to 'wade in' and offer my own suggestions, I waited and watched. Another child joined and said he was bigger and could reach into the puddle. Standing astride it he reached into the puddle and found that he too did not have long enough arms to retrieve the object. Finally, the child who had originally used the colander (having realised that it was an ineffective tool for her purpose) returned with a bucket and began to remove water efficiently. Eventually the water was shallow enough for 3–year–old Amy to reach into the puddle and grasp the trowel with her hand. She raised it into the air and announced triumphantly 'I've got it'! What a collaborative and sustained effort for those children!

Voices from the present

The most powerful voices of the present come from the children themselves as they demonstrate in words, and through the depth of their engagement, how significant mud play is for them:

- Sarah dipped her hands into a large bowl of sloppy mud and lifted them out; she wiped her hands up and down her arms, 'painting' them with mud.
- Joan rolled the sticky clay-based mud into neat balls; she took one and flattened it between her hands, then formed it carefully into a mud

pancake. As she did this she burst into her own song, 'Mud, mud, mud diddy mud . . .'.

- James and Ben, dressed in full waterproofs, sat in a muddy puddle and let the mud ooze through their fingers, silently relishing the feel of the mud; they were completely absorbed in the experience.

- Rose used a long stick to prod at the bottom of a muddy puddle as though she was gauging its depth; she then moved to another puddle and repeated the action before stepping tentatively into the puddle.

- Alex, Helen, and Sam mixed soil, leaves and water in a large bowl and then placed it in the 'oven' to 'cook' in the Mud Kitchen; they explained, 'We've made a chocolate cake, you can have some when it's ready.'

You may consider that different elements of this play are more relevant in different climates and at different times of the year, but each offers its own unique learning possibilities.

Figure 16.2 Pouring from a jug

In the following section I discuss what I believe to be some of the benefits and opportunities of mud play that cause me to agree with White (2012) when she writes 'It seems to me that mud play is one of the most valuable and vital experiences we can provide for children.'

Physical exercise and collaboration

Physical challenges may include carrying containers of various sizes full of mud and/or water. If the containers provided are large (catering-size saucepans, for example), we observe how children work cooperatively to transport the contents, manage the weight and to ensure the contents are kept within the container. As they mix and stir with spoons of different sizes, children exercise the muscles in their arms and back, using the turkey basters and picking leaves to add to the pot children practice and refine their fine motor skills.

Where a setting provides resources for large construction, children often build their own work surfaces for placing containers whilst they mix ingredients, but they may also squat on their haunches or lean over obstacles as they stir their concoctions, using their whole bodies in the intensity of the action.

Benefits to the immune system

The 'hygiene hypothesis' proposed by Ruebush (2009) suggests that the practice in many western, twenty-first century homes of using anti-bacterial products is causing children to grow up with immune systems that have not had any 'exercise'. Just as our muscles need exercise to develop, our immune system needs to be put to work to protect us on a daily basis, so that it is ready for action when needed. Play in mud can provide just such exercise: 'Kids who play outdoors and get dirty are healthier', states Ruebush (2009:65). The benefits of outdoor play throughout the year were recorded in 1919 by Margaret McMillan when she stated: 'the best health records of the open-air nursery are always in winter', going on to say 'Nature never does betray the heart that trusts in her' (1919:33).

Children who are generally in good health benefit from contact with soil, providing that they are also taught good hand-washing techniques when they finish their play.

Communication and relationship building

Observers of children engaged in mud play comment on the complexity of language that is used by the children. It is rare that children do not discuss the reasons for the food they are making, sometimes a birthday party, on other occasions a meal. In any circumstance, the children discuss the ingredients that they are using and the ways in which they are combining them, often telling each other that they need to wait until the meal is cooked before they can eat it. They are applying knowledge from experiences in their kitchens at home, or on other occasions such as cookery programmes they have watched on the television. Attentive observation of children engaged in play, and conversations with parents, can help adults understand the links that the children are making with home, and plan for future activities following these interests.

Mud play and children's well-being

Laevers and colleagues (2005:3) explain 'Well-being refers to feeling at ease, being spontaneous and free of emotional tensions and is crucial to secure "mental health".' They propose that children with high levels of well-being are able to engage more fully with learning opportunities and will have good emotional intelligence.

Christopher Lowry, a neuroscientist at the University of Bristol in England, has researched mycobacterium vaccae, a bacterium found in the soil and believed to trigger the production of the 'feel-good chemical' serotonin in the brain. 'These studies', he says 'leave us wondering if we shouldn't all be spending more time playing in the dirt' (BBC News 2007). I suggest that we should be mindful of Lowry's research and the possible implications of mud play for children's well-being (and consequently for their learning and development) as we plan our gardens.

Deepening involvement

Observers of children at play in mud often note that they demonstrate an intensity of concentration that is undisturbed by even the noisiest jet plane flying overhead – they are completely absorbed in their play. This is what Csikszentmihalyi (2008) describes as a 'state of flow', and when in this state, he proposes, learning for the child is at its best. He asserts that such intensity of involvement is achieved when the challenge of the task and the skill of the child are well matched. You might describe the child as being 'in the zone'.

In mud play, children can determine the level of challenge themselves by, for example:

• wading through deeper mud or puddles
• adding more mud to make the bucket heavier to carry
• making the pattern of flowers or pinecones on the mud pie more complex.

Thus they maintain a state of flow.

Conclusion

Play in mud offers children opportunities to develop and hone physical skills, be creative, engage in experiments, re-create experiences of cooking from other experiences within or beyond the setting, and to explore 'real-life' mathematics and science.

In mud play, children feel a sense of agency as they mix and transform earth and water. They demonstrate their creativity as they discuss recipes, perhaps recording them on a slate or wipe board, and share 'food' with their friends. Their bodies are exercised physically as they transport heavy loads, and their immune systems are 'exercised' through contact with the soil in mud play. The skills children develop in this exciting and fun-filled environment are foundational for their future learning and development.

Questions for further thinking and reflection

1. Reflect on the section entitled One hole, three case studies. As you reflect, consider what each account of the children's play tells you about their experience and learning. What might you have done to enhance/extend the play (if anything)?
2. How might you respond when a child adds worms to the soup and mixes them roughly? How does your response support the child's learning?

Resources for mud play

- *Books* – provide a selection of fiction and non-fiction books about mud play. Include laminated recipe cards outdoors and recipe books in your book area.
- *Mark-making resources* – provide chalkboards, slate tiles, or dry wipe boards for children to record their own recipes.
- *Clothing* – have children dress in all-in-ones for wet and muddy play, either provided by parents or by the activity provider.
- *Containers and utensils for mixing* – acquired from charity shops or donated.
- *Ingredients* – availability of mud, sand, water, and other potential ingredients: gravel, herbs, blossom, and other non-toxic plant materials.
- *Storage and changing* – a place for storing wellington boots and muddy outdoor suits.
- *Cleaning* – model washing up is part of the fun of the activity; further excitement may be added if you provide a hosepipe with a showerhead.

- *Information leaflet for parents* – include reasons why you are offering mud play as part of your play opportunity. (I have found it helpful to include information about ways to remove mud from clothing!)

Consider where you will place your resources: do you want them to be contained in one area of the garden or are you happy for children to be able to transport them and use them in all areas?

References

BBC News (2007) Dirt exposure 'boosts happiness' [Online]. BBC News. Available from: http://news.bbc.co.uk/1/hi/health/6509781.stm [accessed 8 January 2016].

Burbank, L. (1922: 91) *The Training of the Human Plant*. New York: The Century Company.

Csikzentmihalyi, M. (2008) *Flow: The psychology of optimal experience*. New York: Harper Perennial.

DfE (Department for Education), (2014) *Statutory Framework for the Early Years Foundation Stage*. Runcorn: Department for Education.

Froebel, F. (2013) *The Education of Man Edited* (Vol. 1). London: Forgotten Books.

Laevers, F. (Ed.) (2005). *Well-being and Involvement in Care Settings. A Process-oriented self-evaluation instrument (SiCs)*. Brussels: Kind & Gezin. Available at: https://www.kindengezin.be/img/sics-ziko-manual.pdf [accessed 17 March 2017].

McMillan, M. (1919), *The Nursery School*. London: Dent and Sons Ltd.

Montessori, M. (1988), *The Discovery of the Child*. Oxford: Clio Press.

Ruebush, M. (2009) *Why Dirt Is Good: 5 ways to make germs your friends*. New York: Kaplan Publishing.

Peanutsroasted.blogspot.co.uk. (2016). *Roasted Peanuts: October 2010*. Available at: http://peanutsroasted.blogspot.co.uk/2010_10_01_archive.html [accessed 18 Aug. 2016].

Twain, M. (1882) *The Prince and the Pauper*. Boston, MA: Osgood and Company.

White, J. (2012) Make a Mud Kitchen for Mud Day – new guidance published today! [blog post]. *Jan White Natural Play*, 11 June. Available at: https://janwhitenaturalplay.wordpress.com/category/events/ [accessed 13 June 2016].

White, J. and Godfrey, M. (2015) Enabling Environments: Mud kitchens – magic mixes *Nursery World* 14 June. Available at http://www.nurseryworld.co.uk/nursery-world/feature/1152017/enabling-environments-mud-kitchens-magic-mixes [accessed 17 March 2017].

Chapter 17

'Because we like to': young children's experiences hiding in their home environment

Carie Green

Chapter introduction

Carie Green is an Assistant Professor in Graduate Education at the University of Alaska Fairbanks in the USA. In this chapter, she researches 3- and 5-year-olds' hiding places and experiences in their home environment. She found that children have many kinds of hiding places serving various purposes in their lives. This includes a sense of comfort and security, and opportunities for play and creativity where young children are recognised as active agents in creating their own culture and place in the world. Therefore early childhood educators are encouraged to consider the significance of hiding places for young children's development in their own practice.

Introduction

A fascination with hiding begins at a very young age, emerging as infants innocently engage in the game of peek-a-boo with a parent, sibling, or adult caregiver. As young children grow and develop, their hiding game becomes more sophisticated, more abstract. In a more complex version of "hide and seek" young children take ownership of the game in creating and/or adjusting their own rules (Corsaro 2005; Gillespie 2006). But why are young children so fascinated with hiding? The purpose of this paper is to expand the limited research on young children's hiding and their hiding places through exploring children's experiences and perspectives. Drawing from findings of a larger qualitative study of children's special places (Green 2011, 2013a), the intent of this paper is to encourage early childhood educators to consider the "physical world socialization of a child" and the role of hiding in the development of young children's place identity (Proshansky and Fabian 1987, p. 22).

Theoretical framework

This study was shaped around contemporary sociological theories of childhood, particularly in recognizing children as active agents who are creating and constructing their own culture and places in the world (Corsaro 2005; Qvortrup et al. 2009). This research recognized the "unique contributions that children make to their own development and socialization" through their interactions with adults and each other, as well as children's interactions with their physical environments and "persistent attempts to gain control of their lives" (Corsaro 2005, p. 5, 134).

In recognizing the significance of place in children's everyday lives, this research was also informed by place identity theory. As a substructure of self-identity, place identity considers the "physical-world socialization" of a child (Proshansky and Fabian 1987, p. 22). Whereas physical environments are recognized as "unfolding backdrop(s) for ongoing personal and social events" of children's everyday lives, these environments, or places, "provide a rich set of cognitive and emotional associations . . . that resonate with our sense of self" (Devine-Wright and Clayton 2010, p. 268). Place, in this sense, is not separate from, but inclusive of psychological, socio-cultural, and environmental aspects (Low and Altman 1992; Scannell and Gifford 2010). Psychological aspects include the personal meanings that a child holds towards a place, including affective, cognitive, and behavioral components (Scannell and Gifford 2010). Sociocultural aspects refer to how social norms, culture, and ideologies influence human–place relationships, including activities attributed to particular places (Low and Altman 1992). Environmental aspects assume that certain physical features such as size, tangible, or imaginative aspects create certain people–place relationships (Low and Altman 1992). Early childhood is recognized as a significant period when more stable aspects of one's place identity are formed (Chawla 1992; Proshansky and Fabian 1987). Therefore, this research considers how place significantly contributes to children's construction of culture and their individual identity.

Related literature

Although anecdotally one could argue that hiding is a natural part of early childhood and to some extent, a recurring activity in children's everyday lives, the phenomenon of hiding from a child's perspective has not been thoroughly explored. Some suggest that hiding has evolutionary origins, noting that hiding is an activity in which both humans and animals participate (Bruner and Sherwood 1975; Clarke 1999; Groos and Baldwin 1898/1976; 1901). Groos and Baldwin (1898/1976) proposed that children instinctively hide because of a natural inclination to hunt and gather for survival.

More contemporary theories of hiding view it as a developmental phenomenon. Bruner and Sherwood (1975) suggested that hiding aids understanding of object permanence.

In viewing hiding as a social phenomenon, Gillespie (2006) described hiding as a "social institution that has many levels of complexity" (p. 91). As children develop, so does the complexity of the game. Initial stages of hiding appear to begin in stationary forms, such as peek-a-boo (Clarke 1999; Gillespie 2006). Then, as children become mobile, it may transition into games such as "I'm-going-to-get-you" (Clarke 1999, p. 77). When children first begin to hide, they fail to fully differentiate the perspectives of other players (Gillespie 2006; Peskin and Ardino 2003). However, as children develop they grow in their ability to take on different perspectives (Gillespie 2006), and begin to create their own rules to make their hiding activities more complex (Clarke 1999; Gillespie 2006).

This social view of hiding relates to Corsaro's (2005) "as if" assumption. Specifically, by adults treating young children "as if" they are "socially competent" and "capable of social exchanges," children move from limited, responsive participants, to initiators or directors of a game, to eventually adjusting or creating their own rules (p. 18). Moreover, Corsaro's (2005) concept of "secondary adjustments" is useful for understanding how children collaboratively attempt to evade or bend adult rules in order to gain control of a game or routine (p. 42).

In considering children's perspectives, Hart (1979) noted that elementary-aged children prefer places in the natural environment to hide from parents and siblings when they are in trouble. Fjørtoft (2001) contends that natural playscapes (i.e. bushes, shrubs, and trees) lend themselves to preschool-aged children's hiding activities. Children also prefer quiet and isolated spaces to be alone (Skånfors et al. 2009) and explore their environments (Hart 1979). "Within a preschool setting, children hid in closets or between furniture in order to gain space to be alone, while small groups of children jointly constructed spaces to exclusively play with each other (Skånfors et al. 2009).

While the literature points to some of the psychological, socio-cultural, and environmental aspects of children's hiding activities, no study, to my knowledge, has specifically explored children's perspectives and experiences in their hiding places within their home environments. Therefore, this study addresses the following research questions: (1) How do young children experience hiding places in their home environments? (2) How do children use hiding places to actively construct their own culture and place identity?

(3) How do sociocultural and environmental contexts influence young children's hiding activities?

Methodology

This research utilized an interpretive qualitative approach in which the researcher was "interested in understanding the meaning people have constructed, that is, how people make sense of their world and the experiences they have in the world" (Merriam 2009, p. 13). Meaning was mediated through the researcher as the primary instrument. The strategy was inductive: the researcher gathered different kinds of data to describe a phenomenon, in this case, children's hiding place experiences. Rich descriptive data were collected in two phases, occurring at school and in children's homes, through methods aimed at including children in the research process as opposed to methods done to children. Additionally, the researcher engaged in reflexivity throughout the research in considering how personal biases and experiences as well as adult/child positioning may influence data collection and interpretation (Punch 2002). Multiple interactive methods were used in order to provide children with several opportunities to talk about, represent, and share their hiding place experiences.

Refer to Green (2012) for additional details on the research methods.

Data Collection

The first phase included thirty-one 3 to 5-year-old children (15 girls and 16 boys) at a preschool in a small university town in the Rocky Mountain region of the United States. Data collection began with a puppet show to introduce the study to the children and to help establish a positive, non-threatening relationship with the children (Green 2012, 2013b).

A children's book, *My Own Special Place,* was designed specifically for this study and was used to introduce children to the concept of special places and to prompt discussions of their place experiences

After the book discussions, children were invited to create artistic representations of their places and further share about their place experiences. As Isenberg and Jalongo (2014) explain, art is a language by which young children communicate, "children learn to express themselves through art by interacting with their environments" (p. 103). The children could choose from four different developmentally appropriate modes to represent their places, including: drawing, painting, molding, and building with blocks. Because their artistic abilities varied significantly, the contents of the representations were not analyzed. Rather, the verbal descriptions expressed by the children were used as data for this research.

The second phase included home visits with eight children and their families, three boys (Robert, John, and Caleb) and five girls (Sara, Emily, Fern, Lisa, and Tesa). Two pairs of siblings participated: Sara and Caleb, and Fern and Lisa. Five of the six families were white and considered middle-class, while one family identified itself as Hispanic and held a lower socioeconomic status. Home visits began with a place tour with children serving as tour guides, showing and describing all of the places that they considered important. Additionally, informal interviews with children occurred during the tours when the researcher posed questions and listened intently to the children as they described their hiding places and activities.

Informal interviews were also conducted with parents during the home visits to provide insight regarding the nature of how children engaged in their hiding places in their everyday lives. Parental data was not used to provide voice for the children; rather it provided possible explanations as to why children seemed to prefer certain places.

All data collection activities were video-recorded and transcribed for analysis purposes. Preliminary analysis was conducted immediately following each data collection activity, where the researcher jotted down observational notes, emerging themes, and patterns that connected new data to previously collected data. In this way the researcher aimed to stay "on top of" the data through checking what was coming in and trying to identify where the data may be leading (Grbich 2007, p, 31). Second, domain coding (Saldaña 2009) was utilized for categorizing and quantifying children's hiding place locations. These locations are used as categories in this article to present children's experiences of hiding, as talked about at school and/or shown during place tours. Third, children's experiences in each hiding place location were grouped together to show common themes (i.e. hiding with stuffed animals) in order to demonstrate children's shared and individual experiences. In this way, rich descriptive data are presented to capture how children engage in their hiding places and how their independent and social activities may relate to the construction of their place identity. Finally, the psychological, socio-cultural, and environmental influences of children's hiding experiences are discussed and related to the research literature and place and childhood theories.

Hiding places

How do young children experience hiding places within their home environments? Table 1 includes children's descriptions in some of their most popular hiding places. Children's experiences hiding are further explored in the sections that follow.

In the closet

The closet was the most common hiding place mentioned and shown by children.

Many children ventured to the closet alone but some also hid in the closet with siblings or pets. Others mentioned hiding in the closet with stuffed animals, dolls, and favorite toys, such as *"Lincoln Logs"* or "flashlights." Hiding in the closet offered children a sense of control as one girl remarked, "I hide in my closet and take clothes down . . . I make a mess . . . my mom and dad says pick those clothes up and I say no!" Perhaps, as illustrated above, part of the fascination with hiding in the closet was the opportunity to avoid or bend adult rules (Corsaro 2005).

Under the covers

Several children mentioned hiding "under my blankets" or how they liked to "pull blankets up on top of the bed." Hiding "under the covers"

Table 17.1 Children's experiences in their hiding places

Hiding place	Children's comments
In a closet	"I hide in my closet and take clothes down . . . I make a mess . . . my mom and dad says pick those clothes up and I say no" (3-year-old girl) "I bring my night light toys in there with my sister" (4-year-old girl) "My special place is to bring Thunder (dog) in my closet" (3-year-old boy)
Under blankets	"I snuggle up in my bed underneath the blankets" (3-years-old girl) "Under my blankets, I like to lay and look at the stars" (4-year-old boy) "I like to hide in my bed. I like to read books and I read books with my babies" (4-year-old girl)
Under a bed	"I like to take my Barbie under there. Mom does not know that I am there" (4-year-old girl) "I like to hide under the guest bed" (3-year-old girl) "I go under the bed and underneath bears and babies. There's a cookie monster" (4-year-old girl)
Under a tree or bush	"In the bush . . . I like to do is hide. I like to go there with friends" (3-year-old girl) "Me and Jocelynn, run in the tree" (4-year-old girl) "It's really fun under the tree . . . We bring some toys at the park and play with them" (4-year-old girl)
Behind a couch or chair	"I go in back of the couch by the heater" (4-years-old girl) "I play behind the couch with babies" (4-year-old girl)
Under a table	"Caleb and me like to go under the table. We just hide . . . Once we were playing monsters under the table and Caleb found us" (4-year-old girl) "I go under the table when mom is cooking" (3-year-old girl)

Other mentioned or shown hiding places: in a toy box, under a trampoline, blanket tents, spaces behind or between furniture, in a playhouse, in a car, behind a door, upstairs loft, a bathroom, inside a cupboard or cabinet, brother's room, behind curtains, in Daddy's office provided children a cozy space to "snuggle up" with stuffed animals, as a girl described, "I like to take all of my stuffed animals under the covers."

Others mentioned "under the blankets" as a place to play with "toys and puzzles," "read books," or play with "babies." One boy mentioned that he liked hiding under the covers because he could "lay and look at the stars."

Another girl talked about "bear places." "Not real bears," she clarified, "in my room and on my bed . . . one bed on the bottom and one on the top. I have a bunk-bed . . . underneath babies and purse blanket pillows. I go under the bed and underneath bears and babies."

Another child mentioned how she hid under the covers from "mommy's vacuum." This hiding place provided a sense of security from objects, or events that made her nervous.

Yet none of the children mentioned hiding under the covers with parents or an adult, indicating that this kid-only space plays a significant role in children's construction of their own culture and place (Corsaro 2005).

Sara and Caleb hid in 18 different places during their place tour, many of which included blankets. The children went up and down the stairs to retrieve blanket after blanket from their bedroom in order to construct a large bed on the living room floor.

"They love blankets, blankets and pillows," their mother explained, "They would much rather get a blanket for Christmas than a toy."

Sara and Caleb involved blankets in many other hiding activities, including tucking into a cabinet under the stairs, concealing themselves in a toy box in their playroom, hiding behind a window curtain, sliding under a comforter at the end of their parents' bed, and venturing into a dark bathroom with flashlights and toy plastic vampire teeth.

Hiding was something that Sara and Caleb chose to do. It also appeared to be a way for them to create their own rules and gain control (Gillespie 2006). The children exercised "secondary adjustments" through requesting access to hiding places and their parents had deemed as "off limits." (Corsaro 2005, p. 42).

In addition, Caleb and Sarah's use of blankets in hiding was associated with a desire for physical "warmth" and a sense of security. Sara's favorite place was hiding behind the couch, next to the heater vent with a blanket over her; the children also hid behind the couch when they were "nervous of strangers," as explained by their mother.

Under the bed

In addition to under blankets, many children referred to hiding under a bed. Whether it was under their own bed or someone else's bed, as one girl explained, "I like to hide under the guest bed," and three others mentioned hiding "under my mom's bed".

"I take my *Barbie* under there," one girl said in referring to her hiding place under her mother's bed, "Mom does not know that I am there." Her comment, once again, points towards children's attraction to secret hidden spaces where they could make themselves inaccessible (Skånfors et al. 2009, p. 105).

Later during the home visit, John clarified his favorite hiding place, stating, "I like to play under Kyle's bed." (Kyle is his baby brother).

"Almost every morning when I go get Kyle, his little brother, he goes under there," his mother explained, "Are you going to go show her how you fit under Kyle's bed?"

"John, what do you like to do under there?" the researcher asked again.

"Play cars," he said in a high voice, still hidden.

"Do you bring your cars under there?" the researcher asked.

"Yes and Kyle's cars," John answered, referring to a bin full of large play cars beside the crib. He then disappeared behind the brown bed skirt one last time before lifting it up and scooting out from underneath the crib.

Like many of the other children's hiding places, John's hiding place became a secret space where he was free to play. Separate, yet within close proximity to his mother, this space provided John with the opportunity to explore his place identity (Proshansky and Fabian 1987).

Discussion

Social and Psychological Aspects of Children's Hiding Activities

How do children use hiding places to actively construct their own culture and place identity? Through hiding, children claimed their own spaces and gained a sense of control in their home environments, a place predominantly structured by adults. Throughout each of the children's place tours, it was apparent that children did not want, nor invited, parents or other adults (including the researcher) to enter into their hiding places. Rather the children were constructing their own child culture within their claimed spaces. Novel places, such as inside a parent's closet and under beds, even beds where they could not fit, offered children opportunities to engage in their own play activities, exercise creativity, and gain a sense of autonomy.

Parents were frequently surprised by their child's choice of hiding places, at times expressing a contradicting opinion about where their child's favorite place was located. For instance, Lisa and Fern's mother argued against her daughters' selections of places stating, "no you do not," when Lisa crawled under the art easel and Fern tucked between the wall and her dresser. Likewise, Robert's mother was in a state of disbelief over his attempt to crawl under his bed; she stood aside and watched as Robert persistently attempted to lodge his body into the tight space underneath. As Corsaro (2005) noted one of the most significant features of children's construction of their own culture is found in their "persistent attempts to gain control of their lives" (p. 134). In this way, hiding provided a means for children to gain control over spaces in a predominantly adult-structured environment.

John's hiding place under his brother's crib was located within close proximity to his mother, which allowed him to observe what was happening while engaging in his play. Likewise, Sara's hiding place behind the couch in the family room allowed her to listen in on family conversations while remaining inaccessible. In addition to playing and gaining physical warmth, she used her place to process feelings when she was upset.

Furthermore, children were attracted to hiding places that offered them a sense of comfort and security. These "comfy" places often included blankets and other stuffed animals that were cozy, soft, and warm. Indeed, this study points to the importance of familiar and comfortable settings, which support children in developing their place identity (Pro-shansky and Fabian 1987). Therefore, it was not surprising that many of the items that children considered special accompanied them to their hiding places. Furthermore, some children choose to hide when confronted by uncomfortable situations, such as from "mommy's vacuum" or from "strangers". Once again, this suggested that hiding places provide children with a sense of comfort and security.

While children sometimes preferred to hide alone, hiding was more often than not characterized as a social activity (Clarke 1999; Corsaro 2005; Gillespie 2006). The children enjoyed the act of hiding and having others seek them. Parents indicated that children had learned the basic structure of hide and seek from mothers or fathers, siblings, and friends. In this way, children were treated "as if" they were fully competent and able to play the game (Corsaro 2005). Sara and Caleb demanded access to hiding places that had been previously forbidden, exercising Corsaro's (2005) concept of "secondary adjustments" through bending parent rules (p. 42). In this instance, their mother allowed the children access to forbidden places. Thus, this enabled the children to gain control.

Socio-cultural and environmental considerations

How do socio-cultural and environmental contexts influence young children's hiding activities? The children in this study came from predominantly white, middle-class families positioned in a western, privileged culture. While the positioning of the study within a predominantly white, middle-class, westernized culture might pose a limitation, especially in assuming that findings may be similar in other cultural and geographical contexts, there were, within the study's context, some notable differences in children's hiding experiences. For instance, Sara and Caleb's hiding place experiences appeared to be related to their family's lower socio-economic status, parenting style, and the physical structure of their home. Within their home setting, there appeared to be a lack of structure and rules, or if there were rules they were not always enforced. This was noted in the physical mess and disorder of the home. The homes of the other eight children appeared much more orderly and some spaces were designed specifically for children's use. Future research might explore children's hiding experiences within different geographical contexts (e.g. children living in an urban versus rural environment) or further investigate children's hiding activities within various socio-cultural contexts (e.g. children living in poverty or from minority families). A quantitative research study could also be conducted to analyze and compare trends in children's hiding across these different contexts.

Conclusion

How can findings from this study be applied to early childhood education? While the importance of bridging the home and school cultures is well recognized (Allen 2007). It is also important for early childhood educators to understand the significance of children's hiding places and activities. Specifically, educators should consider how through hiding, children are actively constructing their own culture and place. Children need to be able to claim their own places, for it is within these special spaces in an adult-structured world that children gain control and construct their own place identity. Hiding places play a significant role in children's lives by allowing them to socially engage with adults and peers and negotiate their own rules, engage in play and creativity, and find comfort and security. With that said, this study revealed distinct differences between children's connections to place and hiding activities in a healthy-structured home environment versus a messy, disorderly setting. While this study recognizes children as active agents, adult caregivers and educators need also consider the significance of providing structured and intentional learning environments that promote children's place connections and support them in constructing their own identity.

Questions for further thinking and reflection

1. How might the findings of this study impact on planning for children's development and learning in early years settings?
2. What aspects of health and safety might need to be considered in planning for young children's hiding places in early years settings?

References

Allen, J. B. (2007). *Creating welcoming schools: A practical guide to home-school partnerships with diverse families*. New York, NY: Teachers College Press.

Bruner, J. S., & Sherwood, V. (1975). Peekaboo and the learning of rule structures. In J. S. Bruner, A. Jolly, & K. Sylva (Eds.), *Play: Its role in development and evolution* (pp. 277–285). New York, NY: Basic Books.

Chawla, L. (1992). Childhood place attachments. In I. Altman & S. Low (Eds.), *Place attachment* (pp. 63–86). New York, NY: Plenum.

Clarke, L. J. (1999). Development reflected in chase games. In R. S. Riefel (Ed.), *Play contexts revisited* (pp. 73–82). Stamford, CT: Ablex Publishing.

Corsaro, W. A. (2005). *The sociology of childhood* (2nd ed.). Thousand Oaks, CA: Sage.

Devine-Wright, P., & Clayton, S. (2010). Introduction of the special issue: Place, identity and environment. *Journal of Environmental Psychology, 30*(3), 267–270.

Fjørtoft, I. (2001). The natural environment as a playground for children: The impact of outdoor play activities in pre-primary school children. *Early Childhood Education Journal, 29*(2), 111–117.

Gillespie, A. (2006). Games and the development of perspective taking. *Human Development, 49*, 87–92.

Grbich, C. (2007). *Qualitative data analysis: An introduction*. Thousand Oaks, CA: Sage.

Green, C. (2011). A place of my own: Exploring preschool children's special places in the home environment. *Children, Youth, and Environment, 21*(2), 118–144.

Green, C. (2012). Listening to children: Exploring intuitive strategies and interactive methods in a study of children's special places. *International Journal of Early Childhood, 44*(3), 269–285.

Green, C. (2013a). A sense of autonomy in young children's special places. *International Journal of Early Childhood Environmental Education, 1*(1), 8–33.

Green, C. (2013b). Puppets as an interactive tool for teaching. *Focus on Teacher Education Association for Childhood Education International (ACEI), 12*(3), 1–2.

Groos, K., & Baldwin, E. L. (1976). *The play of animals*. New York, NY: D. Appleton. (Original work published in 1898).

Hart, R. (1979). *Children's experience of place*. New York, NY: Irvington.

Isenberg, J. P., & Jalongo, M. R. (2014). *Creative thinking and arts-based learning: Preschool through fourth grade* (6th ed.). Upper Saddle River, NJ: Pearson.

Low, S. M., & Altman, I. (1992). Place attachment: A conceptual inquiry. In I. Altman & S. M. Low (Eds.), *Place attachment* (pp. 1–12). New York, NY: Plenum Press.

Merriam, S. B. (2009). *Qualitative research: A guide to design and implementation*. New York, NY: Wiley.

Peskin, J., & Ardino, V. (2003). Representing the mental world in children's social behavior: Playing hide-and-seek and keeping a secret. *Social Development, 12,* 496–512.

Proshansky, H. M., & Fabian, A. K. (1987). The development of place identity in the child. In C. S. Weinstein & T. G. David (Eds.), *Spaces for children: The built environment and child development* (pp, 21–40). New York, NY: Plenum Press.

Punch, S. (2002). Research with children: The same of different from research with adults? *Childhood, 9*(3), 321–341.

Qvortrup, J., Corsaro, W. A., & Honig, M. (2009). *The Palgrave handbook of childhood studies.* New York, NY: Palgrave Mcmillan.

Saldaña, J. (2009). *The coding manual for qualitative researchers.* Thousand Oaks, CA: Sage.

Scannell, L., & Gifford, R. (2010). Defining place attachment: A tripartite organizing framework. *Journal of Environmental Psychology, 30*(1), 1–10.

Skånfors, L., Löfdahl, A., & Hägglund, S. (2009). Hidden spaces and places in the preschool: Withdrawal strategies in preschool children's peer cultures. *Journal of Early Childhood Research, 7*(1), 94–109.

Chapter 18

Using digital resources to document young children's everyday moments

Karen Horsley

Chapter introduction

Karen Horsley, Lecturer in Early Years at The Open University, draws on her study using photographs to listen to children and find out about their experiences in their day nursery and at home. The project considers the different relationships children have with practitioners and family members and how talking about photographs that children have taken provides insight into their interests and preferences. The project also considers the use of technology and the way in which it can be used to support children's and practitioner's reflection.

Introduction

> We can be known only in the unfolding of our unique stories within the context of everyday events.
>
> (Paley, 1990:xii)

Participatory approaches using digital resources to listen to young children's voices and perspectives have become more significant as children are increasingly seen as 'experts in their own lives' (Langsted, 1994; Clark and Moss, 2011). This chapter introduces the beginnings of conversations and reflections from a small exploratory project in a day nursery in the South East of England. We included the use of a digital camera to listen to one child and his view on the world, at home, through the photos he chose to take independently and the stories he chose to tell about them. We built on the nursery's practices of viewing the camera as a 'vehicle for communication' in 'making learning visible' (Milne and Garnett, 2015:67) with children as citizens with a right to be heard from their own perspectives. This emphasis on relationships, dialogue and the child's voice and experiences draws on a socio-cultural view that all learning is profoundly social and contextualised (Rogoff, 2003; Lave and Wenger, 1991).

Listening and participatory approaches

Participatory photography supports children in creating and documenting *their own* powerful learning stories (Clark and Moss, 2011; Kervin and Mantei, 2011; Kervin, 2016). The combination of the child's photos and narrative (verbal and non-verbal) have been used together in photo-elicitation which positions the child's photos as central to a shared discussion over a short time period (Rose, 2011).

The study also draws on approaches used by the charitable organisation PhotoVoice (2016). The concept of 'photovoice' for sustained participatory action research was originally developed by Wang and Burris (1994, in Wang, 1999) and photovoice aims to:

1. record and reflect their communities strengths and concerns
2. promote critical dialogue and knowledge about personal and community issues through large and small group discussion of their photographs
3. reach policymakers. (Wang, 1999:185)

The use of photovoice has the capacity to stimulate dialogue for change, as well as children developing their own stories and knowing those of others. Photovoice is a 'highly flexible tool that crosses cultural and linguistic barriers, and can be adapted to all abilities' (2016). It therefore has potential for inclusive practice, though the use of a camera as a participatory tool for engaging young children is not unproblematic (see Waller and Bitou, 2011). However, in this study the photos are central to understanding the child's everyday life and Michael's voice is evident through the choices he has made in the photos he has taken and the subsequent discussion about what they mean to him.

Introducing Michael*

Michael is 4 years old, and lives with his mother, father and 4–month–old sister. They are a very close, loving family where humour is shared, which is reflected in Michael's photos, actions and discussions as you will see in the extracts from the study with myself, Emma, Michael's keyworker and his mother.

Michael was asked whether he would like to talk about his photos and where. He chose the room of his usual nursery session, while the other children and staff played in the communal area outside. Michael talked about a self-edited selection of twenty photos, many of which were of his sister in bathing, dressing and feeding routines either pictured by herself or with their mother. There were also many 'selfies' with Michael's face pulled in all directions. Other photos conveyed household items, such as the front door, and Michael led the discussion about his toy white bear and a photo of a plant. These selection of photos 'evoke the affective materiality of social life' (Hunt, 2014, cited in Rose, 2016:316) and bring the 'everyday' more to the fore (Rose, 2016).

Michael: That's my baby sister.
Karen: She's looking up at you?
Michael: She's getting ready for her bath.
Michael: That's my sister's plant in her room
Emma: Is it a special plant?
Michael: Yes, she had it when she was a baby. Mummy gave me one too.
Emma: What's that one Michael?
Michael: In my bath [bath tidy across the bath].

I found looking at the selection of photos taken that there were many that focused on horizontal and vertical lines, for example, the bath tidy, the front door, the plant and one of a key tidy.

Figure 18.1 Photo of the plant taken by Michael in his sister's bedroom

Figure 18.2 White Bear

Michael: That's White Bear, my special bear, I had when I was a baby.
Mother: Why is White Bear called White Bear?

Michael shrugs and his mother pauses.

Mother: 'We asked you what to call him and you said "white bear" so
             that's what we called him . . . You had the same blue bear too but
             white bear is smaller than blue bear because white bear is your
             favourite bear and you took him everywhere.'
Michael: [changing the subject] That's my favourite picture of my baby
             sister [on the bath mat looking up].
Karen: And those are mummy's toes in the corner of the picture!
Michael: No, they are my toes!
Michael: I like that one too [one of several of his mother cuddling his
             sister]. Mummy's hair is like a fringe! [his mother's hair was falling
             onto the baby's forehead].

There was a pause in the conversation as Michael's attention was drawn to some
toy animals, Emma noticed the changes of time frame and lighting in the photos.

Emma: What time period did Michael take the photos over?
Mother: About a week.

Michael's mother added that Michael had found the nursery's 'child-friendly' camera difficult to use because he couldn't just pick it up. He had to keep asking how to use it and he got frustrated.

Practitioners: what did we learn together? Implications for practice

Michael's discussion of his own photos helped to illuminate his everyday life and especially how important his family are together with key personal objects and his environment. Einarsdóttir (2005:527) reflects, '[Children] are the experts, the ones who know about the pictures, and they decide through the pictures what will be talked about.' Michael also demonstrated that he could combined old and new technologies as he built a Lego city after he had finished talking about his photos. He also incorporated dressing up as his father in his job during the discussion as well. Rose (2016:328) comments that this more detailed context may not be visible in photos, and therefore we 'have to think quite carefully about the relation between the visible and the social'.

Considerations of the interrelationships between the visible and the social are integral to practice in the nurseries of Reggio Emilia and Pistoia in Northern Italy. Stories start from the child; they are shared and woven into the daily life of the setting, as they have a tradition of drawing on documentation for explicitly celebrating the life of the child now, and for learning about ourselves and others (Barrs, 2006). As Rinaldi notes:

> . . . documentation . . . is seen as visible learning as a construction of traces (through notes, slides, videos and so on) that not only testify to the children's learning processes, but also make them possible because they are visible, for us this means making visible and thus possible, the relationships that are the building blocks of knowledge.
>
> (Rinaldi, 2006, in Hartley, 2015:60)

So digital resources offer a valuable medium in documentation and the development of relationships, which brings everyone together in a range of creative learning that may draw on the valuable 'everydayness' of children's stories and experiences. Digital resources (including audio too) have possibilities for capturing and reflecting on these in nursery books, on the walls, the theatre and more.

It also became evident that in the study's setting the staff too have rich stories – the walls hold stories from both children's and adults'

learning. Rachel, an Early Years practitioner, likened our discussions
to the communal nurseries in Reggio Emilia and the emphasis there on
the 'hundred languages of children' and the attention to the aesthetic
environment (Edwards, Gandini and Forman, 1998). As a group
we reflected on the use of cameras to look at children's experiences
and surroundings with 'fresh eyes'. Rachel said she often notices the
unexpected, for example, unusual shapes in the environment or berries for
'volcanic jam' in a place no one looks. She reflected on children imagining
roaming horses and feeding them with a big bag of pretend carrots in
unlikely places. These observations on the use of reflecting on digital
resources exemplify the significance of the 'everyday' contexts of Michael's
experiences in a community with others.

Ethical considerations

Rose (2016) highlights the centrality and dynamics of relationships
between all the research participants. My concern was Michael's consent
throughout and I was aware of not being familiar to him. Punch (2002,
in Einarsdóttir, 2005) highlights being sensitive to children's interests,
capacities and feelings, and being at ease with the adult researcher. Not
knowing the child enabled me to listen without prior knowledge, whilst
his keyworker Emma offered familiarity. Michael was asked where he
wanted to talk about his photos in recognition of a sense of space and
place being important in framing the context for him feeling comfortable
and safe. Fraser (2004, in Einarsdóttir, 2005:525) suggests the need to be
flexible and negotiate 'child–friendly methods'. Humour, too, seemed to
be a possible element: Michael captured humour in most of his photos,
suggesting that humour is valued at home as part of his communication
and learning. Walsh and colleagues (2011) found humour and knowing
children well over time as helpful in developing contexts that support
learning and the development of relationships.

Multiple voices in this study prompted further thinking about how
to use digital technology in future projects considering family digital
literacies where children learn first and foremost (Plowman and McPake,
2011). Here, Michael is used to using his mother's iPhone to take photos
independently. Also, a disposable camera was deliberately avoided as images
cannot be copied and it was important to show that Michael's photos and
experiences were not disposable. Lily, another Early Years practitioner,
added that it may be beneficial for adults to develop more professional
photographic skills for documenting, communicating and reflecting on
children's learning together.

Inclusive practice

The use of photos and dialogue works towards inclusive practices where everyone's voice can be heard through stories that support learning, even if the process feels 'uncertain', and we embraced this aspect. Megan the nursery Manager commented:

> We don't know what we will find out but I think this is about understanding children's views and feelings, to see their world view and learning in the wider world including all cultures. The most important part is the process and celebrating each child's life and their experiences. Using the camera and talking, we can slow down to listen. Sometimes all of us need to slow down and listen to children. To see the familiar and unfamiliar to children. As adults, we need to be open to everything the child teaches us – they are our educators as we get to know children and create memories together. Children have different ways of thinking and constructions of the world. It's about the heartbeat of children.

Conclusion

This small exploratory project has drawn on photo elicitation and photovoice as methods in a broader toolbox of supporting children as architects of their own visual stories. Adults get to know the stories children bring with them into nursery, and in Paley's words (1990:xi), 'connect everything that happens in this nursery school classroom' and 'draw invisible lines between the children's images'. Digital technologies act as a mediator or shared resource helping adults, in inclusive practice, to slow down and listen, to draw the invisible lines and make connections within and between all children's everyday moments and stories. Relationships are integral and may be enhanced through the creation of visual pedagogical documentation in many forms, for example, wall display, stories, books, theatre, whether these are in individual learning stories or community resources.

The sharing of photovoices or visual stories through digital resources offers the possibility of developing new creative ways of understanding children's lives, and, perhaps more importantly, genuine reflection and learning about their perspectives on everyday moments for building relationships, community and pedagogy.

Questions for further thinking and reflection

1. What are the potential opportunities and challenges in using digital resources to capture children's perspectives?

2.   Do you think participatory photography can help to make children's perspectives about their lives more visible? Are there any problems with this?

Notes

★   All names have been changed.

Further reading

Edwards, E., Gandini, L., and Forman, G. (eds.) (1998) *The Hundred Languages of Children: The Reggio Emilia approach advanced reflections.* Greenwich, CT: Alex Publishing Corporation.

Milne, W., and Garnett, W. (2015) 'Making learning visible through the use of new technologies' in Wharton, P. and Kinney, L. (eds.) *Reggio Emilia Encounters. Children and adults in collaboration.* Abingdon: Routledge.

Rose, G. (2016) *Visual Methodologies. An introduction to researching with visual materials* 4th edn. London: Sage

References

Barrs, M. (2006) The creative community of Pistoia, *Teaching Thinking & Creativity, 8*(1): 18–27.

Clark, A. and Moss. P. (2011) *Listening to young children: The mosaic approach.* London: National Children's Bureau Enterprises Ltd.

Edwards, E., Gandini, L. and Forman, G. (eds). (1998) *The Hundred Languages of Children: The Reggio Emilia approach advanced reflections.* Greenwich, CT: Alex Publishing Corporation

Einarsdóttir, J. (2005) Playschool in pictures: Children's photographs as a research method, *Early Child Development and Care, 175*(6): 523–541.

Hartley, B. (2015) Powerful images, visible learning, in Wharton, P. and Kinney, L. (eds) *Reggio Emilia Encounters: Children and adults in collaboration.* Abingdon: Routledge.

Kervin, L. (2016) Powerful and playful literacy learning with digital technologies. *Australian Journal of Language and Literacy, 39*(1): 64–73.

Kervin, L. and Mantei, J. (2011) This is Me: Children teaching us about themselves through digital storytelling. *Practically Primary, 16*(1): 4–7.

Langsted, O. (1994) Looking at quality from the child's perspective, in Moss, P. and Pence, A. (eds) *Valuing Quality in Early Childhood Service: New approaches to defining quality.* London: Paul Chapman.

Lave, J. and Wenger, E. (1991) *Situated Learning: Legitimate peripheral participation.* Cambridge: University of Cambridge Press.

Milne, W. and Garnett, W. (2015) Making learning visible through the use of new technologies, in Wharton, P. and Kinney, L. (eds) *Reggio Emilia Encounters. Children and adults in collaboration.* Abingdon: Routledge.

Paley, V.G. (1990) *The Boy Who Would be a Helicopter: The uses of storytelling in the classroom.* Cambridge, MA: Harvard University Press.

PhotoVoice (2016) Available at: https://photovoice.org/ (accessed 17 March 2017).

Plowman, L. and McPake, J. (2011) Seven myths about young children and technology. *Childhood Education, 89*(1): 27–33.

Rogoff, B. (2003) *The Cultural Nature of Human Development.* Oxford: Oxford University Press.

Rose, G. (2016) *Visual Methodologies. An introduction to researching with visual materials,* 4th edn. London: Sage

Waller, T. and Bitou, A. (2011) Research with children: Three challenges for participatory research in early childhood. *European Early Childhood Education Research Journal, 19*(1): 5–20. doi:10.1080/1350293X.2011.548964 (accessed 17 March 2017).

Walsh, G., Sproule, L., McGuinness, C., and Trew, K. (2011) Playful structure: A novel image of early years pedagogy for primary school classrooms. *Early Years, 31*(2):107–119.

Wang, C. (1999) Photovoice: A participatory action research strategy applied to women's health. *Journal of Women's Health, 8*(2): 185–192.

Chapter 19

Count on play: the importance of play in making sense of mathematics

Linda Pound

Chapter introduction

Linda Pound, an early childhood consultant and author who has published extensively, emphasises how children's play makes sense of mathematics. In her chapter, she gives examples of everyday play situations that can be linked to mathematical explanations. She explains how this is important in supporting children's future learning. She considers the significance of children being able to create and investigate through ideas and discovery promotes flexible, playful and challenging thinking. She argues that mathematics is about life and providing rich and enabling experiences is key to understanding mathematical concepts.

Introduction

> Mathematics is not about number but about life. It is about the world in which we live. It is about ideas. And, far from being dull and sterile as it is so often portrayed it is full of creativity.
>
> (Devlin 2000:76)

Of course mathematics is about number – and shape and measurement, but understanding depends on foundations which go beyond those obvious components. Play and creativity are not words that are commonly used in relation to the development of mathematical understanding, yet they are fundamental. This chapter sets out to demonstrate the importance of both play and creativity in helping children to make sense of mathematics. It begins with a snapshot of playful activity. It then considers the role of pattern, problem-solving and spatial awareness, ending with a focus on mathematical thinking – or playing with ideas.

Counting on play

> We are all of us, at all ages, already highly skilled mathematicians. We just haven't often learned it in our mathematics lessons.
>
> (Lewis 1996:17)

The following examples give a snapshot of activities in a North London children's centre. There are three main areas – one for babies, a second for toddlers (mainly 2-year-olds) and a third room which acts as a base for 3- and 4-year-olds. During the course of a week, forty-eight children attend the centre. In addition to the normal free hours, some families pay fees for wrap-around or full day care, while others are given free places because of particular needs. The centre is situated in a very diverse part of London.

- Zac – In the baby room, babies are moving – crawling on the floor, climbing up the steps and ramp of the mini-gym for a different view of their world. Sixteen-month-old Zac attempts to run down a gentle slope at the end of the garden – approaching it cautiously at first, stopping when his feet reach the slope and gradually getting braver and bolder. Others are exploring sand while some are embarking on imaginative and symbolic play – feeding a doll or sharing a book.
- Leah – In the toddler room, a group of 2-year-olds are cutting paper into increasingly small pieces. Some begin to glue them onto another piece of paper. On the carpet – Leah, 19 months, lines up animals around the edge of the block trolley lid. A copy of *Dear Zoo* has been placed on the rug – as this is a familiar activity for her.
- Peter – Amongst the 3- and 4-year-olds in the garden, a group race around the perimeter of the garden on bikes and scooters. Another group in a sheltered corner are building a train with hollow blocks and chairs borrowed from their room. Inside, Peter is making tickets. In the wet sand tray, someone has created a track and cars have been left there mid-journey.

Playing with pattern

Many of the children described above, like Leah with the animals, were engaged in creating order. Others were intent on gaining sufficient experience to make sense of their world – identifying patterns of behaviour, patterns in the rhythm of the day or year, patterns in the space around them. For many mathematicians, pattern is what mathematics is actually about.

The brain likes pattern because it creates order and regularity, enabling us to deal with large quantities of information. Throughout life, this remains the case. Traffic experts seek to prevent accidents by looking at patterns of mishap. Psephologists look at patterns of voting behaviour to predict the outcomes of elections.

Despite its central place in the world of mathematics and life in general, pattern receives scant attention in many early years curricula. Providing opportunities to explore, notice, discuss and describe pattern is actually a foundational aspect of maths, best done playfully. Bringing to children's attention the vocabulary of pattern will help them to become aware of its many different aspects in songs, stories, pictures, the natural world, clothing and so on.

Interventions in playing with pattern

Adults have a vital role to play in helping children understand and use pattern. This will occur where children are offered a rich range of pattern making resources including a wide variety of natural materials, everyday objects such as keys and clothes-pegs, as well as structured materials such as Pattern Blocks. It will be supported where adults talk to children about pattern, including where patterns are occurring and introducing descriptive vocabulary.

Problem-finding/problem-solving

> Children need to become more than adders and dividers. Society needs 'seekers and solvers of problems and makers of new mathematical meanings.
>
> (Worthington and Carruthers 2006:222, citing Wilkinson 1998)

Teachers often feel that problem-solving should be left until children have 'covered the basics'. But this is to misunderstand the nature of human learning and of mathematics. Just as many mathematicians claim that maths *is* pattern, so others claim that it *is* problem-solving. Humans are born problem-solvers, but we are also born problem-seekers since a problem is not a problem unless you want to solve it! When adults determine which problems children should work on, all too often children are not engaged. However, they will spend long periods working at something they want to solve. For example, the group of children building a train spent most of the session making decisions, trying out arrangements of blocks and chairs, identifying and solving their problem. Schiro (2004:171) argues that 'finding problems to solve is an important phase of the problem-solving endeavour' and that children need to learn 'to identify mathematical problems in their world that might be worthy of solution'.

While successful problem-finding depends on our innate curiosity, problem-solving requires a wide range of experience, modifying strategies that have worked in similar situations. As they progress, children will learn to persevere and to work both systematically and intuitively. Learning to check as you go along can save a great deal of frustration if teddy's bed does not fit, or your den collapses. Many children create challenges for themselves – repeating a puzzle which has taken considerable effort but faster. Or, like Zac, they may gradually increase the risk or level of challenge.

Interventions to support problem-finding and solving

Adults' key role in supporting children in becoming 'seekers and solvers of problems' is to ensure that they think flexibly. Play has a vital role, as it allows children to imagine a range of solutions and rehearse ideas. Adults help children to become better at problem-solving by talking to them about how they've solved problems and any other similar problems they've dealt with. Their role is also to check for progress – monitoring and nurturing perseverance, planning, systematic exploration, and use of relevant tools such as tape measures or timers.

Playing in space

> When we open our eyes each morning, it is upon a world we have spent a lifetime learning to see. We are not given the world: we make our world through incessant experience, categorization, memory, reconnection.
>
> (Sacks 1993:71)

The lifetime in which children are learning to see their world is remarkably short. From their unique and limited experience, they attempt to remember, construct rules and connect with the world of others around them. This is a highly complex process. Attempts to curtail it – to hurry children through these experiences – are counter-productive. The way in which children naturally manage this enormous task is through play.

Current research is providing insights into the strong link between spatial awareness and mathematical understanding, including number (Davis et al.

2015). The way in which children make sense of the space around them (Sacks 1993; Davis et al. 2015) includes:

- *experience* – exploratory play is key to gaining the rich experience of the world necessary to mathematical understanding.
- *imagination* – mathematics is a highly abstract subject. Abstract thought involves imagination, visualising things that are not there or that could not exist, but are suggested by discussion, image, story or sound.
- *categorization* – in their play children naturally seek to categorise. Heuristic play, for example, provides experiences in which children may begin to group and sort objects. Big and little is probably the first category to emerge, but young children's categories can surprise adults which is one reason why tidying up is not always straightforward. Four-year-olds often use narrative as a category, grouping things like a bus, tree, dog and chocolate biscuit, because they all relate to visiting their grandmother's house, for example.
- *connecting and reconnecting* – every experience lays down a pathway in the brain and thus creates a memory. Concepts develop and change as experiences overlay each other and form a complex system of neural connections in the brain. These support human creativity, enabling us all to construct ideas from both what is seen and how experiences are represented. This may be through talk, drawing, dancing, play or any one of 'the hundred languages of children' (Edwards et al. 2012).
- *figuring* – a great word to use in this context since it has so many mathematical connotations – symbols, calculations, digits, shape, diagram, pattern, sequence of movements and logic. For Whiteley and colleagues (2015), figuring in relation to the development of spatial reasoning involves two distinct processes: representing and puzzling over what is seen. The process of transformation from one mode of representation supports creativity – that is, making unusual connections in the brain.

Interventions to support spatial reasoning

Physical movement is crucial to spatial reasoning – moving freely and boldly indoors and out, gaining a sense of independence and agency. It enables children to locate and connect spaces, navigating and mentally mapping their way, and provides experiences which will develop concepts vital to mathematical understanding such as balance, symmetry and scale.

Talk to encourage children to see things in their mind's eye may include some games and activities that promote the use of imagination.

What does an ant's bed look like? What will this flattened box look like when I put it together again? Imagine this piece of material folded in half. Supporting children's natural drive to make marks and to represent experiences enables them to compare, construct, deconstruct and reconstruct concepts. This may be seen in building and knocking down blocks, in cutting paper and sticking it on things. Representations of mathematical ideas may be seen in making train tickets, building tracks in the sand and in domestic play.

Playing with ideas

> People think it's about numbers but for mathematicians it's all about concepts and logical reasoning . . . and there's the enormous role of intuition.
>
> (Villani, quoted by Cadwalldr, 2015)

Because maths is such an abstract subject, it is often taught in ways that draw on concrete objects such as shells and counters, fingers and sets of mathematical apparatus such as Multilink and Numicon. However, precisely because it is abstract, it must also be taught in ways that promote abstract thinking. This requires social contact and input from all available senses and channels in a rich and enabling environment.

Estimation is widely regarded as a process that comes after children have learnt the basics, but the truth is that children are able to estimate long before they can count. We know that in the first year of life, babies can match a small number of sounds to the same number of objects, can detect errors when a small number of toys are added to or taken away from another group of toys, and are more interested in numerosity than objects – preferring, for example, to link two buses to two teddies – rather than linking two buses to three buses. By the time estimation is introduced into the curriculum, children have already internalised the idea that mathematics is all about getting the one right answer – not guessing.

Subitising

Recognising a small group of objects – rather than counting them individually – is known as subitising. We subitise when we notice three uneaten chocolates or when we spot the dice pattern for five. In their early years, children are frequently told by adults to count – not guess – and this can lead to the view that guessing is not part of the mathematical process, and the ability is lost. Referring to it as 'intuition', mathematician Cédric Villani underlines its importance.

Subitising is involved in 'counting on'. Children who are successful at this are able to hold a number in their head – while counting on. In a study by Macnamara (1996:125), a 5-year-old boy who could subitise groups of nine or ten objects rapidly is described as 'see[ing] some and label[ling] them with their size through subitising, and then count[ing] on and add[ing] the rest'. Those who lose their ability to subitise struggle to add 3 to 21. They may faithfully count out 21, adding 3 and starting again at 1 to come up with an answer. They do this because they have forgotten how to count on – believing that only when they have counted all will they achieve the right answer. Structured apparatus such as Numicon is based on subitising, emphasising standard patterns. However, not all numbers we meet in life conform to these patterns, so children need to be presented with numbers in a wide range of forms.

Guessing

In a review of cognitive development, Goswami (2015) underlines the importance of understanding that numbers are approximations of quantity. The brain loves pattern and is good at subitising. It is good at estimation – or approximation – something we do a thousand times a day as when we cross the road or cook a meal. Guessing encourages playful approaches reducing the stress and tension associated with coming up with a right answer. It helps to ensure that children draw on 'hunches' or intuitions, making use of connections in the brain. It gives children and adults an insight into others' thinking and may encourage the development of good ideas.

Interventions to support playing with ideas

Encourage children to guess first! Nurture imaginative play since it is a vital component in abstract thinking and a helpful step in helping children to understand the use of symbol systems. Present materials which challenge existing thinking and conceptual understanding – large objects that are light, small objects that are heavy. Above all encourage humour – it supports learning and is often absent from maths talk.

Conclusion

Everyday things hold wonderful secrets for those who know how to observe and tell about them.

(Rodari, in Castagnetti and Vecchi 1997:12)

Mathematics is about life – it should not be confined to carpet time or sets of structured apparatus. Its playfulness and creativity should permeate every area of provision and learning and are essential for mathematical understanding. Rich and enabling experience is key – especially physical experience. Maths is about ideas and discovery, and this will be supported by resources and discussion which promote flexible, playful and challenging thinking. Guessing must be a part of this! And it must also be about exploring symbol systems – children creating their own and investigating those that are part of our shared experience. Mathematical understanding will be enhanced when we help children to observe and tell others about those 'wonderful secrets'.

Questions for further thinking and reflection

1. Look at the resources available to the children you work with – indoors and out. How do they support mathematical development?
2. Reflect on an extended conversation you have had with a child recently (or ask a colleague to observe you). Did you play with ideas – asking open-ended questions and using humour?

Further reading

Carruthers, E. and Worthington, M. (2011) *Understanding Children's Mathematical Graphics: beginnings in play* Maidenhead: Open University Press

Davis, B. and the Spatial Reasoning Study Group (2015) *Spatial Reasoning in the Early Years: principles, assertions and speculations* Abingdon: Routledge

Pound, L. and Lee, T. (2015) *Teaching Mathematics Creatively* 2nd edn Abingdon: Routledge

References

Cadwalladr, C. (2015) Cédric Villani: mathematics is about progress and adventure and emotion *The Observer* 1 March www.theguardian.com/science/2015/mar/01/cedric-villani-mathematics-progress-adventure-emotion (accessed 17 March 2017).

Castagnetti, M. and Vecchi, V. (1997) *Shoe and Meter* Reggio Emilia, Italy: Reggio Children.

Davis, B. and the Spatial Reasoning Study Group (eds) (2015) *Spatial Reasoning in the Early Years: principles, assertions and speculations* Abingdon: Routledge.

Devlin, K. (2000) *The Maths Gene: why everyone has it but most people don't use it* London: Weidenfeld & Nicolson.

Edwards, C., Gandini, L. and Forman, G. (2012) (eds) *The Hundred Languages of Children: the Reggio Emilia experience in transformation*, 3rd edn Santa Barbara, CA: ABC-CLIO LLC.

Goswami, U. (2015) *Children's Cognitive Development and Learning* York: Cambridge Primary Review Trust Research Briefing 3 http://cprtrust.org.uk/wp-content/uploads/2015/02/COMPLETE-REPORT-Goswami-Childrens-Cognitive-Development-and-Learning.pdf (accessed 17 March 2017).

Lewis, A. (1996) *Discovering Mathematics with 4- to 7-year-olds*. London: Hodder and Stoughton.

Macnamara, A. (1996) From home to school – do children preserve their counting skills? In P. Broadhead (ed) *Researching the Early Years Continuum* Clevedon: Multilingual Matters.

Sacks, O. (1993) A neurologist's notebook: to see and not to see *The New Yorker* 10 May pp. 59–73.

Schiro, M. (2004) *Oral Storytelling and Teaching Mathematics* London: Sage.

Whiteley, W. Sinclair, N. and Davis, B. (2015) What is spatial reasoning? In Davis, B. and the Spatial Reasoning Study Group (eds) *Spatial Reasoning in the Early Years: principles, assertions and speculations* Abingdon: Routledge.

Worthington, M. and Carruthers, E. (2006) *Children's Mathematics: making marks, making meaning* London: Sage.

Chapter 20

The role of art education in children's development

John Oates and Nóra I. Ritók

Chapter introduction

John Oates is a Senior Lecturer in Developmental Psychology at The Open University. He works closely with Nóra Ritók, who is the founder and director of The Real Pearl Foundation and Art School, located in one of the most disadvantaged regions of Hungary. The Foundation supports children and their families in creative art to improve social competences and improve their quality of life. In this chapter, they explain how children become engaged in art activities that support and foster intellectual, emotional and social skills. The foundation works towards developing self-worth and optimism for positive change for children and their families.

Introduction

> If I could I would use art to support personal development in every school and in every adult community. Art is a unique human activity. With it we can effectively reach areas which help everyone to create a higher quality of life for themselves. It strengthens the individual and the community better than anything else.
>
> (Nóra Ritók, Director, Igazgyöngy Alapítvány)

Igazgyöngy Alapítvány (The Real Pearl Foundation) is an independent, charitable organisation working near the eastern border of Hungary, in the county of Hajdú-Bihar. In this part of Hungary, there are high levels of unemployment, concentrated especially in the large number of small rural communities, some of them quite isolated. This area is part of what is known as the 'Észak-Alföld' (Great Northern Plain), which has a very low population density and is not intensively farmed, nor is there much industrial development, except in and around the major city of Debrecen, so the opportunities for employment are very limited.

The Foundation focuses on supporting integration and enhancing the future prospects of children, mostly 'Roma', from families who have lived for generations in these conditions of extreme poverty. The work is informed by a complex model of effects, developed on the basis of experience, which takes creative activity as its starting point and is applicable to adults as well as children. The complexity of the issues linked with coordinated development strategies lies at the core of the model. It is based on three main elements:

- education
- family care, and
- development of the community.

These encompass crisis management, developing self-preservation skills, job creation and the creation of cooperation between the statutory services, especially, but not restricted to, social work, education and health.

The basis and starting point is visual education. Even though the art sessions are separate, after-school activities, the main goal is not narrow preparation for specialised education (although each year there are several pupils who choose this further education path). Rather, art education is seen as important first and foremost for the development of social competence in a broad sense. The sessions are conducted in an integrated manner, where the children can learn the rules of coexistence and cooperation, in the context of activities where the positive emotional basis embodies a sense of achievement and joy in shared experiences.

Background and context

The communities with which the Foundation works are disadvantaged in many ways: by their isolation, which means that travel to access services is difficult; by poverty associated with unemployment and associated factors which have multiple impacts on families, and by prejudiced views which act against the integration of different groups. Within the communities, one way of describing their fragmentation is to talk about 'Roma' and 'non-Roma' people, since this is one of the main 'splits'. But the term 'Roma' is problematic, although it is widely used, and indeed marks serious social and policy issues in Hungary. This is because it is used to lump together many different groups, with different histories, ethnic origins and lifestyles. But what these groups share, in this area of Hungary, is a host of challenges to living comfortable lives, and real difficulties in giving their children opportunities to better their lives. Many families struggle to achieve even the basic necessities of life;

adequate diet, secure, warm and dry housing, sanitation and water supply, and access to health care and education are all compromised. Poverty and these associated problems, along with repeated traumas and disruptions that are all too common, make it hard for people to plan long-term and to give children a stable, supportive upbringing that allows them to gain the life skills that they need. So these families, without additional help, find themselves segregated, isolated and discriminated against. And the consequence is that children from these backgrounds find it hard to integrate into the schooling system, and indeed with other state services. Leaving school at the earliest opportunity (at 16 years of age), or being held back by one or two years within the school are all too common.

Developing skills that are lacking

A major obstacle to integration is that, as a consequence of their disrupted family lives, children's social skills are often at a very low level, and they do not receive enough positive support for their development at the level of the family, the school or even at the level of society. Personal skills, self-confidence and self-respect are underdeveloped, and a strong and positive sense of self-identity is often lacking. So their capacities for cooperation are weak, their tolerance and solidarity among themselves are low, their group identity is fragile.

There has to be a serious consideration of compensating for a whole range of issues in the case of the children who come to the Foundation with multiple and complex disadvantages. They show a shortfall in sustaining and regulating attention, fine motor control, synthetic and analytic thinking, identifying emotion and interpreting metacommunication from others. Their graphical representation capacities are also undeveloped; they lack technical knowledge and their repertoire of forms of visual expression of ideas is very limited.

Case-study: Bözsi (pseudonym)

Bözsi's home is a squat in a two-room mud-brick house in poor condition, in a tiny settlement 10km down a dead-end road. Her father is illiterate, often drunk and aggressive. Her mother suffers from ill-health, and struggles with providing motivation, food, clothing and care for the four children who are still living with her. Bözsi, 8 years old, lives in a family in deep poverty, full of conflict.

Although school segregation is illegal in Hungary, Bözsi's school is de facto segregated, with only Roma children, and her teacher is prejudiced against Roma. Bözsi has been held back a year, as is common practice, and she is now in a class with younger children.

But when Bözsi draws and paints at the Real Pearl Foundation, she loves it. Something in her is able to produce really positive images. She often role-plays being a primary school teacher who likes Roma children and helps them to learn. So in some way, this enables her to create fantasies of a better life that help her to survive.

The Foundation's core approach is to develop exercises which, step-by-step, reveal and repair weaknesses, such as those affecting Bözsi, while they give the children a sense of achievement, and reinforce self-confidence and self-esteem. This is a conscious pedagogical work, which is individually tailored, strengthening the sense of self-efficacy, and takes into account each child's interests, development and personality. These is no 'one-size-fits-all' but instead, highly personalised involvement. For Bözsi, this has meant a greater integration into her schoolwork and will hopefully mean that she will not continue to be isolated and held back.

For preschool children (up to 6 years old), the starting point is visual games, initially with gross motor activities, which then lead towards using paper with rhythmic poems, songs, with tools that easily leave a trace,

Figure 20.1 Blue head

building up their repertoire of patterns, reinforcing the interpretation of visual messages. And for children in the first years of school, such as Bözsi, the basis is also games, experiencing and reproducing a unique synthesis of imagined and real things, along with encouraging the expression of individual attitudes. Stereotypical, 'clichéd' formulations are avoided, and individual voices are brought out, so that in this work, diversity becomes an asset.

Encouraging motivation

Motivation flows from this individual tailoring. If a child only loves to draw cars, he will be encouraged to use themes that always include cars, and his visual development can be pursued in this line. If the task is the representation of interior space, he can draw a car parked in a garage. If it is human movement, then it can be filling the fuel tank, or car repair. If it is observation of natural forms, then it can be a truck transporting logs or apples. If it is outdoor space, then it can be a car driving on a winding road. In visual education, it is not the theme that is important but rather the skill the educator would like to develop and teach, and this can be done most easily and successfully if a theme is chosen which ensures the child will be motivated in the activity. Compared to the constraints of imposed subjects, this gives tremendous freedom, because everyone can draw what they like! There is never any imposition of sterile still-life drawing or boring form analysis. Instead, creation is matched with individual interest; this has the most positive developmental impact.

Compensatory exercises

The Foundation has developed some very specific types of exercises which can compensate for skills that are lacking, by giving a strong sense of success while they are being completed. For the development of fine motor skills, a number of graphic exercises are used. Generally, children work on paper with very ambitious, large-scale movements, since they are not able to use fine graphic signs, which will be crucial in their development towards more detailed work. They can only be guided towards finer movements with very carefully tailored technical solutions. This is also of great importance not only in visual education, but also from the point of view of writing skills. We frequently use line structures in the drawings which are actually writing elements, and the first graders can practice the movements in bigger forms, decoratively, with the chosen thematic approach. The use of these different techniques is guided by the children's age and level of development.

Figure 20.2 Győri Péter

The teachers know the challenges of the different techniques, and they know how to avoid them in their projects to guarantee the children's success.

Visual memory, observation skills, developing the sense of symmetry, continuous collection of patterns, awareness of colour selection – these all help children to develop learning skills during their creative activity. The fact that they achieve success in this activity continuously enhances their self-image – it proves to them that they are able to work wonders, and this positive feeling affects their education in other subjects as well. They are able to pay attention for longer, to concentrate, to remember, to think, even in other contexts.

Attention and concentration

Nowadays, in this fast-moving and loud world, children want everything right away; they finish everything quickly, and what isn't intense enough doesn't have the power of engaging them and does not evoke enough motivation for the task. Children are no longer so used to sustained, intensive school work; they finish it rapidly, up to the point where it begins to mean something to them, and it is very difficult to encourage them to extend their repertoires of expression and representation.

This issue presents itself even more in those children where at home everything is loud as well, where instructions are powerful, often aggressive; where there is little or no culture of conversation, nor of storytelling; where neither the physical nor the emotional environment supports intense, extended daydreaming or thinking. In these contexts, there is no need to pay attention to anything for more than ten minutes, where there are no rules to obey, and the instinct of survival is dominant. This specific world created by poverty does not favour the development of the skills which schooling values and builds upon. When this was realised, work started consciously on exercises which can help with this issue.

Children are guided through multi-level creative processes, where there is always an element that creates additional awareness either thematically or technically, which 'uplifts' the whole project in level, with steps that have to be followed, because this is only way that the child's interest can be captured and harnessed to progress. In this way the child can feel a real sense of success on completion. There are several exercises, which are multi-field images, or organised along an 'image in image' composition. These exercises help with the development of the ability to grasp and express the essential, to concentrate, to code in visual messages, which results in a surprisingly effective development of thinking abilities.

Art work and subject knowledge

Building on the basic idea that 'I can draw something only if I have knowledge about it', this is interpreted broadly as linking artwork with intellectual development, so that, by using a thematic approach, inter-subject integration is fostered as well. For the Foundation's art teachers, understanding the knowledge base of other subjects helps to visualise other knowledge and to internalise it.

The classic saying 'What I hear – I forget, what I see – I know, what I do – I learn' (Confucius, 551–479 BC) has been amply demonstrated in the Foundation's work. The children internalise more deeply knowledge that they visualise this way, far more than reading it in a textbook, or solving problems in a workbook.

A sustained, individualised focus on compensating for skills that are lacking helps greatly to enhance the motivation of children and the expression of their personalities in their artwork. This approach to developing individual attitudes and visual communication fortunately coincides with international trends in children's art education. Igazgyöngy Foundation pupils gain hundreds of awards every year from international art competitions, where only the quality of the children's drawings is judged, where the jury has no knowledge of the social background of the children who prepared them.

Visual education and the development of social competencies

The development of the other crucial domain – social competencies – is also important from the point of view of fostering integration. For this, a cooperative method is used, based on the organisation of learning, where large-scale (sometimes mural) artworks are created together, in groups. This collective creative work gives a shared sense of success, strengthens group identity, develops the ability to divide labour, and later, in the social spaces, the artworks multiply their positive effect.

The starting point is collective 'construction' pictures. For example, each person represents themselves as a tree, draws it, cuts it out, and then a collective forest of them is glued in place, or each one prepares their own 'fairy fish that grants wishes', which are placed in the collective 'class-river', etc. Or a collective village in the mountains is created, and each child creates a house (their own), and a public building (which is how the difference between the two categories can be learned), or each one draws a fairy vehicle, and they are assembled together in a big common space.

Here the central point is to build a new system, where everybody is involved, and the visual effect works much stronger in this way than with individual works. The strong effect, the positive feelings engendered, link up with an enhanced sense of belonging, of togetherness, of playing a part of the whole.

Collective creation

The next advance is towards collective creation. Here, more serious cooperation is needed: to divide the task, to discuss and debate, to compromise, to adapt, to express different interests. Here, the children are given thematic exercises, in which they have to start with fact finding and research, and then prepare within the topic their own personal approach.

Then they form groups, and assemble the elements of the individual drawings in a new composition. They have to decide which elements to include from which drawing, what will be the main pattern, and how the other elements are related to it. It is important that something from the drawing of each pupil is included in the collective composition. This often leads to serious discussions, where they can practice reasoning, persuading and compromising. If they reach a consensus, they prepare an outline plan, and then create the drawing on a wall, paper or canvas. They fix the lines with permanent media, then give it an atmosphere through an overall colouring scheme. Then they paint the work, constantly paying attention to the distribution of who does what, so that each person works on what they do best. Then they enhance the surface with graphic symbols.

Wonderful creations are made this way, in groups of four, six, eight, or ten, depending on the size and nature of the surface to be covered. When completed, every creation contains an element drawn by each person, everybody feels it as their own, and they are proud of having been part of the group which created it. This method of collective creation develops integration skills better than anything else. It embodies the individual ideas, the adaptations, the division of work, the practice of decision making and the highest level of cooperation. The finished artwork gives a collective joy, which builds up an astonishing sense of belonging. These works, also because of their size, have great significance as decoration of the school, and spread the message of collective creation in the community.

Involving parents

In the opportunity-creating model of Igazgyöngy Foundation, it is a basic principle to aim to minimise the factors that weaken the benefits of education. It can be clearly observed that the positive benefits of schools are often weakened or negated by the home environment, which is organised according to completely different values, in a specific miserable lifestyle inherited through generations. That is why it is seen as so very important to work with the parents as well, making them partners in the development of their children, and compensating also for the skills that they did not receive either from their own schooling or their home environment. In the Foundation's Szuno project, drawings by the children are then embroidered by the mothers, sisters and grandmothers onto small pieces of fabric, which are then sewn into everyday objects by those who have also learned the art of sewing through the project. Bags, pillows, toiletry bags, mobile phone holders and other things, useful in the kitchen or in the household in general, are made for sale, giving work and income to families where neither job nor training opportunities are available to enable them to improve their lives. This development across generations has effects in several ways: making the children proud, since it is their artwork that is embroidered by their parents, and it makes the mothers proud, since they are working with their children's artwork (with self-worth and self-confidence building for both).

Conclusion

While having art at its core, the work the Igazgyöngy Foundation is broad in its scope and aims, and in understanding how children can best be engaged in art activities that support and foster the development of their intellectual, emotional and social skills. By analysing carefully each child's profile of abilities and using themes that start from their specific interests, motivation and learning are maximised, helping them to develop better their capacity to maintain attention and effort. These are crucial for benefiting from formal education. Through working in groups, and experiencing success, social skills (important for social integration) and self-esteem are nurtured. In the context of the Foundation's wider work with parents and communities, the negative effects of poverty and discrimination can be overcome and a greater sense of self-worth and optimism for positive change instilled in children and their families.

Questions for further thinking and reflection

1.   What are the key messages that you will take away from reading about the Pearl Foundation and the work Nora is doing with children and families?
2.   Are there any connections between the Foundation's work and your own approach or ethos in supporting creative art with children?

Further reading

Eisner, Elliot W. (2002) *The arts and the creation of mind*. New Haven, CT & London: Yale University Press.
Ritók, N.L. & Bodoczky, I. (2012) 'The positive influence of art activities on poor communities' *International Journal of Education through Art*. Volume 8, number 3, pp. 329–336.

Chapter 21

'My leaf is smiling at the whole world': exploring creativity through learner-led projects

Lee Robertson

Chapter introduction

Lee Robertson, head teacher at the Histon Early Years Centre (HEYC) and member of the Cambridge Early Years Teaching School, in Cambridge, England, explores the value of learner-led projects where children are encouraged to develop their creativity through dance, music, movement and creative exploration of natural resources. The chapter analyses an example of practice, an extended project where children explored their nursery's garden to find a 'gift' which evolved into a dance based on children's observations and reflections about leaves on the trees and on the ground.

Introduction

This chapter examines a project undertaken at the beginning of an academic year, with a group of 3-year-old nursery school children. It is an example of our philosophy and approach, and explores the manner in which we, as practitioners, have to address and deal with the ongoing balance between child-led exploration and adult direction in everyday practice. As a nursery school, we only have a single year to engage and learn with our children before they move on to the next stage in their educational journey. During this time, we seek to support their exploration of the new and exciting world that they have been introduced to, outside of the familiarity of their home environment. This chapter provides an outline of how the team at HEYC encourage children to develop their creativity and support their independent learning through observation, documentation, dance, music, movement and their creative exploration.

Our beliefs and values

In our setting, the inclusive practice of holistic sharing results from the fact that for several years we have been a member of the Cambridgeshire

Culture initiative. Membership commits the setting to explore and develop learning through cultural and creative references and stimuli. As part of this commitment, the Centre has commissioned specialist teachers of music and dance to work alongside the children to explore their creative emotional development. This collaborative working partnership is influenced by the principles of the Reggio Emilia preschools.

It is important to understand the reasoning behind the term 'influenced'. As educators, our role is not to replicate observed learning but to interpret its messages and own the practice which then develops as a result. It is an 'influence' and not a practice, because the interpretation has to belong to the individuals who aspire to support child–centred and child–led practice through observation, dialogue, reflection and understanding. At the heart of this belief is the importance of 'the image' of the child; this is gained from observing the interaction between each other, the foci of the impetus and the collaboration of the adults. The role of the adult practitioner is to nurture and steer the social journey and cohesion of the group. The purpose is to create a dialogue between the children. To refer to Reggio Emilia, a dialogue is used to not only describe a way of conveying meaning about something, but includes encompassing invention of new direction, thought and experiences not previously considered in conscious thought. Following this influence, HEYC promotes a creative and reflective pedagogy where all are involved in becoming active, vibrant, competent and creative learners.

Learner-led projects: movement and dance

At HEYC, we passionately believe in a holistic and child-centred approach to learning. We build our beliefs upon the open–ended spiral concepts associated closely with the Reggio Emilia approach. Our philosophy builds upon the view that 'play is the work of children.' Jean Piaget, and pioneers such as Maria Montessori and Susan Isaacs, all, in their own time, identified this lynchpin as fundamental in their research, when studying children's development and learning. We hold the view that it is children's play that is the foundation of physical, social, emotional and verbal progression required by the revised Early Years Foundation Stage Curriculum in England (DfE, 2014). It is wise to note that Paley (2004:2) asks what is to be made of 'today's revision of priorities in our nation's early childhood centres, where lessons have begun to replace play as the centre piece of community life'. Our belief is to maintain the worth of play and expressive development through our physical interpretation and storying. The dance that the children have co-created after visiting the garden in the example below, is a potent and distilled version of child's play which reminds us of Vygotsky's famous quote: 'In play the child is always behaving beyond his age, above his usual everyday behaviour: in play he is, as it were, a head above himself' (Vygotsky, 1978:74).

Vygotsky viewed play as an important tool to support children's intellectual and social development, emphasising the way children's imagination could be linked to developing confidence through practising skills. In the example of the project, we see how children are exploring their environment, using their imagination and reflecting their learning through their thoughts and actions.

An outdoor 'gift'

It had developed into a bright crisp October morning, having rained during the night. Twelve nursery school children, five girls and seven boys, all of whom have celebrated their third birthday, are eager to explore the garden area. This year, we have planned our theme around the exploration of natural materials and we had agreed with the children to find something special, a gift from the outdoor environment, to share with the other children in the class.

The children follow the path which leads them around the garden. They remain together to begin with, secure in their mutual support. Initially, they see grass, stones, trees, flower beds. The adults follow, observing interactions between the children. After a short time, Patrick and Elise discover a large puddle and run off from the group to explore this further. They splash and jump into the water. Patrick finds a large spoon and begins to stir the mixture, whilst Elise collects some bark from a dish and drops it into the 'soup'.

Other children also explore small environments within the garden. Alison and Karen are moving between the sunlit patterns on the floor, running purposefully from one shape to the next. Kevin and Robert climb a grassy mound, enjoying the fact that they can see the whole garden from this vantage point. Elliot shouts from the other side of the climbing frame that he has found a feather. The others start hunting for feathers and squeals of delight accompany each new discovery.

Four children have all settled around the edge of the flower bed and have collected a set of stones and pebbles. They examine these and start arranging them, indirectly making patterns. They are sorting them into agreed groups, working cooperatively and to an agreed purpose. The adult observes their interactions closely as they discuss which pebble belongs where, and how they should arrange them.

Emma is to one side of this group. She is standing under a large tree, shading her eyes from the sunlight and staring intently up at the tree. She seems oblivious to the shouts of the other children, and she has not joined the feather hunt or the pebble sorting, despite knowing some children in both groups.

Jayne, a practitioner within the team, approaches Emma, but does not say anything. She waits to see if Emma wishes to direct any engagement or conversation. 'It is sad, that one', says Emma.

'Why do you think that Emma?' asks Jayne.

''Cos it is', she responds, 'would you be sad?'

'I never thought of trees being sad', replies Jayne.

'Not the tree! The leaf . . . there . . . it's sad.' Emma points to an isolated leaf on one of the lower branches of the tree, then motions to another one lying on the ground by the trunk. 'So is that one, under the tree.' She then shifts her gaze: 'Look' – she points to the area of the garden, where an eddy of wind is causing a group of leaves to blow around – 'all its friends are together and dancing in the sun over there.'

Emma looks up at the branch again. She walks over to the tree and picks up the leaf she had previously noticed on the ground by its stalk and runs towards the other leaves. There she picks up another leaf and starts twirling around, laughing.

Emma holds her arms up high above her head, looks up and shouts over to Jayne, 'My leaf is smiling at the whole world!'

Other children join Emma and also play with the fallen leaves. Some begin to explore and notice the changing hues; others are still exploring around the area, but the experience Emma has caught offers a potential 'wow moment'. The adults skilfully invite the others to explore the leaves, encouraging the children to watch the movement the leaves make through the air when they are tossed up and left to fall to the ground. The children are all charged to look for one special leaf . . . there are no defined characteristics outlined, each child has the opportunity to make a good choice, their choice, no leaf is better than another – all are different and equally special.

Once inside, the children are invited to share their 'gifts' with their peers. They explain the collection and then are encouraged to show how the leaves moved outside in the wind and interpret the experience of falling to the ground. The group hold their leaves aloft in their hands and begin to move; swirling and whirling, round and round, holding the leaves high – the beginning of the dance of the leaves 'which smile at the whole world'.

The significance of movement and dance

Many experts have written about the importance of whole body movement and non-verbal communication skills to truly express meaning. Filipa, our own specialist, does not offer dance in the sense of following a sequence of steps and repeating them until the movement is rehearsed and learnt. The skill is in ensuring that the children achieve an awareness of their own body movement, not only within the space and area that the 'dance' is performed, but more importantly within their own physical space, and head space – to know what their body can do in interpretation to a given stimuli, and begin to grasp the process of being responsible for, and in control of, their own learning.

Trying to balance, to move one foot independently from the other, to achieve a preconceived desired goal is really very difficult. Running is fun, but stopping is hard, changing direction, being still, stretching fingers and toes, making a conscious connection and contact through positive touch to another individual. Paley (2004:18) observes that young children have a greater need to be in physical contact with each other: 'When nothing more dramatic came to mind, they maintain contact by grabbing at one another, anything to keep connections alive.'

The realisation that a visual image – in our example, a leaf – can be processed and interpreted into a series of controlled movements is phenomenal and deserves considered discussion and debate. Once an adult learns to trust the children to offer their interpretation of either an object or an emotion, extraordinary responses can be observed. Children have the ability to hone in and link with feelings and responses without inhibitions. Understanding, reflecting, having awareness and celebrating children's interpretation of movement, dance and music are influences which we aspire to maintain when considering creative interpretation.

Filipa explains that the way she achieves this is 'by drawing upon a range of arts practices to foster and inspire the "making processes" of interpretation and expression'. Inclusive and creative dance requires observation of the elements of movement. Then, through choreography, the dance specialist interprets the thoughts and feelings expressed by the children. This in turn facilitates their understanding of themselves and how they fit within the environment, through movement and dance. With our young children, we observe 'wow moments' as they realise they are steering their bodies to tell the story of their leaf.

As the project developed over the weeks, we used movement, interpretation and expression to understand the essence of being a leaf in the environment. The children repeated, revisited and refined their dances.

They watched each other and performed collaboratively together to 'feel' their interpretation. They documented and shared their stories of their leaves and acted out those personal scenarios both in dance sessions, but more importantly, within their free-flow child-centred opportunities within the classroom. Here, like Paley (2004:1), we observe the importance of fantasy play: 'The only age group in school that is always busy making up its own work assignments'. We are charged to find out what this play is all about – as the children are actually creating their independent learning as they go along. In their play, very little has long-term reference, very little is repetition of a pre-learned formula. The children wrestle with and finally arrive at the discovery for themselves.

Finally, family members were invited to share the children's 'performance'. Some were surprised that they were not witness to a 'production', but most were moved by what was being shared with them by their youngest family members. The interpretation was fundamental, conceptual, intuitive and meaningful. The visual collective of all the 'leaves' joining together in the swell and rotation in a spiral towards the ground, was impactful and very emotional. Observing the children's interpretation was immensely moving, with individual children beginning from separate points in the room and following their own journey, until, ultimately they slowly converged with one another and followed a circular movement, which became tighter and closer in unity until all fell slowly to the floor.

Outcomes and implications

In the same way as Reggio Emilia preschools function, we promote learning environments which support the emotional and creative development of children as the basis for effective learning. Van Manen (2016) suggests that projects give opportunities for collaboration and thoughtful interpretation of children's needs and we, the adults in their company, need to co-construct with children foundations for learner-led engagements. One of the key elements here is the capturing and documentation of rich learning moments; otherwise they pass unrecognised and are very hard to share.

The influence of Reggio Emilia preschools reinforces that pretending and imagination enable us to ask 'what if?' questions. The role of the educator is to confirm joint understanding of learning through reflection and observation, constructing and co-constructing common themes and understandings together in collaboration with the interest of the children within the group. We are often asked 'we understand that this was a really enjoyable set of activities, but what did it achieve?' Our documentation and record keeping offers a comprehensive response.

The outdoor gift project has:

- reinforced the necessity to ensure comprehensive and accurate record keeping, in order to ensure that we do not miss 'wow moments' and that we can record an individual child's progress over time, via observations, notes and photographs
- enabled the identification of measurable and quantifiable development in children's abilities in motor skills and whole body movements
- allowed children to develop their problem-solving skills by sharing thoughts and discussion
- enhanced language and negotiation skills via discussion and debate
- increased mark-making capabilities through the drawing of pictures to support understanding and the annotation of their photographs
- enhanced the children's desire to collaborate – both in practical activities and within their language use, in order to 'tell their story'
- established an understanding of the structure of stories, i.e. 'one day we went . . .'
- engaged children to make the connection between thought and the ability to create
- enhanced children's willingness to share observations and imagination through movement and dance, as well as through words
- provided children with a concrete and visible 'memory', offering a springboard to move towards the next step in their learning.

Conclusion

This chapter has explored our philosophy and approach towards children's play and creativity, and the use of movement and dance to support children's interests. Through the example, we have highlighted how practitioners respond sensitively to children, to balance child–led exploration and adult direction in play situations. We encourage children to develop their creativity and support their independent learning through a child–centred approach so that their learning is personal and meaningful. As Paley states:

> If readiness for school has meaning, it is to be found first in the children's flow of ideas, their own and those of their peers, families, teachers, books, and television, from play into story and back into more play. It was when I asked the children to dictate their stories and bring them to life again on a stage that the connections between play and analytical thinking became clear.
>
> (Paley, 2004:11)

This is very much the approach we advocate through our practice and we all face the challenge of how best to build each and every child's confidence, to encourage them to believe in their own ability and to help them to discover their elected method of communication. 'My leaf is smiling at the whole world' are 3-year-old Emma's words. How profound is that?

Questions for further thinking and reflection

1. In what ways do you recognise and value a young child's observations of the world?
2. How do you ensure you offer children confidence to believe in their abilities?
3. What strategies do you use to capture the imaginations of young children?

Further reading

Paley, V.G. (1991) *The boy who would be a helicopter: Uses of storytelling in the classroom.* Cambridge, MA: Harvard University Press.
Kolbe, U. (2005) *It's not a bird yet: The drama of drawing.* Australia: Peppinot Press.
Edwards, C., Gandini, L., and Forman, G. (Eds.) *The hundred languages of children: The Reggio Emilia approach to early childhood education*, 2nd edition. Norwood, NJ: Ablex.

References

Department for Education (DfE) (2014) *Statutory framework for the early years foundation stage: Setting the standards for learning, development and care for children from birth to five.* London: Crown Copyright.
Paley, V.G. (2004) *A child's work: The importance of fantasy play.* Chicago, IL: University of Chicago Press.
Van Manen, M. (2016) *The tone of teaching: The language of pedagogy*, 2nd edition. Abingdon: Routledge.
Vygotsky, L. (1978) *Mind in society: The development of higher psychological processes.* Cambridge, MA: Harvard University Press.

Chapter 22

If you go down to the woods today: young children learning outdoors

Philippa Thompson, Jenny Bulloss and Steven Vessey

Chapter introduction

Philippa Thompson, Senior Lecturer at Sheffield Hallam University, Jenny Bulloss, an Early Years teacher with responsibility for Forest School sessions in a primary school, and Steven Vessey, a student teacher, consider the value of Forest School and how the natural environment can support and enhance young children's experiences. They suggest that Forest School is a way in which children's play and creativity can be nurtured in a risk-benefit environment and provide case studies of children's learning and development through Forest School experiences.

Introduction

The term 'Forest School' has become an integral part of the early years (0–8 yrs) educational landscape, but the term can be interpreted in practice in a variety of ways. This chapter seeks to explore the historical perspective, the ethos and learning theories behind the approach and considerations for practice in England. A definition of this style of outdoor learning stands as a benchmark to consider the many ways in which Forest Schools have developed over recent years. Case studies and links to play and creativity suggest that some interpretations in settings seek to undermine the very ethos that attracted practitioners initially. This chapter returns to the underpinning theories that question outcome-driven practice and attainment-led curriculum. It encourages and challenges thinking to clarify and improve practice and enable reconnection with the outdoors in a positive, risk-benefit environment.

O'Brien (2009:45) suggests a starting point should be an 'inspirational process that offers children, young people and adults regular opportunities to achieve and develop confidence and self-esteem through hands on learning experiences in a woodland environment' (Murray and O'Brien, 2005; Knight, 2013). Forest School first came to England in 1993 from the Danish pre-school approach after a group from Bridgwater College, Somerset made a practitioner-led exchange visit (Bridgwater College, n.d.). Since then, the idea has become increasingly popular pedagogically in early years settings and schools. Prior to this Scandinavian visit, outdoor experiences for young children tended to be introduced by families that had an affinity with being in the outdoors, rather than new opportunities which a Forest School had the potential to offer (Shields, 2010).

Reports in recent years (UNICEF, 2007; DoH, 2011) have highlighted the need for a deeper focus on health and well-being in education, specifically in the early years. This has supported the growth in numbers of settings working outdoors with children aged 3–7 years (O'Brien and Murray, 2007; Knight, 2013). However, practitioners are faced with the contradiction in philosophies of those such as Rousseau, Pestalozzi, Froebel, McMillan and Isaacs against a backdrop of education reform (Education Reform Act, 1988), in which subject content and attainment targets replace children at the heart of education. Current global responses to climate change encourage responsibility for the environment. This has prompted countries such as Slovenia to develop programmes of study from pre-school to university on 'Education for Sustainable Development' (ESD) (Krajnc and Korze, 2013:53). There is still a tension, however, behind how such education should be approached, as well as a lack of expert knowledge and confidence amongst those working with our youngest children.

Approaches to learning outdoors

Practitioners can sometimes raise barriers when learning in the woods is presented as a curriculum opportunity. Chief concerns appear to be pedagogical approaches (Maynard, 2007): lack of environmental knowledge, weather and physical space. It is important for leaders to be confident in responding to these concerns in a considered and educated way. Pedagogical approaches considered in this chapter are those of experiential learning within the context of constructivism and socio-culturalism. They are considered within the discourse of continually changing policy and curricula in which attainment is the driving force.

In England, the Early Years Foundation Stage (EYFS) states that all settings should 'provide access to an outdoor play area or, if that is not possible, ensure that outdoor activities are planned and taken on a daily basis' (DfE, 2014:28). There is no mention here about the quality of outdoor provision or a consideration of systematic development of provision in these settings. Government policy appears not to have taken into account emerging literature considering the principles behind a

Figure 22.1 Child between trees

quality outdoor environment for young children (White, 2014). Malaguzzi considers the environment as the 'third partner' (Smidt, 2013), whilst White and Woolley (2014:30) suggest it could be the 'first teacher' and as such, settings in England are lacking in quality. The woodland is a space that provides many of the elements required for a quality outdoor space, such as an area where children can raise their heart rate and be challenged both physically and mentally (White and Woolley, 2014; Fjortoft, 2004; Fjortoft and Sageie, 2000).

In a Forest School, practitioners and children are learning through and responding to their experiences of the woodland. A rich provision of open-ended materials, rather than the closed experience of a plethora of plastic (Jackson and Forbes, 2015; Goldschmied and Jackson, 2005; Siraj-Blatchford and Sylva, 2004), allows young children's thinking to be spontaneous, versatile and meaningful. These experiences allow young children to develop their play with the adults and children around them. Rather than perceiving children as 'empty vessels', they can be seen as co-constructors of learning (Clark and Moss, 2011), who are given a voice in an often adult-dominated arena (Carr and Lee, 2012).

Rami

Rami is a 7-year-old boy with English as an Additional Language (EAL). He has also been identified by the class teacher as requiring additional behavioural and learning support within the classroom. When completing written work, he looks for constant reassurance that he is completing tasks correctly and raises concerns that he is struggling. Support strategies are in place to help Rami become more independent in the classroom.

A Forest School afternoon was planned for the whole class to participate in. The children took part in a den-building activity where they went into the woods and collected branches, logs and other natural resources. Rami needed no reassurance and quickly became the leader of his group. He shared ideas with his peers, suggesting how the den should be built, and took other children's ideas into consideration. Rami's first attempt at putting the den together was unsuccessful, so questions such as 'Why do you think it didn't work?' were asked. Rami was able to provide opinions and problem-solve to re-build. The Forest School environment allowed Rami to present himself as a self-confident, independent learner with high self-esteem.

Whilst considering the Forest School approach from the position of the child (e.g. Rami) it is also important to consider it from the perspective of the practitioner. The downward pressure experienced by many Foundation Stage classes in England sometimes convinces practitioners that Forest School sessions must become more behaviourist in approach (Skinner, 1980).

Learning theories into practice

In order for policy makers and educationalists to value Forest School, practitioners need to understand and convey the principles of pedagogy that create such a meaningful experience. There are a range of relevant learning theories to consider, one of which being 'experiential education'. According to Kolb, Boyatzis and Mainemelis (2001), Kolb (1984:41) defined experiential learning as 'the process whereby knowledge is created through the transformation of experience. Knowledge results from the combination of grasping and transforming experience.' A consideration of children's 'well-being and involvement' (Laevers, 2002; Clark and Moss, 2011; Carr and Lee, 2012) presents a more child-centred approach. Laevers (2002) also discusses the concept of 'self-organisation' as a key component of experiential learning and one that also is important for adults and children alike. Practitioners face a constant dilemma about whether their approach should be 'curriculum centred' (Wood and Bennett, 2001) or child initiated. When children take charge, it becomes more problematic to identify progression and attainment that is so desired by inspectors and policy makers. As Laevers (2002) identifies, this can be challenging to those faced with an outcome-driven education system with school performance measured by children's attainment.

In terms of the practitioner working with young children, Quay (2003) also refers to experiential education as 'holistic learning', which is sometimes a term more familiar with early years practitioners. Davis and colleagues (2000:65) argue that 'we can only form concepts through our bodily actions', supporting the observations of many in the early years workforce. Being out in the woods constructing dens or lighting fires often relies on child-initiated thinking, with some peer or adult support when required. This is akin to the social constructivist perspective within which Vygotsky's work on the 'zone of proximal development' (1978:84–91) may well be reflected. Of course, it is also necessary to consider that practitioners in the early years do not always have the underpinning knowledge and philosophies to feel confident to allow children to lead their own learning. How many have considered and debated the key issues in approaches to learning both indoors and outdoors?

Figure 22.2 Three children in a forest

Assessment as a creative process

Hedges and Cullen (2006) discuss the heavy reliance on developmental psychology in early years pedagogy, with the result that practitioners focus on ages and stages rather than the more participatory cultural psychology (Walsh, 2005). Forest School challenges practitioners to consider 'wild and adventurous play' (Knight, 2011) as an effective way of learning for young children. Practitioners are also encouraged to consider 'risk benefit' rather than simply 'risk assessment', which becomes a cultural as well as practical challenge. Developing an understanding of 'good risk' and 'bad risk' (Dowd, 2004) and that the two definitions are fluid depending on the individual and environment is key. The following case study highlights the need for practitioners to recognise young children as capable and competent in terms of managing their own risk. In a supportive environment the benefits far outweigh the perceived dangers.

Bug Hotel

A group of 5-year-old children had decided to build a 'Bug Hotel' using small planks of wood, nails and a hammer. Jenaid, Sarah, Emily and Kyle worked in pairs. The adult stood observing. Jenaid and Sarah held two planks of wood together; Emily held the hammer and Kyle held the nail in place. Jenaid said to Emily 'You can bang the nail now, but you have to bang it nicely.' Emily tapped the nail gently with the hammer and the children were constantly communicating with each other to maintain a safe environment and do the job correctly, and changed roles regularly. The children discussed hitting the nail too hard and agreed that the person holding the nail would get hurt. Kyle was curious about what types of bugs might come into the bug hotel; Jenaid responded by saying 'If soil and mud is placed in there, worms will come and stay.' Once finished, the children explored the woodland hunting for insects. Sarah found a worm and placed it into the bug hotel, saying, 'Now you can wiggle in the soil.'

In this case study, there are numerous challenges created alongside the deep-level learning occurring (Laevers, 2002). This experience is not unusual in the Forest School community and an experienced practitioner will know to let children make decisions and mistakes for themselves. Creative thinking, risk analysis, problem solving, working as a team, experiential learning, contact and empathy with the natural environment are key components. Consider this against the scenario of children being told to make a 'bug hotel' with the adult closely supervising turn taking and hammer use.

Practitioners need to convince policy makers and senior managers to see the value in this child-initiated play and support the development of woodland spaces. Documentation is essential and Reggio Emilia (in Italy) and Te Whariki (in New Zealand) provide excellent starting points. Recording the thinking and learning that takes place in the outdoor environment will bring a convincing case that this approach is play in its richest sense. 'Planned and purposeful play' (DfE, 2014) is developed through practitioners who document children's experiences appropriately and being 'an observer, follower, initiator, provider, interpreter and recorder of the narratives being made' (Smidt, 2013:38). The following case study considers how, in a brief moment, a young child can be inspired to create; problem solve; measure; instruct; communicate; manipulate materials; interpret and raise their heart rate.

Ewan

'It's windy' says Ewan (aged 3) as he watches a flag blowing. He observes what the other children are doing while stood next to me. 'I want a flag.' He bends down to the box brought to the woodland by the children and takes some ribbons and scraps of material. 'Wait there', he says and then runs away. After a few moments, he returns with a medium-sized stick. He ties the materials onto the stick and creates a flag. He then uses it to run whilst watching the direction of the wind and following it round.

Moments such as this can be recorded by those who have a deep understanding of a child's development and take time to facilitate learning. This level of documentation requires a depth of understanding from practitioners who see the potential in young children's play.

Conclusion

In summary, Forest School does not require extensive woodland on the doorstep to be a success. What *is* required are practitioners who are willing to learn and challenge their current thinking on how to approach learning with our youngest children. Being in a risk-benefit environment allows children to challenge their thinking and bodies in a way that inevitably leads to a more independent, creative and competent learner than those in risk-averse environments. Involvement with families and communities is also a strong ethos at the heart of the Forest School. If parents can understand the benefits gained from risky and outdoor play, then gradually children will be able to reclaim some freedom. Supporting young children to learn in a playful, experiential way and documenting their thoughts and processes is not without its challenges, but the rewards for all are immense and eventually may even lead to a new-found discovery of the global environment.

Questions for further thinking and reflection

1.   Reflect on what you think it is about the Forest School environment that gives children a 'sense of control and empowerment or agency'? (White and Woolley, 2014). What identities do children construct from their differing experiences of indoors and outdoors?
2.   How could the practitioner best support and document spontaneous, responsive play?

Further reading

Knight, S. (2011) *Risk and Adventure in Early Years Outdoor Play: Learning from Forest Schools.* London: Sage.
Maynard, T. (2007) 'Encounters with Forest School and Foucault: A risky business?', *Education 3–13*, 35 (4), pp379–391.
Tovey, H. (2007) *Playing Outdoors: Spaces and places, risk and challenge.* Maidenhead: Open University Press.

References

Bridgwater College Forest School. (n.d.). Available online at: http://www.bridgwater. ac.uk/forestschool (accessed 17 March 2017).
Carr, M. and Lee, W. (2012) *Learning Stories: Constructing learner identities in early education.* London: Sage.
Clark, A. and Moss, P. (2011) *Listening to Young Children: The mosaic approach*, 2nd ed. London: NCB.
Davis, B., Sumara, D. and Luce-Kapler, R. (2000). *Engaging Minds: Learning and teaching in a complex world.* Mahwah, NJ: Lawrence Eribaum Associates.
DfE (Department for Education) (2014) *Statutory Framework for the Early Years Foundation Stage.* Runcorn: Department for Education.
DoH (Department of Health) (2011) *Start Active, Stay Active: A report on physical activity for health from the four home countries' chief medical officers.* Available online at: https:// www.gov.uk/government/publications/start-active-stay-active-a-report-on-physical- activity-from-the-four-home-countries-chief-medical-officers (accessed 17 March 2017).
Dowd, J. (2004) 'Risk and the outdoor adventure experience: Good risk, bad risk, real risk, apparent risk, objective risk, subjective risk', *Australian Journal of Outdoor Education*, 8(1), pp69–70.
Fjortoft, I. (2004) 'Landscape as playscape: The effects of natural environments on children's play and motor development, children', *Youth and Environments*, 14(2), pp21–44.
Fjortoft, I. and Sageie, J. (2000) 'The natural environment as a playground for children: Landscape description and analyses of a natural landscape', *Landscape and Urban Planning*, 48(1–2), pp83–97.

Goldschmied, E. and Jackson, S. (2005) *People Under Three: Young children in day care*, 2nd ed. London: Routledge.

Hedges, H. and Cullen, J. (2012) 'Participatory learning theories: A framework for early childhood pedagogy', *Early Child Development and Care*, 182(7), pp921–940.

Jackson, S. and Forbes, R. (2015) *People Under Three: Play, work and learning in a childcare setting*. 3rd ed. London: Routledge.

Knight, S. (2011) *Risk and Adventure in Early Years Outdoor Play: Learning from Forest Schools*. London: Sage.

Knight, S. (Ed.) (2013) *International Perspectives on Forest School: Natural spaces to play and learn*. London: Sage.

Kolb, D. A. (1984) *Experiential Learning: Experience as the source of learning and development* (Vol. 1). Englewood Cliffs, NJ: Prentice-Hall.

Kolb, D. A., Boyatzis, R. E. and Mainemelis, C. (2001) 'Experiential learning theory: Previous research and new directions'. In Sternberg, R. J. and Zhang, L. F. (Eds) *Perspectives on Thinking, Learning, and Cognitive Styles*, pp227–47. Mahwah, NJ: Lawrence Erlbaum.

Kranjc, M. K. and Korze, A. V. (2013) 'Increasing experiential learning using ecoremediations in Slovenia'. In: Knight, S. (Ed.) *International Perspectives on Forest School: Natural spaces to play and learn*. London: Sage.

Laevers, F. (2002) 'Forward to basics! Deep-level-learning and the experiential approach', *Early Years*, 20(2), pp20–29.

Maynard, T. (2007) 'Encounters with Forest School and Foucault: A risky business?', *Education 3–13*, 35(4), pp379–391.

Murray, R. and O'Brien, E., (2005) *Such Enthusiasm – A Joy to See: An evaluation of Forest School in England. Report to the Forestry Commission*. London: Forest Research/NEF.

O'Brien, L. (2009) 'Learning outdoors: The Forest School approach', *Education 3–13*, 37(1), pp45–60.

O'Brien, E. and Murray, R. (2007) 'Forest School and its impacts on young children: Case studies in Britain', *Urban Forestry and Urban Greening*, 6, pp249–265.

Quay, J. (2003) 'Experience and participation: Relating theories of education', *Journal of Experiential Education*, 26(2), pp105–112.

Shields. P. (2010) 'Forest School: Reclaiming it from Scandinavia', *FORUM*, 52(1), pp53–59.

Siraj-Blatchford, I. and Sylva, K. (2004) 'Researching pedagogy in English pre schools', *British Educational Research Journal*, 30(5), pp713–730.

Skinner, B. F. (1980). 'The experimental analysis of operant behaviour: A history'. In Rieber, R. W. and Salzinger, K. (Eds) *Psychology: Theoretical-historical perspectives*. New York: Academic Press.

Smidt, S. (2013) *The Developing Child in the 21st Century*, 2nd ed. Abingdon: Routledge.

UNICEF (2007) *Child Poverty in Perspective: An overview of child well being in rich countries*, Innocenti Report Card 7. Florence: UNICEF Innocenti Research Centre.

Vygotsky, L. (1978). *Mind in Society: The development of higher psychological processes*. Cambridge, MA: Harvard University Press.

Walsh, D. J. (2005) 'Developmental theory and early childhood education: Necessary but not sufficient'. In Yelland, N. (Ed.) *Critical Issues in Early Childhood Education*. Maidenhead: Open University Press, pp40–48.

White, J. (2014) *Playing and Learning Outdoors: Making provision for high quality experiences in the outdoor environment with children 3–7.* Abingdon: Routledge.

White, J. and Woolley, H. (2014) 'What makes a good environment for children?' In: Maynard, T., and Waters, J. (Eds) *Exploring Outdoor Play in the Early Years.* Maidenhead: Open University Press.

Wood, E. and Bennett, N. (2001) 'Early childhood teachers' theories of progression and continuity', *International Journal of Early Years Education* 9(3), pp229–243.

Chapter 23

You sing, I sing, we both sing, we all sing

Vanessa Young

Chapter introduction

The benefits for babies of interactions with adults that involve singing are widely acknowledged. In this chapter, Vanessa Young, music specialist at Canterbury Christchurch University, discusses a research project that worked with baby room practitioners to explore ways in which singing and song can influence the development of more intimate interactions between practitioners and the babies in their care. She concludes with practical suggestions for how parents and practitioners can be alert to everyday opportunities to deepen their communications with babies through singing and song.

Introduction

Have you noticed what people often do when they're 'introduced' to a new baby? Something happens to their voice, indeed to their whole demeanour. They might say something like: 'Hello beautiful – aren't you gorgeous? Yes you are . . . oh yes you are . . . oh yes you are!' The voice becomes generally higher and more gentle; certain words are stressed and there are often a number of repetitions. A characteristic of this kind of speech is that it has exaggerated 'ups and downs' in pitch. This 'Infant Directed Speech' (often referred to as IDS) is called 'motherese'. The speech is often accompanied by larger, exaggerated movements of the head and facial expressions.

There is a wealth of evidence that this is universal practice. It happens the world over, in all cultures – no matter what the language. Indeed, Chinese mothers break the rules of their tonal language in order to convey the 'tune' of motherese rather than the words (Powell, Goouch and Werth 2014; Fernald 1989, in Mithin 2005). Why do we do this? It's something that many people do quite intuitively, unaware of the wealth of research evidence that highlights this phenomenon as a crucial part of communicating and interacting with babies. Mother–infant interactions, through singing with their babies, for example, contribute to babies' cognitive development and regulation of emotions, and they support their memory, language learning and attentiveness (Dionyssiou 2009). It seems the reason we all talk like this is that, whilst we may not know this, we do sense that babies are hyper-sensitive to the rhythms, melodies and terms of speech long before they understand the meanings of actual words. Indeed, there is a weight of evidence to show that babies much prefer listening to 'IDS' than to normal speech (Mithin 2005).

The borders between singing and speech are often blurred, particularly for the young child (Welch 2013). 'Motherese' – the simplified and repetitive type of speech, with exaggerated intonation and rhythm, often used by adults when speaking to babies (or pets!) – has an essentially musical character. It can seamlessly slip into what has been called 'singese' (Dionyssiou 2009) or 'infant directed singing'. Singing interactions, when communicating with pre-linguistic infants, seem to be even more effective than speech interactions. This is not a question of playing a CD of nursery rhymes or lullabies, but rather unaccompanied singing. (Babies don't seem as able to process the multiple strands of music found on many commercially produced songs.) Furthermore, experiments undertaken by Fernald and colleagues (in Mithin 2005) showed that non-lexical phrases (those without words – only sounds) were more powerful than those with words ('melody is the message'). Dunbar makes the following observation:

> Singing has an obvious continuity with laughter. It involves exactly the same anatomical and physiological processes: they are both all about breath control, are hard work for the chest wall muscles and diaphragm, and are consequently likely to be an effective mechanism for endorphin activation. Wordless singing (or humming) also shares with both laughter and speech a number of properties including segmentation, articulation, phrasing and synchrony, and this makes it an ideal transition between laughter and full speech.
>
> (Dunbar 2014:156)

The benefits of IDS are found to be not just for the babies in question. The Limerick Project (Corolan et al. 2012) which looked at singing with babies when they were *in utero* found considerable benefits for mothers too. Singing or exchanging vocalisations one to one can be an intimate experience which enabled the mothers to feel closer to their babies; it also developed their confidence in interacting with their babies and to make connections with others – for example, partners or grandparents when they too joined in – and it provided them with an additional tool to use with their babies – to soothe when distressed, or stimulate when listless. By extension, these benefits can also be experienced by practitioners working with babies. Indeed, it is imperative that practitioners seamlessly continue these kinds of interactions with babies when they arrived in nursery settings. Dalli, in a recent keynote address entitled 'Revisioning Love and care in early childhood' referred to the need for [practitioners] to 'rehabilitate' love (Dalli, 2015). This kind of inspiration was at the heart of the Babysong Project.

The Babysong Project

The Babysong Project emerged out of previous important work carried out by Professors Sacha Powell and Kathy Goouch. The project challenged what was perceived as a growing functionalism in baby care, where the overriding goal seemed to be completion of a task, for example, feeding or changing a baby's nappy. The project aimed to develop a closer, more intimate approach to interactions between practitioners and the babies in their care. We adapted the findings of the Limerick project mentioned above to create a theoretical framework for our own project. We entitled this 'The 4 Cs' (see Figure 23.1). During the project, we worked with local baby room practitioners to explore ways in which singing and song could promote these '4 Cs'.

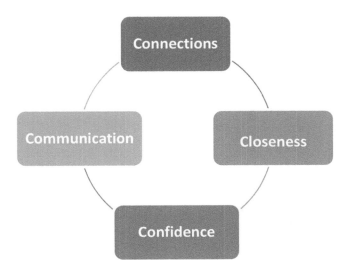

Figure 23.1 'The 4 Cs'

We looked at the importance of making *connections* with: babies, other professionals, parents, the babies' cultures, memories . . . . We explored what it meant for meaningful **communication** to take place between participants and their babies, the babies' parents or carers and significant adults in the baby room. We put a high value on finding opportunities for **closeness** to babies – intimate encounters. Additionally, we wanted to develop **confidence** – not just that of the participants, but also that of the babies in their care.

The soundscape of the baby room

What do babies hear in the baby room? A key starting point was developing this kind of empathetic awareness of babies' aural experiences in the baby room. We asked practitioners to listen carefully, as if from the baby's point of view, to all the sounds that presented themselves to the babies in the course of a session. They created a 'River of Sound' to represent these, which they shared at the next session. One of the things they found surprising was just how noisy the baby room was. This led to discussions as to the importance of 'stillness' for babies; how 'quiet spaces' and 'quiet, intimate moments' could be created, when senses are heightened and when what Karmiloff-Smith (2014) refers to as the 'dyadic gaze' between baby and practitioner is intensified. These kind of scenarios could provide perfect opportunities for closeness and musical communication.

It is important to consider what we mean by musical communication here. During the project, I created a *Spectrum of Vocal Utterances* (Figure 23.2.) illustrating that musical communication could be very broadly defined.

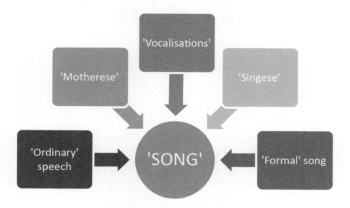

Figure 23.2 Spectrum of Vocal Utterances

'Song' then in this context covers a range of vocal musical utterances. *'Ordinary' speech* can become the musical speech of *'motherese'*. These utterances don't necessarily need words – they can include any sounds that can be made with the human voice (*'vocalisations'*) which in turn can be turned into the extended rhythmic and melodic phrasing that characterises *'singese'* (Dionyssiou 2009). But what about songs themselves? *'Formal' songs* – those that we learn from our culture or that we 'acquire' as finished 'products' – form an essential part of our regular repertoire too. We knew, however, that these were already being sung in baby rooms. What we were particularly interested in were the middle components of the spectrum. We explored *'motherese'* for example, and sought ways to turn ordinary *vocalisations* – through playful, imaginative and spontaneous approaches – into *'singese'* (or 'singing') opportunities, integrating them into regular interactions with the babies. At its most obvious and straightforward, a child who complains about a stone in her shoe for example could be distracted by a quickly improvised melodic chant: 'Ooh aah! I've got a stone in my shoe, a stone in my shoe, a stone in my shoe. Oh no! I've got a stone in my shoe and I don't know what to do – ouch!!'

More subtly perhaps, when a baby yawns, the downward sliding pitch of the yawn itself (a glissando) can be imitated, manipulated and 'played with' in a reciprocal way, creating a musical dialogue between practitioner and baby. In order to promote this kind of approach, it is important to have a clear understanding of this, to move beyond the simple (though clearly important) singing of songs and see the vast range of potential the human voice has in terms of fostering meaningful and musical communication. It is also important to develop the kind of confidence needed to engage in these kinds of interactions. As well as understanding what was involved, we needed to boost the skills and confidence of the practitioners in this kind of spontaneous vocalisation and song making. We sought to do this through practical workshops during the sessions. Participants were then encouraged to apply their learning in their own baby room settings.

Repertoire

It might be surprising to know that even very young babies can have strong musical preferences. In one particularly powerful video clip, the baby unequivocally shows which song she prefers. She smiles and gurgles when her mother sings 'Incy Wincy Spider'. This turns to loud wails and grimaces when her mother switches to 'Lady in Red'. Infants are highly sensitive to the underlying affective message contained within 'songs', both in terms of their musical content (regardless of the lyrics) and the way the song is sung. In technical terms, both the tempo (or speed) of a song, and the timbre (or tone of voice) have been found to be related to specific emotional or affective messages. The true expressive effect is dependent of course on the manner of singing: a loving tone of voice and slow tempo usually conveys soothing or comforting messages, whereas fast, clipped utterances can express excitement, fear or surprise (Tsang and Conrad 2010). One of the key considerations during the project was the choice and application of 'repertoire' (whether improvised vocalisations and singese, or formal songs). Different kinds of 'songs' produce different behavioural responses. For ease of distinction, we referred to these as 'play songs' and 'lullabies'. Lullabies tend to be slow, low-pitched and quiet, whereas play songs are more likely to be fast, high-pitched and loud (or have sharp variations in dynamics). Another interesting distinction is that 'play songs' direct attention outwards to the caregiver whereas 'lullabies' direct attention inwards (Rock et al., in Tsang and Conrad 2010) – an important characteristic in encouraging 'closeness'.

Lullabies or play songs?

So the choice of repertoire seemed to be important. We asked our participants to brainstorm and collate the songs that they commonly used in their baby rooms. The collection was huge in terms of the sheer number of songs sung; however, when asked to categorise them into play songs or lullabies, it emerged that there were very few lullabies. This resonated with previous research carried out by my colleagues who had found that less than 1 per cent of songs were obviously lullabies (Powell, Goouch and Werth 2013). Consequently, we discussed the value of stillness and songs to soothe (vocalisations and improvisations as well as formal songs). Although we heard from practitioners of one or two vignettes of stillness occurring in their baby rooms, it seems that 'closeness', and 'being still' with babies can be problematic. Participants talked about the difficulties of justifying 'stillness', of the need to 'jolly up' and to 'look lively'. One said it was 'hard to find the moments'. We learned that there is great pressure to 'keep busy' and be seen to be so – busyness and activity apparently being an overt sign and presumption of 'hard work'. We hypothesised that opportunities to be still and quiet within these baby room cultures would in practice be compromised by these kinds of pressures. One manager acknowledged that there were Ofsted expectations that every child should appear to be 'engaged' at all times. This of course raises questions about what it means for babies to be engaged, and how we know when they are. Does 'stillness' imply lack of engagement? Just think of how still you can become when completely absorbed in a task.

A key component of our project sessions was developing the understanding and skills of the participants in terms of singing and song; we needed to redress the apparent imbalance between 'play songs' and 'lullabies'. As a consequence, many of the songs I chose for us to work with could be described as 'lullabies', and a number of these were from other cultures (that is, not English-language dependent). An example of this was 'Ho Ho Wateney' – an Iroquois lullaby which was sung as a 'call and response'. At the start of the session, I sang the call without any preamble or explanation, adopting an appropriate 'lullaby' style of singing, and through gesture, invited the participants to join in with the response. I then asked them what they thought the song was about. They all thought it was probably something to do with babies sleeping, or being lulled to sleep. When asked, they were able to clearly identify key features that made it lullaby-like: quiet (dynamics), slow (tempo), sung with a gentle, soothing voice (timbre), a tune where each line gradually got lower (pitch, melodic phrasing, falling cadences), repeated word lines (rhythmic phrases, structure). This was a powerful demonstration of the participants' intuitive musical understanding of 'how lullabies go', and served to reassure practitioners that they did in fact have 'tacit knowledge' (Polanyi 1967, in Swanwick 1988:131–132).

Having seen how lullabies and play songs differed from one another in terms of their key features, the participants then had an opportunity to apply their understanding in a new context. Working in small groups, they had to choose either a play song or a lullaby and find ways of turning the song into the opposite, for example, making 'Rock-a-by-baby' into a play song and 'Humpty Dumpty' into a lullaby without changing the words. On sharing their results with each other, they identified not only what they had done technically to make the change (adjusting tempo or dynamics, for example), but importantly, how this changed the feel, or expressive 'message' of the song. The point about this exercise was that any song can be adapted, changed, 'played with', fragmented – it's not so much the song itself, but the way that it's sung that makes it a lullaby or a play song. This was an important dimension of the project and was designed to encourage the participants to 'take liberties' with the musical materials of song; to adapt them, spontaneously to the needs of the babies and the needs of the situation.

So what can practitioners or parents do to capitalise on the power of singing and song in deepening communications with babies? A key strategy involves awareness and alertness allowing practitioners to look for every opportunity to engage with babies using vocalisations:

- Listen out for and *imitate* any of the baby's vocalisations. Exaggerate, repeat, make bolder. Create a 'musical dialogue'.
- *Take turns* to make up a sound – copy and 'play' with it. (Change it slightly each time in a kind of '*sound ping pong*'.)
- *Mirror* the baby's *actions* and *add* some matching *sounds*.
- *Mirror* the baby's *utterances or vocalisations* (e.g. a yawn) and *add actions* and *gestures*.
- *Play* with sounds. Use an exclamation such as 'Ouch!' or 'Yippee!' or 'No!' or 'Yay!' or 'Ugh!'. *Repeat* in a playful way. *Exaggerate* the pitch/volume/tempo . . . .
- *Convert* instructions or suggestions into '*singese*', e.g. 'Let's go and get some lunch', 'Shall we change your nappy?' Repeat and make into a kind of chant or chorus.
- *Manipulate and change* songs or bits of songs to create different moods, e.g. convert songs – turn play songs into lullabies.
- *Change the song's narrative*, e.g. sing very quietly or very slowly (such as 'Grand Old Duke of York' to create some very weary soldiers) contrasted with something loud and lively.

All this practice, whilst highly desirable, is not without challenges. Its success is entirely dependent on the willingness, engagement and skills of the practitioner in the first instance. A practitioner who was, for example, reluctant to sing or experiment with their voice – that is, 'can't sing, won't sing' – would be problematic. Having a positive attitude to singing or vocal work, and a willingness to go beyond a tired repertoire are, one could argue, more important than musical skills per se. The more generic skills of observation and listening and the ability to communicate effectively with young children are much more crucial here. The practitioner needs these skills together with a confident and perceptive knowledge of the child in order to recognise opportunities for such engagement in the first place, and then to capitalise on those opportunities.

On its own however, having an enthusiastic, motivated, willing, skilled practitioner is not enough. Early years managers themselves have to recognise and value the worth of such activities and actively promote this kind of practice. They also need to understand that such engagement does not always have to be lively and up-beat. Armed with this knowledge, managers should be prepared to justify, actively support and foster moments of stillness and intimacy. Calm, peace, tranquillity, serenity, gentleness . . . these are surely beyond price in our loud, frenetic, action-packed world.

Questions for further thinking and reflection

1. Draw up a list of songs, rhymes that you commonly use, or hear used with babies and categorise them into play songs or lullabies. What does this tell you?
2. Reflect on the communications using singing and song that you have/or have observed – what opportunities could you take to develop your own and others' skills to communicate more effectively with young children?

Further reading

Tafuri, J. (2008) *Infant Musicality: New research for educators and parents*. Surrey, England: Ashgate Publishing Ltd.
Young, S. Lullaby light shows: Everyday musical experience among under-two-year-olds. *International Journal of Music Education*, 26(1): 33–46.

References

Corolan, M. et al. (2012) 'The Limerick Project: An intervention to relieve pre-natal stress' *Midwifery 28 (2012)*, 173–180.
Dalli, C. 'Revisioning love and care in early childhood: Constructing the future of our profession', keynote address at Te Tari Puna Ora New Zealand Childcare Association National Conference, Roturua, 15–17 July.
Dunbar, R. (2014) *Human Evolution*. London: Pelican.
Dionyssiou, Z. (2009) 'Encouraging musical communication between babies and parents: Report of a case study from Corfu'. In A. R. Addessi and S. Young (eds.) *Proceedings of the 4th Conference of the European Network of Music Educators and Researchers of Young Children – MERYC 2009* (313–322). Bologna: Bononia University Press.
Fernald, A. (1989) 'Intonation and communicative intent in mother's speech to infants: Is the melody the message?' *Child Development 60*, 1497–510.
Karmiloff-Smith, A. S. (2014) 'Making conversation with babies and toddlers: Its importance for all aspects of child development', keynote address given at Canterbury Christ Church University's 5th Annual Baby Room Conference, Coin Street, London, September.
Mithin, S. (2005) *The Singing Neanderthals: The origins of music, language, mind and body* London: Weidenfeld & Nicholson.
Polanyi, M. (1967) *The Tacit Dimension*. Garden City, NY: Anchor Books.
Powell, S., Goouch, K. and Werth, L. (2014) *Mothers' Songs in Daycare for Babies*. London: The Froebel Trust.
Swanwick, K. (1988) *Music, Mind and Education*. London: Routledge.
Tsang, C.D. and Conrad, N.J. (2010) 'Does the message matter? The effect of song type on infants' pitch preferences for lullabies and playsongs' *Infant Behavior & Development 33* (2010) 96–100.
Welch, G. (2013) 'The research evidence on singing development in early childhood'. In Welch, G. and Elsley, J. (eds.) *Baseline Assessment of Singing in English Schools*. University of Surrey, Roehampton Institute.

Index